Small Houses

Fine Homebuilding

GREAT HOUSES

Small Houses

The Taunton Press

Cover photo: Jeffrey Dale Bianco
Back-cover photos: top left, Charles Miller;
top right, Joanne Kellar Bouknight; bottom left, Kevin Ireton

TAUNTON
BOOKS & VIDEOS

...by fellow enthusiasts

First printing: July 1992
Printed in the United States of America

A FINE HOMEBUILDING Book

FINE HOMEBUILDING® is a trademark of The Taunton Press, Inc., registered in the
U.S. Patent and Trademark Office.

The Taunton Press, 63 South Main Street, Box 5506,
Newtown, CT 06470-5506

Library of Congress Cataloging-in-Publication Data

Small houses.
       p.   cm.
    "Collection [of articles] from the first 10 years of Fine
homebuilding magazine" – Introd.
    "Fine homebuilding, great houses."
    "A Fine homebuilding book" – T.p. verso.
    Includes index.
    ISBN 1-56158-046-5
    1. Architecture. Domestic – United States.   I. Fine homebuilding.
NA7205.S64   1992   92-10170
728' .0973—dc20   CIP

Contents

Introduction

Small houses have always been popular as vacation cabins and country retreats, but today they are becoming increasingly popular as primary residences as well. Small wonder.

Small houses can be cheaper to build, and they can be built on smaller lots. They require fewer materials to build and less energy to run. They are quicker to clean and easier to maintain. Small houses also appeal to the evolving American household (smaller families, empty nesters, singles) and to the budgets of young first-time buyers, for whom home ownership has become increasingly difficult.

Although small can be beautiful, a small house can also be cramped and unappealing. Even those who want a small house often still want the benefits packaged in a larger house. The challenge faced by builders and designers is how to make a small house feel big enough. This book offers dozens of practical solutions.

The 37 articles in this collection come from the first 10 years (issues 1-66) of *Fine Homebuilding* magazine. They cover a diverse range of houses, all of them under 2,000 square feet. They include new houses and remodels, urban rowhouses and rural retreats, and guest cottages that can double as work studios. Some are superbly designed and engineered, others are simple owner-built creations. There's a playhouse and a tract house and some wonderful advice on how landscaping can make a small house feel larger. Together, these articles give you a big dose of small ideas.

— *The Editors*

Note: One thing that small houses share with large houses is that they can burn to the ground. Such was the tragic fate of the Honda house (see pp. 86-89), which was destroyed in the 1991 Oakland-Berkeley fire.

The Covered Bridge Cottage

This cost-efficient small home accommodates a family and a career

For years our family has admired traditional cottages. They're somehow very personal and warm, conducive to quiet, peaceful times. This seems particularly true of those that have been built by their owners, for such cottages retain an individuality that's not present in today's world of cellular suburban tracts.

I'm a professional artist, and I teach art at a nearby university. I've also done a fair amount of residential design and construction over the years. With one son in college and the other close behind, we realized some time ago that a small, affordable house—a cottage—would make the most sense for our future. Like many families whose children are leaving home, our needs for housing are decreasing. With the freedom to design and build a home and studio for ourselves, we decided to create a house that would balance cottage charm with our active way of life—and minimal budget.

The challenge of small homes—There are many advantages to building small. Fewer materials are involved, and technical problems are generally cheaper to solve. Spans are short and loading is straightforward, so you don't usually need expensive heavy beams or custom hardware. Finally, construction just goes faster. For us, this was especially important. Since the building crew would be my wife Cathy, myself and our two sons Scott and Tim, and all of us but Cathy had to return to school in the fall, we wanted to complete the house during our summer vacation.

Along with their advantages, though, cottages have some drawbacks. We faced a classic one at the outset: what to do with all the stuff we had collected over the years. Designing lots of storage space is one way to minimize this prob-

lem, but simply getting rid of unnecessary furnishings helps a lot, too.

Designing a small house or cottage is challenging because spaces need to be so efficient. The most difficult problems to overcome are the loss of privacy and the increase in noise levels. It's hard to find solitude in a cottage, particularly when you share it with others. Often when you open the door to a small house, you've seen all there is to see. And if not, a glance up into the inevitable loft usually finishes the view. Because interior spaces are condensed, the noise of dinner under way in the kitchen can easily intrude on a phone conversation happening just about anywhere else in the house. If the lot is also small, it's difficult to insulate yourself from activity outside—the neighbor's kids playing in the yard, the traffic on the street.

Developing a program—One of the very first things I do when designing a house is to get an idea of the amount of time its owners will spend at home, and of the kind of activities that take place there. Making a simple calendar is most helpful in trying to record the typical week. On the calendar, I block in the amount of time spent and activity performed in different areas of the house. Then I make an inventory list of all the "no-we-can't-part-with-that" furniture and possessions. Later on, when I begin sketching plans, I scale out the larger items on this list and put them on the sketches. This suggests certain kinds and shapes of spaces, and I can begin to think in terms of room function and size. I like to make some quick calculations at this time of basic materials costs to double-check standard price-per-sq.-ft. estimates to see if my design is in the financial ballpark.

In going through this process for ourselves, we found that informal family living, private spaces for all, and my need for a home studio would be important elements of the design. Most of our time together is spent near the kitchen. Informal discussions, eating and some evening television are the usual activities. This suggested a very small but efficient space for two to four people. My work requires easels, storage for paints and canvases, and plenty of natural light, but most importantly a sense of privacy and separation. It followed that each space would be individually tailored to each person's needs. In nice weather, we like to be outside as much as possible, so a large deck was important.

Working with the site—Our lot is on a high bank of the Willamette River, which meanders through the fertile farmland of Oregon's Willamette Valley. We were lucky to find the site (which included a 100-year-old granary), because the State's Willamette River Greenway now limits development within 250 ft. of the river. But because our site had an existing structure on it, they let us build the house.

We owned the land for a couple of years before we started construction, and during the summers before had been able to install the septic system and well. These were major factors in determining where the house would go, and were largely beyond our control—the county sanitarian told us where to locate them. We

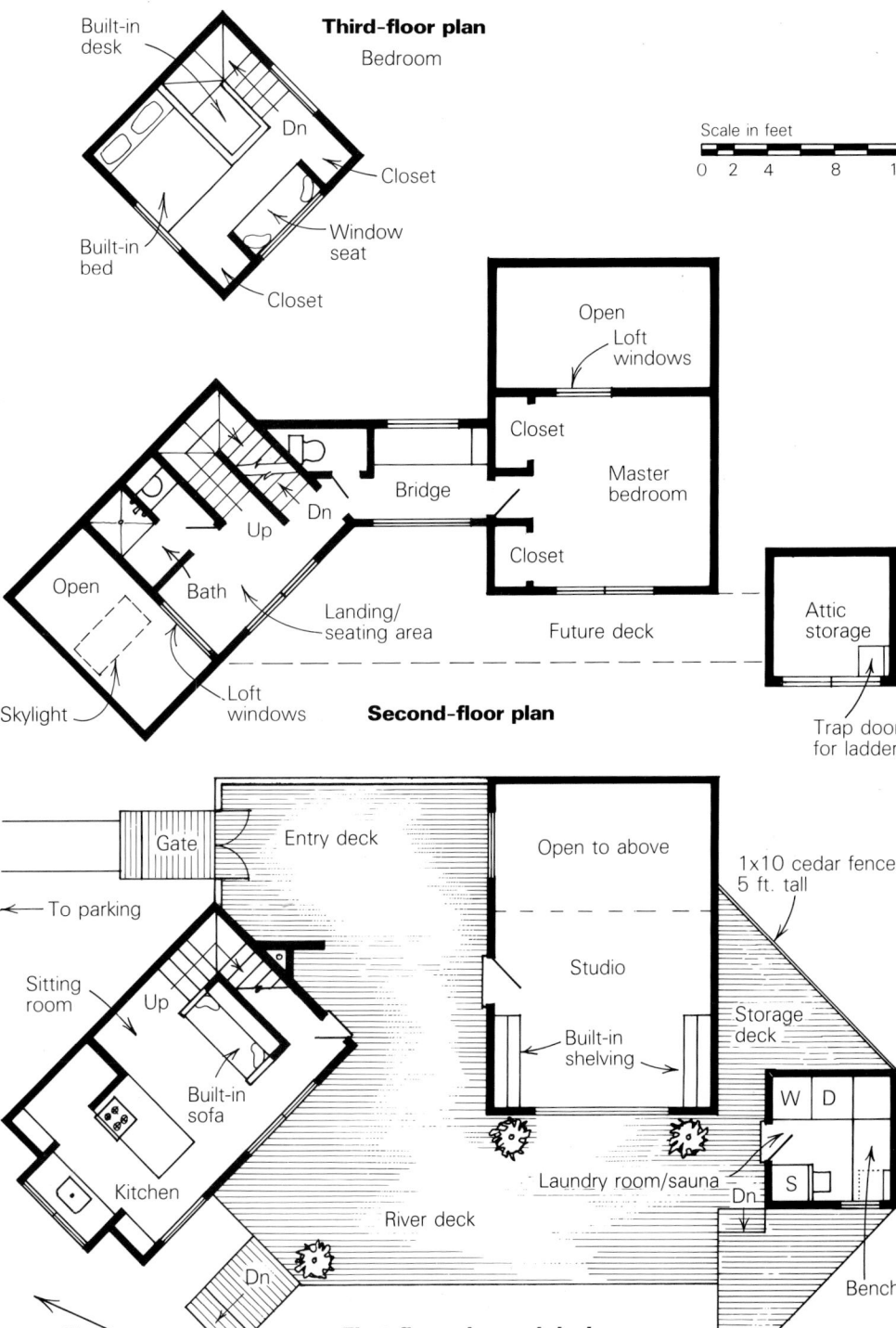

gave about 8,500 sq. ft. of the old granary to a local salvage yard in exchange for having them dismantle the building and clear a building site. Not too surprisingly, they quickly took the best and most usable lumber and left us with a huge mess to clean up.

After we cleared the debris, we decided to leave some of the structure's 32-ft. wide by 125-ft. long concrete floor in place, and use it as our driveway. But some of it had to be removed so we could add some landscaping. We rented a concrete cutter and went at it. The difficulty came when we tried, to no avail, to break the slab into smaller pieces with sledgehammers. Finally we resorted to using a jackhammer, and in two days we were able to break up an area 10 ft. by 80 ft. We removed and stacked the broken pieces in a rubble wall along the driveway, and backfilled behind it with several loads of sandy

loam. It later became a raised planter, and we saved the cost of pouring a new driveway.

Once these predetermined aspects of site development were complete, we made a detailed plot plan of the property, including where it was shaded, where it was sunny and where the major views were. This inventory of the site began to suggest the placement of the structure, and helped to define the building area.

Fine-tuning the design—I wanted to make sure the windows in the house would frame the best views of the farmland, the river and the mountains beyond. I also wanted to take advantage of the warmth of the winter sun. With 2-ft. stakes and a lot of string, we began by identifying the approximate locations of ground-floor rooms. With a partial wall of stakes and string we screened the imaginary entry deck, and hid any view of the river from the approach to the house. Our goal was to arrange the approach so the focus would be on the architecture. After turning the corner on the deck, one would be greeted with views to the river.

Once we had the building roughly where we wanted it, the process of framing the views began. I had sketched certain landscapes I wanted to frame, and working from this plan, we drove 8-ft. long 2x2 stakes into the ground where I thought the edges of window openings should be. With string, we then tried to establish the upper and lower limits of the view from each window. By sitting on a stepladder inside the room areas, we could approximate the view from inside the finished house, and someone else could move the string or the stakes as needed. By turning the kitchen at a 45° angle to the studio, all the 6-ft. door and window openings would face the winter sun. Once we had everything where we wanted it, I took dimensions and began drawing up the plans.

Thinking small, living big—With careful planning, the problems inherent in small structures can be minimized. Though it includes only 648 sq. ft. of living space and 200 sq. ft. of studio space, our cottage feels a lot bigger. Opening it to the view was important in making the house feel larger, since we visually "borrowed" space from the outdoors.

Building up did a lot for the house, too. It gave each room a view and offered the ultimate privacy of having no room adjoin any other. It also helped us to make the most of our tight budget since it minimized the amount of foundation and excavation required. And since the house covered less of the lot, we gained badly needed flexibility in locating the structure. The vertically oriented plan adds considerable interest and mystery to the interior of the house, too, and ensures that a single glance around doesn't reveal everything.

A small house is difficult enough to design, but my need for studio space at home complicated things considerably. I originally thought that my studio would have to be located in a separate building, but I didn't want to be too far removed from family activities, either. Instead, I located the studio in a separate structure and connected it to the house with a covered "bridge." The studio occupies the entire first level, while the master bedroom is located in the loft above. The studio can double as a living room when we're entertaining. Clients who come out to visit don't feel as though they are intruding on our living space.

The bridge isn't wasted space, though. It's a limited-use area between two high-use areas, and acts as an effective sound buffer between them. I built in counter space along one wall with drawers underneath, and the area serves as a study, a sewing room and a place for phone conversations (top photos, facing page). The bridge also provides cover for the walkway below—you can walk between the studio and the kitchen area without getting rained on.

The kitchen/family area was designed to be an informal meeting space, and we wanted it to be quick to heat. We kept the floor space to a minimum and the materials simple and inexpensive (photo facing page, bottom left) with open shelves for accessible storage. The water heater is pushed back under the stairwell as far as possible, and removable shelves in front of it have become a handy pantry. Instead of a door, we used a cloth cover on the pantry to let the excess heat from the water heater into the living

From *Fine Homebuilding* magazine (June 1986) 33:48-52

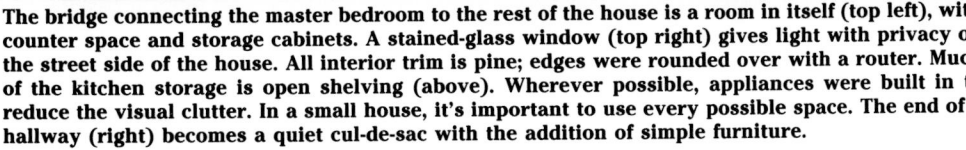
The bridge connecting the master bedroom to the rest of the house is a room in itself (top left), with counter space and storage cabinets. A stained-glass window (top right) gives light with privacy on the street side of the house. All interior trim is pine; edges were rounded over with a router. Much of the kitchen storage is open shelving (above). Wherever possible, appliances were built in to reduce the visual clutter. In a small house, it's important to use every possible space. The end of a hallway (right) becomes a quiet cul-de-sac with the addition of simple furniture.

area. A small kitchen can feel larger if you don't call attention to the appliances, so we built them in wherever possible.

The countertops are different heights for different activities. Near the sink they're 38 in. high, near the stove 34 in., and the rest are 42 in. high. Between the kitchen and sitting room are the higher countertops, where they help to block the visual clutter around the sink. Some of those "no-we-can't-live-without" objects and collectibles we put on a large shelf over the

kitchen shelves and sink, as well as on shelves above the built-in sofa. A window box houses the kitchen sink and was a nice way to enlarge the space without actually adding square footage to the floor area.

To give the illusion of a larger space, we vaulted the kitchen ceiling and opened it to the second-story landing in front of the bathroom (photo above right). In order to control the flow of heat and noise between the two areas, we sealed the opening with hinged windows of

laminated auto safety glass. These can be opened so that we can hoist furniture upstairs, rather than forcing it up the narrow winding stair.

We heat each room with an individually controlled electric baseboard heater, since electric heat is relatively inexpensive in the Northwest. In addition, heat from the studio woodstove flows through shutters to warm the master bedroom above.

When the overall design concepts were worked out, we took a hard look at how the house would have to be built. Our budget was very limited, which meant that we would have to use readily available and inexpensive materials. We set aside about $20,000 for materials only, and allowed enough extra to pay Scott and Tim a fair wage; Cathy and I would donate our labor. By being responsible for every phase of construction, we were able to keep our final cost around $24 per sq. ft. of living area, including the outside decks and kitchen appliances.

Design changes as work progressed—I always feel a certain excitement when the framing begins, very much like beginning a new painting. When I am making a painting, I continually re-evaluate the work and quite frequently change my initial thinking. For me, building a house is very much the same. The boys and I continually looked at shapes and directions, the sizes of windows and doors, textures, balance and light.

The house, as it went together, did change. As we framed the third story (where we weren't able to apply the strings-and-stakes method), a distant and unexpected view of 11,000-ft. Mt. Hood convinced us to install a new window to capture this sight. At another time, we made a mid-course correction in the plumbing. We had originally laid out the upstairs bathroom in a way that would route the waste lines through the stairwell wall that formed the back of the built-in sofa downstairs. It occurred to us that visitors might not appreciate the sound of rushing water behind their heads, but it was hard to find an alternate route for the plumbing. We finally decided to run the line outside the house, and box it in.

A simple structure—We began construction by digging out the footings and crawl-space areas by hand. We were able to be very clean and precise with the excavation, with little disturbance to the site. A cat or backhoe wouldn't have been much faster, and would have been considerably more expensive. For the founda-

tion, we used 8x8x16 split-face concrete blocks. The longest span for the first floors was only 14 ft., so we used 4x8 joists 24 in. o. c. with a ¾-in. T&G plywood subfloor, glued and nailed. With no posts or intermediate support, the work of framing the floor went quickly.

Wall framing was, for the most part, standard for our relatively mild climate: 2x4 studs 16 in. o. c. with ½-in. CDX plywood sheathing. The siding is #2 cedar shingles, which we purchased from a local shingle mill. Installing them with 7 in. to the weather instead of the typical roofing exposure of 5 in. helped to reduce their cost. We already had a compressor so we bought a small staple gun and used ¼-in. by 1¼-in. staples to put up the shingles. The labor savings more than offset the cost of the gun.

To make shorter work of framing the second and third floors, we installed exposed beams of Select 4x8 fir, 24 in. o. c. We nailed in 2x8 blocking at the wall line, bringing the face of the blocks out from the wall line by about an inch (photo below). This made a solid surface for the drywall to butt against, and allowed us to avoid cutting the rock to fit around each beam. Over the beams we laid 1x8 T&G #2 and #3 pine, glued and nailed to the beams. This was covered with ¾-in. T&G plywood, and all upstairs floors and stairs were covered with commercial-grade pad and carpet. With open-beam ceilings, this helps to keep the noise down.

All roof pitches on the house are 12/12. I like steep roofs for several reasons—they will last longer than roofs of a lower pitch, they give us much more interior headroom upstairs against the short side walls, and cutting the rafters and trim is easy.

Working on such a steep pitch can be dangerous, especially for two teenagers, so I finally figured out a safe and easy way to get the job done. I cut all the plywood roof sheathing into 2-ft. by 8-ft. pieces, and we sheathed and roofed the house from inside. Carrying all materials up the stairs instead of up a ladder made the job

easier, too. We first stapled down a length of the plywood at the eaves, then laid our paper and began working the three-tab asphalt shingles up a couple of rows at a time. When the shingles reached the top edge of the plywood, another length of 2-ft. wide plywood went down and the process was repeated. We completed one side of a roof at a time, and the only time we had to be out on the roof was when we reached the ridge, and that was safe to straddle.

Interior finish materials—Just about everything inside the house that is wood is pine. We ripped 1x12 #2 and #3 pine into shelves, cabinet fronts, drawers, window casements and trim, and eased the edges with a ¼-in. radius router bit. Interior doors are made of glued-up 1¼-in. pine blanks (sold in lumberyards as inexpensive tabletops). They worked well when we needed to cut an arch or make an odd size. They also made good desks and closet enclosures.

We gave all wood surfaces a thin coat of latex paint watered down enough to allow the grain of the wood to show through (one part paint to about five parts water). This raised the grain slightly but not enough to bother us. In traffic areas we added a coat of satin polyurethane. A satin finish isn't usually recommended for surfaces that get a lot of wear, but we like the way the finish aged. On the kitchen and studio floors, we used the same latex wash; after a thorough sanding, we applied four coats of satin polyurethane. Using the buff wash over all wood surfaces, including the ceilings, gave a much softer and lighter feeling to the small spaces, and was an inexpensive finish.

Laundry and sauna annex—We don't care much for the noise made by washers and dryers, so after the house was complete we decided to build a separate but nearby building for them. To get the most out of our limited budget and small space, we decided to use this 8x8 laundry room as a sauna. I put a shower in the corner and built long, high bench seats to enclose the washer and dryer. Another bench, somewhat lower, doubles as a laundry sorting table. We installed a standard sauna heating unit and have been most pleased with the operation. A window toward the river and the adjoining deck makes cooling down a soothing experience. We might have stopped there, but we realized that Scott would most likely be home during summer months. We built an attic storage area above the laundry room, with access through the laundry room, up a ladder and through a trap door. Scott can use this space on brief visits. We included a 6-ft. by 4-ft. window facing the river. Eventually we hope to tie this space to a second-story deck that will allow access to the house at this level.

We were initially concerned about the possibility that heat and humidity generated by the sauna would damage the inner workings of the washer and dryer. But we exhaust the room after each use, and we have not had any problems with the equipment. □

As a time-saver, 2x8 blocking was let in to the exposed ceiling beams during framing, and was made to overhang the plane of the wall slightly. Later on, drywall could simply be butted to the underside of the blocking instead of being laboriously cut to fit around the beams.

Richard Robertson is an artist and teacher when he's not designing and building small homes.

A Superinsulated Saltbox

An affordable, energy-efficient apartment and workspace built to traditional lines

by Howard Faulkner

Architects, designers and builders are frequently asked to combine living and working space for clients in one building. As our economic base shifts from industry and manufacturing to service and information, there are more people who can work at home. Personal computers certainly have something to do with this trend. With over 50 million of them currently in use, people are not just alphabetizing recipes.

Here in Maine, where I work as a university professor, students and recent graduates have trouble finding reasonably priced homes, as do young professional couples just starting out. Having some spare room on my lot and a desire to experiment with designs for residential and business use, I decided to build a garage and workspace with an apartment above. Apart from enjoying extra income from the rent, I'd have the pleasure of solving some timely design problems.

Energy efficiency was an important design factor. I had just completed a year's sabbatical studying superinsulated design and construction throughout the U. S. and Canada. I didn't need to be convinced about the value of building an extremely energy-efficient house, but I was concerned about keeping costs under control.

Design goals—I sat down at the drawing board in November of 1983 with a list of requirements for the house. It had to have about 750 sq. ft. of living space, including two bedrooms, and 900 sq. ft. would be devoted to studio/work area, storage and garage space. I wanted to incorporate state-of-the-art structural and thermal design to ensure low operating costs, and to keep construction costs below $30/sq. ft. This meant I'd have to use off-the-shelf materials and make sure all work and materials conformed to code. I'd also have to provide the safe levels of ventilation required in a tight house. Once finished, the house would have to look nice, and be acceptable in a traditional New England community. Also, the design would have to permit easy layout changes so the house could be adapted to fit the needs of tenants.

The design I came up with (photo and drawings, below) is a 30-ft. by 30-ft. saltbox with living space upstairs and garage, storage and workspace on the ground level. The 10-ft. by 30-ft. workshop can expand into one or both garage bays, or part of the downstairs can be used as living space. Upstairs, there's a full bath, two bedrooms and an open dining/living/kitchen area. A deep closet in the kitchen holds a washer and dryer.

Foundation and ground floor—My original plans called for a 4½-ft. high, poured-concrete frost wall set on a concrete footing. When excavation began, plans quickly changed. The backhoe operator hit a granite ledge with his first bucketload. Fortunately, we didn't have to spend extra time and money blasting our way below the frost line. After discussions with our building inspector and the regional representative for the American Plywood Association (P.O. Box 11700, Tacoma, Wash. 98411), we decided to use a permanent wood short-wall foundation. This wood-frame foundation, we discovered, is ideal in many situations where a masonry foundation isn't possible or practical.

After excavating to depths ranging from 14 in. to 22 in., depending on bedrock location, workers packed down a base of ¾-in. crushed stone and leveled it. At the lowest part of the excavation, a drain was installed with its outfall 50 ft. away from where the building would stand.

Following the standards of the National Forest Products Association (1619 Massachusetts Ave. NW, Washington, D. C. 20036) for permanent wood foundations (particularly their Technical Report #7), we used 0.60 CCA (chromated copper arsenate) treated lumber to build the short walls. We framed them with 2x6s spaced on 16-in. centers, and used single top and bottom plates. CCA-treated ½-in. plywood was used as exterior sheathing. As shown in the drawing on p. 15, a heavyweight polyethylene moisture barrier, held in place by a treated 1x6 wear strip at grade, keeps water away from the wall.

After the 2-ft. high treated wall was framed and sheathed, workers laid treated 2x8 sills on the compacted, leveled gravel, and tilted the walls into place on top of them. This level sill acts as a footing, spreading the load of the wall. To steady the walls until the concrete floor was poured, temporary diagonal braces were nailed to the top plate and to posts driven into the ground outside the foundation. The 2x8 sill was stabilized by adding gravel along both inside and outside edges.

After we laid down a heavy-duty, cross-laminated moisture barrier, 1-in. extruded polystyrene insulation was placed inside the short wall. Then a 4-in. thick reinforced concrete floor was poured. To make a

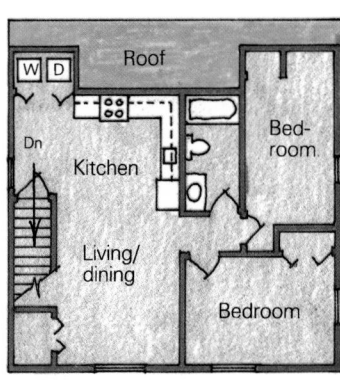

First floor

Workshop — Sink — Plumbing chase — Two-car garage — Up

Second floor

W D — Roof — Dn — Kitchen — Bedroom — Living/dining — Bedroom

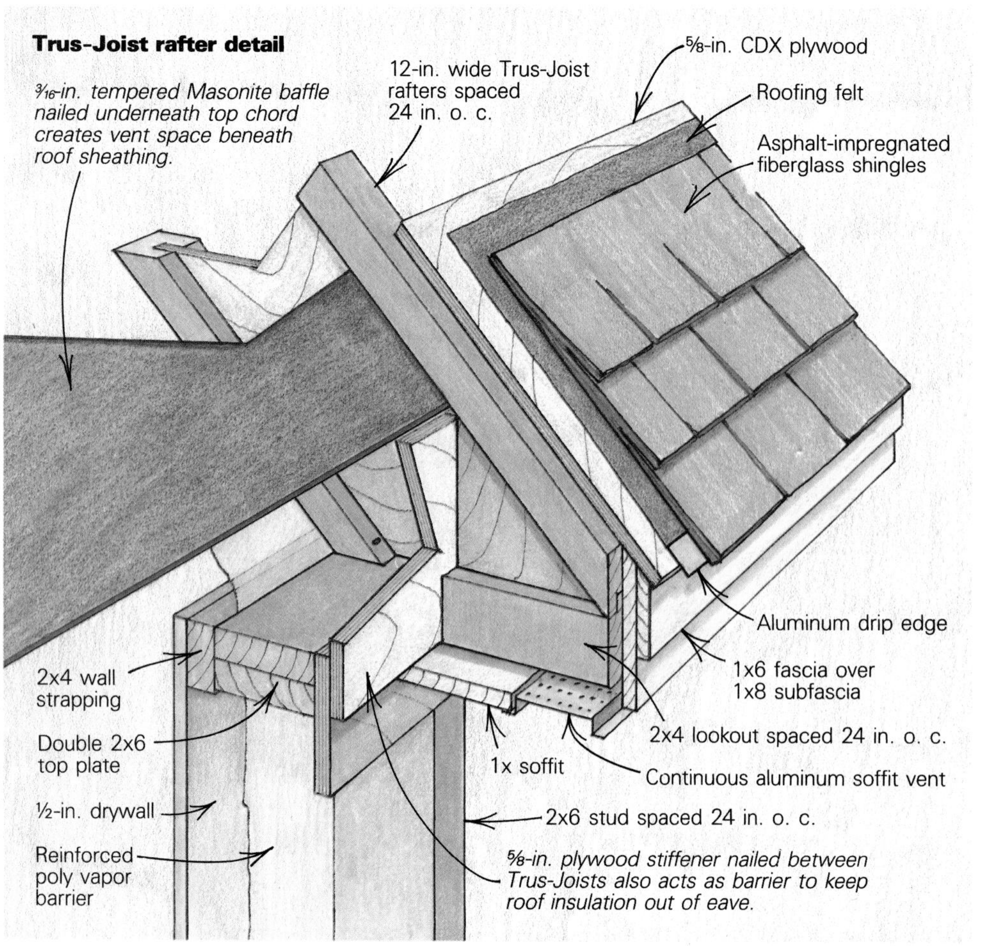

Trus-Joist rafter detail
3⁄16-in. tempered Masonite baffle nailed underneath top chord creates vent space beneath roof sheathing.
12-in. wide Trus-Joist rafters spaced 24 in. o. c.
5⁄8-in. CDX plywood
Roofing felt
Asphalt-impregnated fiberglass shingles
Aluminum drip edge
1x6 fascia over 1x8 subfascia
2x4 lookout spaced 24 in. o. c.
Continuous aluminum soffit vent
1x soffit
2x4 wall strapping
Double 2x6 top plate
½-in. drywall
Reinforced poly vapor barrier
2x6 stud spaced 24 in. o. c.
5⁄8-in. plywood stiffener nailed between Trus-Joists also acts as barrier to keep roof insulation out of eave.

strong connection between walls, floor and backfilled soil at grade, the concrete extends into the stud bays of the short-wall foundation.

Wall and roof framing—The first-floor walls were framed with 2x6s on 24-in. centers. The 5½-in. stud width allows enough room for R-19 fiberglass batts, which were friction fit between the studs. On the high side of the saltbox, a pair of 12-in. wide Trus-Joist I-beams (TJIs) extends atop the wall the full length of the house. You might call the pair of beams an extended header, since its primary purpose is to provide a strong span across a pair of garage doors. These prefabricated trusses have 1¾-in. by 1½-in. laminated chords and a ⅜-in. plywood web. Following the recommendation of the manufacturer (Trus Joist Corp., 9777 W. Chinden Blvd., P.O. Box 60, Boise, Idaho 83707), we glued and nailed 1x6 stiffeners across the full width of the web every 24 in.

Trus-Joists were also used as second-floor joists and rafters. My aim in making extensive use of these structural members was to make the actual construction go faster and easier, saving money in the process. All TJIs used in the house were 12 in. wide and 24 in. o. c. This simplified ordering and also made it possible to get a good bulk price from the local distributor. Compared to 2x12 joists with similar span capabilities, TJIs are much easier to handle because they're so light (a 30-ft. long TJI weighs only about 45 lb.). Also, there are no crowns, bows or other imperfections to contend with. The 12-in. width can accommodate up to R-38 in unfaced fiberglass batts, and the ⅜-in. thick web minimizes thermal conductance from exterior to interior surfaces.

Floor TJIs were spaced on 24-in. centers and then decked over with ¾-in. T&G plywood. To achieve a higher level of insulation in the second-floor walls, I adapted a Canadian superinsulated wall design commonly referred to as *wrap 'n strap* (drawing, facing page). This system is less expensive and quicker to build than a double-wall system, but offers some of the same advantages. Total R-value is 25.

The first step in building a wrap 'n strap wall is to frame a 2x6 wall, with the studs 24 in. o. c. After the exterior sheathing is applied (we used ½-in. CDX plywood), the stud spaces are insulated with unfaced fiberglass batts (R-19). Then a high-quality vapor barrier (we used Tu-Tuf, made by Sto-Cote Products, Inc., Drawer 310, Richmond, Ill. 60071) is installed against the inside edges of the studs. Even though the poly is extremely durable because of its cross-laminated reinforcements, I like to call it a *vapor retarder* rather than a vapor barrier. The latter term implies a level of impermeability that isn't realistic, at least at this point in tight-house technology. A strong, properly installed vapor retarder will substantially reduce the chances of moisture damage in wall, ceiling and floor cavities.

After the poly is installed, the inside of the wall is strapped horizontally with either 2x4s or 2x3s. They're located on 24-in. centers from the top plates to the bottom plates, and around window openings. The 1½-in. thickness created by the strapping holds an extra R-5 of fiberglass insulation and also keeps all electrical wiring on one side of the poly. A 2-in. to 3-in. space is left at appropriate locations in the strapping at floor level to bring the wiring up vertically from the TJI cavity below. These spaces are then covered with sheet-metal plates to protect the wiring from drywall nails. Shallow metal electrical boxes have to be used in all exterior walls.

Since no penetrations of the poly are necessary, air-leakage potential is significantly reduced. The only holes that require caulking are those made in the floor sheathing to bring the wiring upstairs. The floor vapor retarder is actually the ¾-in. T&G plywood sheathing, which is normally laminated with a waterproof glue that locks out moisture. The sheathing was glued to the TJIs, and all T&G joints were caulked.

Once the walls were framed and sheathed, the roof went up easily. On its long side, 28-ft. TJI rafters were set in place in one piece. Had we used dimensioned lumber for rafters, this part of the framing would have been far tougher.

All rafters were installed on 24-in. centers, in line with 2x6 wall studs. As shown in the drawing at left, the lower chord of each truss bears directly on the top plate of the wall, and plywood stiffeners were nailed in place between TJIs at the eaves. These also act as baffles, preventing insulation from settling over the soffits and soffit vents. A second baffle, cut from 3⁄16-in. tempered hardboard, was nailed to the undersides of the top chords. This baffle, which extends several inches above the attic insulation level, creates an air channel that connects the ventilated soffit to a continuous ridge vent.

There are two ceilings in the upstairs living area. Over the living/dining/kitchen area, there's a low-pitch cathedral ceiling, which gives this space a more open feeling. Over the bath and bedroom areas, the ceiling is flat. Three layers of 6-in. thick by 24-in. wide fiberglass batts installed between and over the 2x6 ceiling joists bring ceiling R-value to 57. When this insulation was installed, care was taken to stagger the joints and to alternate the direction of each layer to reduce convective heat loss.

Since this particular site has a spectacular view of Mt. Washington to the northwest, 70% of the upstairs window area faces in this direction. These windows are Quad-pane units from Weather Shield (Weather Shield Window Corp. Medford, Wis. 54451). The rest of the upstairs windows are Weather Shield Tri-pane units.

Heating and ventilation—To determine heating requirements, I used the HOTCAN II computer program from Canada's National Research Council. (Now called HOT-2000, this software is available from The Energy Efficient Building Association, c/o Northcentral Technical College, 1000 Campus Drive, Wassau, Wis. 54401.) The program told me that only 1.77 kw of electricity would be needed to keep the upstairs living space comfortable, so I used electric radiant heat in the form of ESWA heat film. (No longer available, a substitute, FLEXWATT, is available from FLEXCELL CORP., 2380 Cranberry Hwy., West Wareham, Mass. 02576.) This resistance heater consists of a thin film conductor path sandwiched between two layers of polyester film.

ESWA film comes with a factory-installed lead wire 15 ft. long. It can be stapled in place, and

From *Fine Homebuilding* magazine (August 1986) 34:67-69

each room can have its own thermostat. ESWA is meant to be used beneath drywall, and I chose to install it just above the ceiling drywall. With no baseboards or heat registers in the floor or walls, this heating system (which totalled 2.2kw) wouldn't get in the way of furniture.

The one constraint on the use of ESWA (or any other heating source) has to do with high-temperature degradation of poly vapor retarders. Studies at the Swedish Royal Institute of Building Sciences indicate that prolonged exposure to heat in excess of 140°F can damage some polyethylene sheet material. In order to prevent this, I separated the ceiling poly from the heat film. First, 1x3 furring strips were nailed across the ceiling joists on 24-in. centers. Then R-3.75 extruded polystyrene insulation (¾ in. thick) was tacked up between the 1x3s where the ESWA film was to be placed. Finally, the heat film was stapled to the furring strips, and the drywall was installed (drawing, right).

Downstairs, the garage and workshop are heated by an Empire model 235 direct-vent propane gas heater (Empire Stove Co., 918 Freeburg Ave., Belleville, Ill. 62222). This unit, which is rated at 35,000 Btu, delivers heat more quickly than the ESWA panels, an important feature given its intermittent use.

Limited space and energy conservation were determining factors in choosing a system for domestic hot water. I opted for a pair of Heatrae model 7000 electric tankless heaters (no longer available, a substitute is available from W.W. Granger Inc., 1-800-521-5585). Located under the kitchen sink on the wall between the kitchen and bathroom, these units were installed in series, so that the water to be heated passes through both heaters. Tankless heaters are economical because they draw electricity only on demand.

Based on studies done on other superinsulated homes, I projected an air-change rate of between .10 and .12 per hour from the upstairs living space. With a house this tight, some form of mechanical ventilation is required. I specified a Nutone model AE-200 heat-recovery ventilator, (now sold by Honeywell USA, 1985 Douglas Drive North, Golden Valley, Minn. 55422). Installed in the ceiling, this unit exhausts stale air from the bathroom and kitchen and supplies a balanced amount of fresh air to the living room and master bedroom. Since the volume of the living space is quite small, the exchanger can operate in the 80 to 100 cfm (cubic feet per minute) range for only a few hours each day and still provide comfortable, clean air at about 45% relative humidity.

The bottom line—The house was finished in the summer of 1984, and occupied shortly thereafter. I rented the apartment to a young couple, and they operate a sign-painting business downstairs. Construction costs totalled $39,750. This doesn't include the lot, but it does include well and septic. The cost of the building breaks down to about $35 per sq. ft. for the upstairs apartment; the 900-sq. ft. lower level came in at $15 per sq. ft.

As I'd hoped, the house has been inexpensive to heat. From September 1984 through April 1986, the average monthly electric bill was just under $60 for all appliances, lighting, cooking, hot water and heat (at $.08 per kw). Experience of two full winters indicates that the apartment's space-heating costs are less than $120 per season in this 8,000 degree-day climate.

My predictions about the popularity of a garage apartment with workspace seem to have come true as well. This project received an Energy Innovation Award from the Maine Office of Energy Resources in July of 1985, and soon after this, my design won an award in the U. S. Dept. of Energy's National Energy Innovation Competition under the D.O.E.'s Technology Transfer '80s program. □

Howard Faulkner is a professor of architectural design at the University of Southern Maine. For details about plans and specifications, write him c/o University of Southern Maine, School of Applied Science, Gorham, Maine 04038.

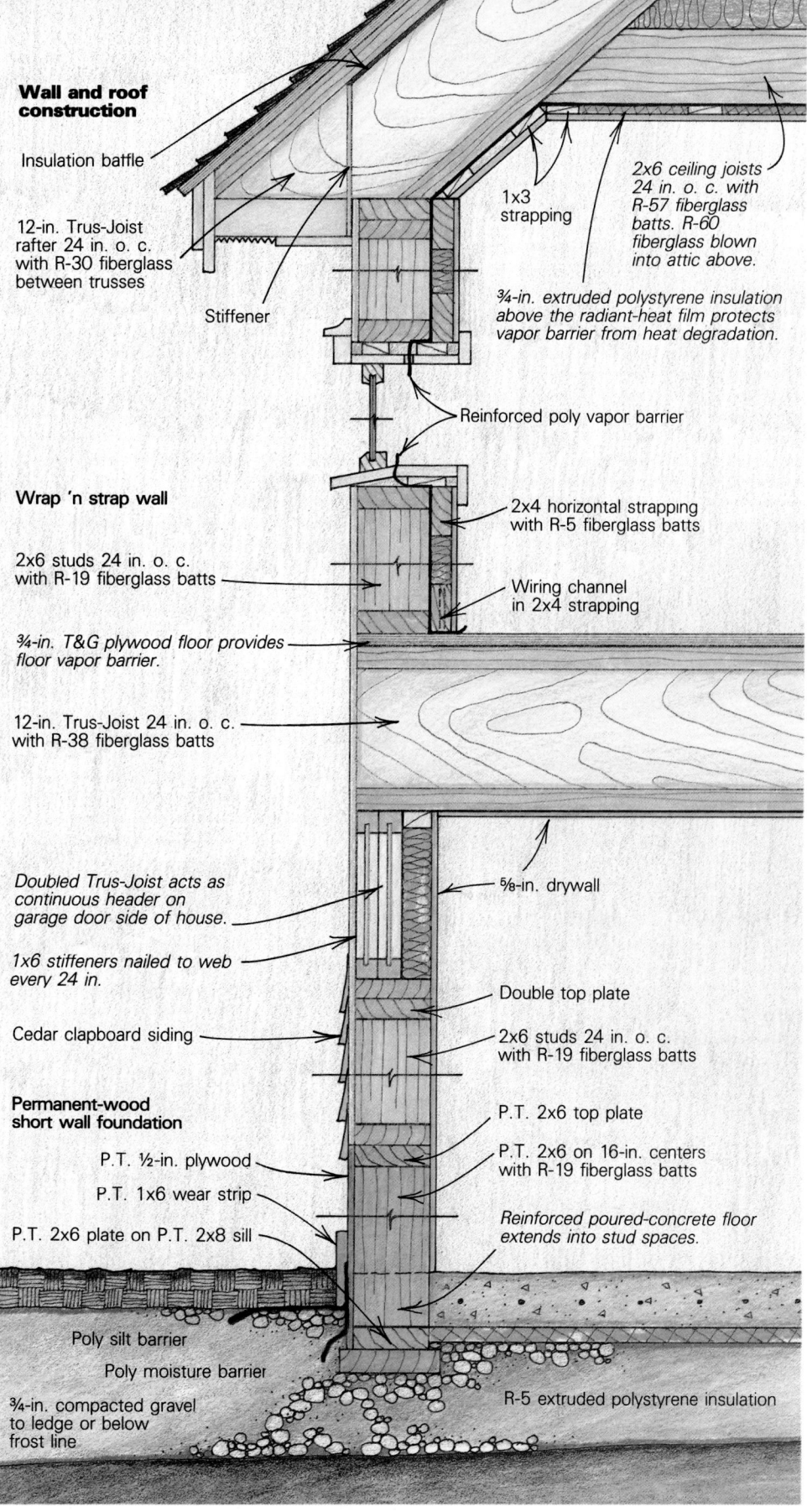

Wall and roof construction

Insulation baffle

12-in. Trus-Joist rafter 24 in. o. c. with R-30 fiberglass between trusses

Stiffener

1x3 strapping

2x6 ceiling joists 24 in. o. c. with R-57 fiberglass batts. R-60 fiberglass blown into attic above.

¾-in. extruded polystyrene insulation above the radiant-heat film protects vapor barrier from heat degradation.

Reinforced poly vapor barrier

Wrap 'n strap wall

2x6 studs 24 in. o. c. with R-19 fiberglass batts

¾-in. T&G plywood floor provides floor vapor barrier.

12-in. Trus-Joist 24 in. o. c. with R-38 fiberglass batts

2x4 horizontal strapping with R-5 fiberglass batts

Wiring channel in 2x4 strapping

Doubled Trus-Joist acts as continuous header on garage door side of house.

1x6 stiffeners nailed to web every 24 in.

Cedar clapboard siding

Permanent-wood short wall foundation

P.T. ½-in. plywood

P.T. 1x6 wear strip

P.T. 2x6 plate on P.T. 2x8 sill

Poly silt barrier

Poly moisture barrier

¾-in. compacted gravel to ledge or below frost line

⅝-in. drywall

Double top plate

2x6 studs 24 in. o. c. with R-19 fiberglass batts

P.T. 2x6 top plate

P.T. 2x6 on 16-in. centers with R-19 fiberglass batts

Reinforced poured-concrete floor extends into stud spaces.

R-5 extruded polystyrene insulation

Tract-House Transformation
Making a cramped house feel roomy—without adding on

by Stan Malek

The story starts back in August of 1988, when I purchased a three-bedroom straight ranch. It sat on a half acre of land in a flat development built in the early 1970s. The development is full of what one sees across the country: low budget, high-profit spec houses, where quality, craftsmanship and variety are sacrificed. With the exception of paint colors and roof styles—some have hip roofs, others gables—all the houses on the one-quarter-mile cul de sac are identical.

The developer not only skimped on the houses, but stripped the development of all surface loam, leaving very little natural vegetation. The impression one gets is of a barren and flat midwestern road with classy air force-base housing placed on either side.

The 960-sq. ft. house I bought was laid out as one small box next to another, with a hallway running down the center (floor plan, p. 19). The most striking feature of the interior was its darkness. All rooms had dark-stained casings, baseboards and doors. Some of the walls had been covered with dark paneling, while others had either been wallpapered or painted with ugly colors. The 8-ft. high ceilings had been sprayed with textured paint and decorated with artificial beams, also stained dark (top right photo, p. 18). Dark cabinets lurked in the kitchen and bathroom (photo right). It was a very rigid and confining layout; a hip roof covered the maze.

Though I had bought the house as an investment property, I planned to live in it for a while so I wanted to transform its depressing interior. The one limitation was money; my $8,000 budget meant that an addition was out of the

question. The challenge, then, was how to make a small house feel larger without adding on.

Vaulted ceilings—Much of my work as a designer involves the use of visual techniques to make small spaces seem larger. By using the entire volume of a house (adding headroom instead of floor space), by choosing bright interior colors, and by adding natural light and well-placed light fixtures, I can create illusions of a grand scale. These techniques let me transform my own house from a dark and dingy arrangement of little boxes into a lively, bright, and visually spacious new home. And because the labor was my own, I completed the project within my budget.

The centerpiece of my design was the vaulted ceiling. The original roof had been framed with 2x4 wood trusses, 2 ft. o. c. After tearing out the old ceiling and rerouting the existing

A fresh coat of paint and some new skylights are the only hints of the transformation within this tract house (photo above). The difference between old and new was particularly dramatic in the kitchen (photos below and right). Cabinets and appliances were painted to save on replacement costs.

wiring, I removed each truss, one by one, leaving the existing top chord, and sistered a 2x8 rafter to each chord. I vented the hip by drilling six ½-in. holes at the intersection of each jack rafter with the hip rafter. This allows air from the lower hip bays to rise to the ridge and out through the ridge vent.

I installed a pair of collar ties every 4 ft., nailing them to both sides of every other rafter (large photo, p. 18). Doubling the collar ties emphasizes their structural function; leaving them open gives a lighter feeling to the ceiling space than would have been possible had I boxed them in somehow.

I also attached a double 2x6 collar tie to the common rafter at each end of the house. I secured this to the first collar tie that spanned the house's width with lag bolts and construction adhesive. I continued this pattern the entire length of the house, filling the intersections with laminated 2x6 blocking. The result is a crosslike framework that visually and structurally joins the house from side to side and from end to end. The collar ties are the first thing people notice as they enter the house. The crosslike pattern is repeated in details throughout the house, as in the basement stair surround (photo, p. 19) and kitchen tile floor (photo facing page).

Walls and ceilings—I stripped off all the old wallpaper and dark paneling. I also removed the fake brick veneer below the kitchen-wall cabinets. Then I renailed the walls and recoated them with joint compound.

All walls and new ceilings were painted with Pro Mar 200, a top-grade latex semi-gloss pure white

paint from Sherwin-Williams (101 Prospect Ave. NW, Cleveland, Ohio 44115; 216-566-2000). I sanded down all the woodwork—doors and windows as well as trim and cabinetry—and primed it with two coats of stain killer. I finished the woodwork with Pro Mar 400, an oil-base semi-gloss. The color I chose was an off-white with a light-brown hue. The hue blended well with the overall color scheme of the house, which is brown and white. The outside of the house is two-tone brown with a rose color to highlight the details (top photo, p. 16). I kept the existing carpets, which were a light brown in color, and installed in the kitchen a white vinyl floor with a brown border (photo previous page). The white tiles add brightness to the space, while the dark-brown border emphasizes and defines the kitchen area. I kept the existing cabinets and appliances and had them repainted to save on costs. Luckily for me, a friend in the auto-body business was willing to come to my house to spray paint the appliances with acrylic enamel. I painted the hardware throughout the house a semi-gloss black.

The importance of lighting—Natural light brightens small spaces and reinforces the sense of spaciousness created by the vaulted ceilings. I introduced natural light by installing venting skylights in every room. I used APC venting skylights because of their low cost and reliability (APC Corp., 50 Utter Ave., Hawthorne, N. J. 07506; 201-423-2900). The skylights also allow heat to escape during the summer.

The bedrooms are isolated from the living area and from each other by partitions that rise from the level of the old ceiling plane to the new ceiling (drawing facing page). The placement of these walls created several soffits. I installed indirect track lighting on these, hiding the lights wherever possible behind plants, planter boxes or books. Most lighting in the house is either Halo track lighting (Halo Lighting, Cooper Industries Inc., 400 Busse Rd., Elk Grove Village, Il. 60007; 708-956-8400), facing upward, or Lightolier's black verti-groove recessed lighting (100 Lighting Way, Secaucus, N. J. 07096-1508; 201-864-3000), facing downward. The only exceptions are a cord-hung white glass globe in the hallway and a Lightolier hanging lamp over the kitchen table. At night the walls and ceilings are awash in light, helping to approximate the daytime brilliance. Harsh glare is eliminated because the lights are out of sight.

The soffits above the kitchen area help define a more intimate activity within a larger vertical space. Plants overflow from the soffits, adding color to the space and helping to clean the air. They also soften the hardness of the edges and the whiteness of the walls.

Unity through details—The base of the kitchen table is an abstracted version of a classical column (photo previous page). It was built from #2 pine and painted to match the house's colors. The tabletop is 3½-ft. dia. bronze-tinted

Photo: Staff

Removing the ceilings introduced some breathing room (photo above) into a formerly stifling interior (photo above right). White paint and natural light brightened the living room and kitchen considerably. The open collar ties emphasize the living area's feeling of spaciousness.

From *Fine Homebuilding* magazine (August 1990) 62:46-49

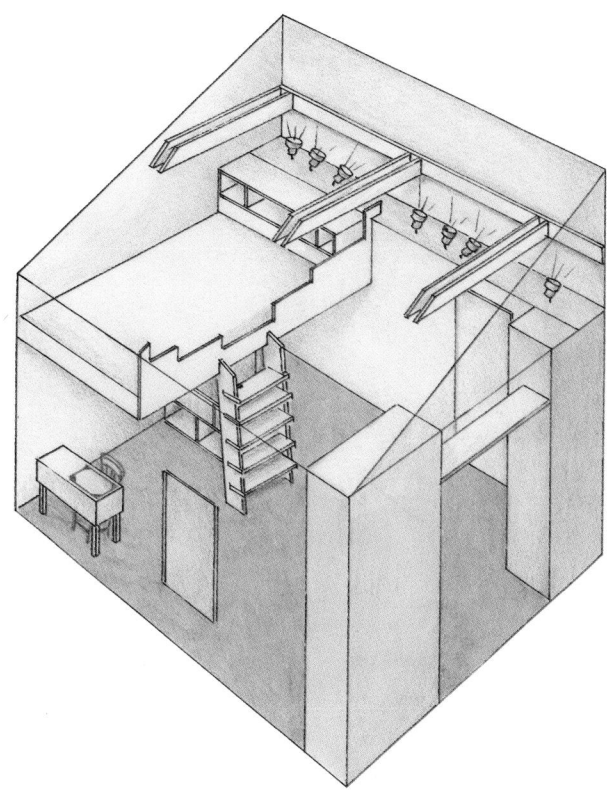

NORTH

Screen porch

Bath

Bedroom

Kitchen

Design studio

Bedroom

Living room

glass. The bronze tint blends with the house's overall color scheme.

The living room is an extension of the kitchen. These two spaces are tied together visually and physically by the vaulted ceiling and the collar ties. Two hip rafters trisect the ceiling into three separate planes. Black contemporary sectional furniture defines the space and controls traffic. It also contrasts with the whiteness of the walls. Wall prints and plants add color and enhance the scheme. The coffee table is a smaller version of the kitchen table, with a 3-ft. dia. bronze-tinted glass top.

The hallway to the bedrooms acts as a transitional space. Its low ceiling plane reinforces the dramatic effect of the vaulted ceilings elsewhere. I framed a narrow soffit 6 ft. 10 in. from the floor, and its narrow, long horizon lines make the hallway look lower and longer than it really is; that strengthens the contrast between it and the living areas. A round hanging lamp moderates the soffit's sharp edges. It also reinforces the ceiling lines as the hallway's focal point.

In the bathroom, I kept the existing tub, toilet, sink and vanity top. I made new pine cabinet doors and painted them the same off-white as the rest of the woodwork. I also installed new pine shelving, added a full-size mirror to make the space look larger, and installed the same white floor tile I had used in the kitchen. The soffit plants thrive on the bathroom's humidity, get plenty of light from the skylight, and add color, a bit of nature and oxygen to the space.

The bedrooms are similar to each other and to the rest of the house, with vaulted ceilings, operable skylights, exposed collar ties and indirect lighting. The front corner bedroom serves as my design studio. The soffit ledge above the door has become a bookshelf for my architectural manuals (they also disguise the track lighting).

My own bedroom is where I realized the most efficient use of limited space. It's a small, 10-ft. by 10-ft. room off the midpoint of the hallway (drawing above). I built a bunk bed with a bookshelf headboard halfway up the wall, leaving valuable space below for a desk, a bureau, a bookshelf, some storage units, and a clothes pole. This design increased the room's usable space by more than a third. □

Stan Malek is an architectural renovation specialist. He is founder of The Malek Group, in Granby, Massachusetts. Photos by author except where noted.

Opening up the old stairwell (bottom right photo, facing page) visually enlarged the living room and kitchen (photo above). The crossed balusters match the intersections of the open collar ties. The steps will be painted or carpeted and the basement remodeled into additional living space.

Escape from Manhattan

A Catskill retreat shaped by thoughtful massing and a simple plan

by Jeffrey Dale Bianco

Four weeks into the start of our new architectural practice, my former partner, Neal Zimmerman, took a day off. Much to my surprise, he returned the next day with our first custom residential commission.

Neal had traveled three hours on a "busman's holiday" to visit his good friends Ken Haas and Jackie Costello. They were about to close on a country house in New York's Catskill Mountains—their retreat from Greenwich Village. Luckily for them, Neal offered to inspect the house. During a brief walkthrough with Ken, Neal observed major foundation and structural problems. Ken withdrew his offer for the property (which subsequently was condemned) and asked Neal if we would consider designing a new weekend retreat for them instead. With that in mind, they embarked on

a tour of the area, looking for a building lot that satisfied three criteria: dramatic views, privacy, and access to public roads and utilities. They found just what they were looking for—a six-acre parcel in a new subdivision that commanded a dramatic 270° view of the Catskills.

Unfortunately, they discovered that the lot and the adjacent comparable properties had just been sold to a spec-house builder. Ken made an offer for his preferred lot and was rejected because the builder, Adam Cyrek of Country Elegance, Inc., wanted to sell a spec house with it. Neal and Ken visited Cyrek and toured some of his completed projects. While they found the houses to be well built, Ken's heart was now set on a custom home.

The solution was a compromise. Cyrek agreed to build a house of our design on the

lot with the best view. In return, we agreed to design the house as a variation on one of Cyrek's typical models so that he wouldn't have to alter his methods drastically to build it. Because we found Cyrek's workmanship and use of materials to be acceptable (stuccoed block foundations, 2x6 wall framing, pressure-treated decks, stained cedar clapboards over OSB sheathing, and Andersen windows), we designed around the 26-ft. by 36-ft. footprint of Cyrek's "La Crosse" model.

A site-sensitive plan—When Ken first visited our office, he brought with him a stack of window manufacturers' product literature showing floor-to-ceiling and gable-end infill glass. I realized that a glass wall represented Ken and Jackie's vision of their weekend retreat. Unfor-

Photos above and facing page: Jeffrey Dale Bianco

tunately, the best views on the site are to the north and northwest (especially in the winter after the trees shed their leaves). I had a vision of my own—Ken and Jackie huddled under a wool blanket in the corner of the room most distant from the glass, shivering and cursing me. We convinced Ken that an equally spectacular panorama could be framed with a continuous horizontal band of double-glazed casement windows, reducing heat loss considerably without sacrificing the view. This detail became the *parti*, or unifying scheme of the building plan.

Ken and Jackie gave us a space budget of approximately 1,250 sq. ft., encompassing an eat-in kitchen, a large combination living/dining room, a guest room that Jackie would also use as a writing room, a three-quarter guest bath (toilet, sink and shower), a master-bedroom suite with a full bath, and a walkout basement that could later be finished into additional living space. Neal and I were determined to develop a site-responsive floor plan that would organize these rooms as simply as possible to squeeze the most out of the available square footage (drawing next page). We placed the kitchen, living/dining room and guest room on the first floor, with the living room oriented to the northwest and wrapped with casements to soak up the view (photo next page).

The main entry faces southeast and consists of two adjacent doors—one opening into the kitchen and the other serving as a private entry into the guest room. The entry is shielded by the house from the winter storms that typically blow in from the north. The kitchen and guest room are linked by a pair of pocket doors to allow a choice between privacy and open circulation. Upstairs, the master-bedroom suite lies directly above the kitchen and guest room. A 2½-ft. square cased opening with operable shutters in the bedroom's north wall draws heat, light and a little ambience from below.

A prowed roof— Building massing and particularly rooflines have the principal impact on a house's image. Given the small stature of this building, we hoped to maximize that impact. We began by designing a simple gable on the entry side of the house, presenting on approach the iconographic image of "home" (photo facing page). This gable end also yielded a large surface area for glazing and solar gain.

Cyrek's typical spec house has an 8-in-12 pitch roof. We convinced him and our clients that a tall roof pitch (14-in-12), although more costly, was needed to increase headroom on

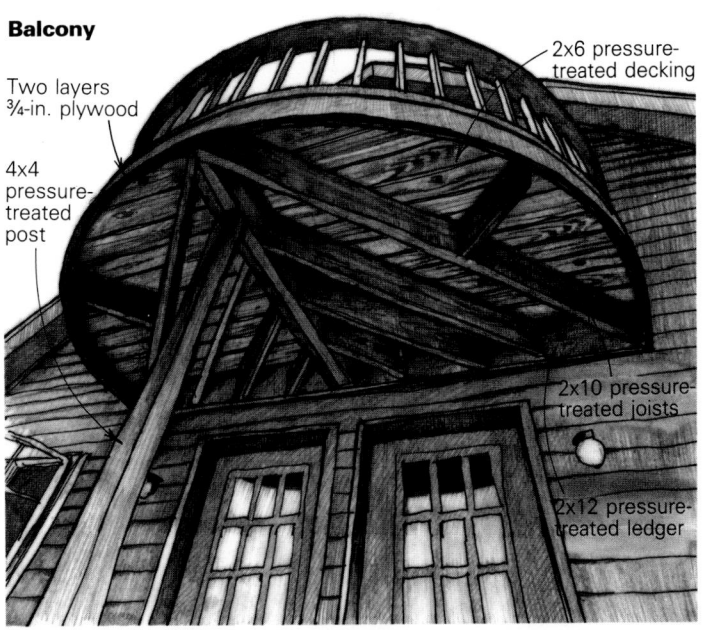

Balcony

Two layers ¾-in. plywood

4x4 pressure-treated post

2x6 pressure-treated decking

2x10 pressure-treated joists

2x12 pressure-treated ledger

On approach, the house, with its symmetrical gable end and semicircular front porch (photo facing page), presents a classic image of "home." The generous use of south-facing glazing in the front elevation encourages solar gain, and the split entry allows access to both kitchen and guest room. Out back (photo above), a hip roof deflects winter storms, while casement windows collect views of the Catskills.

the second floor and to create the proper proportions for the front elevation. We added two dormers symmetrically on the gable, one on either side, which increased the floor space in the master bedroom (top photo, p. 23).

On the north side of the house, we sliced off the gable to create a hip roof, thus reducing the volume of the conditioned space in the living room while creating a prow to deflect the north winds (photo above). This also created distinctive massing in that the front, back and sides of the house each have a distinctive elevation.

Finally we added a semicircular balcony off the master bedroom to provide access to views and to complete the composition of the front façade. This also allowed us to add a significant amount of south-facing glass on the second floor by using sliding-glass doors.

Cyrek wanted to frame this balcony by cantilevering the second-floor joists. However, I

generally prefer to have a balcony "added on" for an improved weather seal by nailing a single flashed ledger to the sheathing as opposed to having a series of cantilevered joists penetrate the building envelope. This add-on method uses less pressure-treated lumber than would the cantilevered method (because cantilevered joists would be pressure-treated both inside and outside the building line). As a bonus, it creates an interesting herringbone pattern from beneath as joists intersect decking (drawing left).

My logic won out. The balcony is supported by a ledger and by a 4x4 post near the midpoint of its periphery. The balcony is such an integral feature of the façade that we echoed its diameter for the tile hearth in the living room.

Working out the hips— The rest of the framing was essentially straightforward 2x stick construction, except for the cathedral ceiling over the living room. In this case I chose a slight complication of construction to accomplish a simplified interior design. Early in the history of the design, we drew the hip roof at a 12-in-12 pitch. There was to be a large structural column—sort of a central mast—to support the intersection of the main ridge beam and the two hip rafters. I figured the column could incorporate the boiler flue, tie into the stair railing and, with the woodstove backed up to it, act as a white backdrop for the black stove pipe. Everyone else, however, felt that a column would obstruct the open living room, so we agreed to explore other ways to carry the roof.

Back at the drawing board, I reduced the pitch of the hip roof to 10-in-12 and increased its span so that the hip rafters and ridge beam converged directly over and were supported by the north wall of the master bedroom. I then drew the dormer gables at a 10-in-12 pitch to mirror the pitch of the hip roof. This not only eliminated the need for a separate load-bearing post to support the roof, but it also looked better both inside and outside.

However, the solution was not without problems. I didn't think Cyrek would view the use of ponderous steel beams or flitch beams for hip rafters as a minor variation on his typical house. The use of wood trusses, space frames (3-D structural frames) or collar ties to support the roof would make Cyrek equally uncomfortable and obstruct the open space above the living room.

So I sought advice from Bill LaPointe of Santo Domingo Engineers, who suggested the use of laminated-veneer lumber for the two

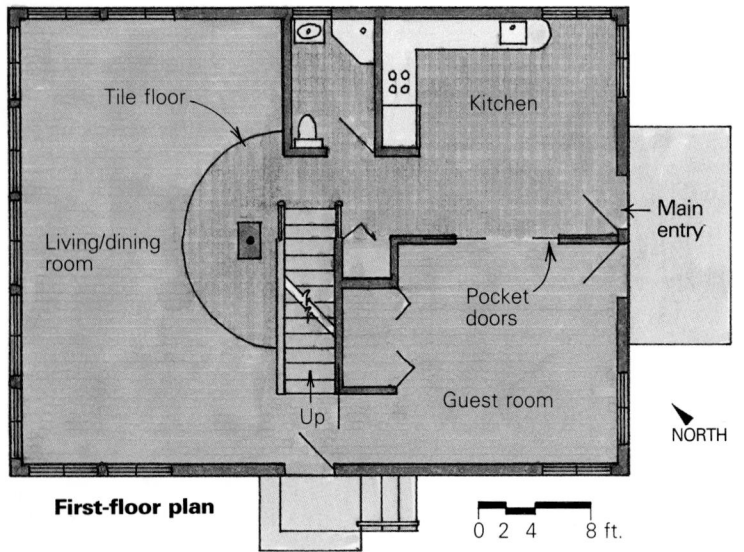

The living room blends aesthetics with energy efficiency. It's wrapped with double-glazed casement windows to capture the views to the northwest, while its hip roof reduces the volume of the conditioned space and deflects the northerly winds.

hip rafters. I mention this for good reason. I took three years of structural design in architecture school, am fairly technically oriented and am licensed by the states of New York and Connecticut to design structures. Nevertheless, I routinely call upon the expertise of engineering consultants—after all, they do this type of work eight hours a day. In this case, I also asked LaPoint to review all the specs, not just the roof span, and he downsized some of the framing members to save on materials where I had been more conservative.

Scored stucco, textured shingles—Cyrek's typical house sits on a stuccoed concrete-

block foundation, just the type of visually solid base we wanted beneath this house. Our only modification to Cyrek's foundation was to call for the scoring of the stucco on a 2-ft. by 2-ft. grid, which added visual interest to the large exposed foundation walls (photo, previous page).

The other exterior upgrade we requested was the use of Georgia-Pacific's Summit brand architectural, laminated-fiberglass shingles (Georgia-Pacific Corp., 133 Peachtree St., 20th Floor, Marketing Services, Atlanta, Ga., 30303). Though these shingles are more than twice as expensive as standard fiberglass shingles, they produce an appealing shadowline that comple-

ments this roof perfectly, plus they're warranted for 30 years instead of the usual 20 years.

Cyrek typically provides continuous eave and ridge vents, and he chose the products on this job. The hip rafters have holes drilled at the top to vent the hip roof.

A stock interior—The interior features a simple palette of materials. The floors in the kitchen and bathrooms are paved with 6-in. by 6-in. American Olean Pale Gray quarry tiles (1000 Cannon Ave., Lansdale, Pa. 19446). On the main floor, the tile is continuous in the kitchen, bathroom and hall, bleeding into the living room to serve as a semicircular hearth for the

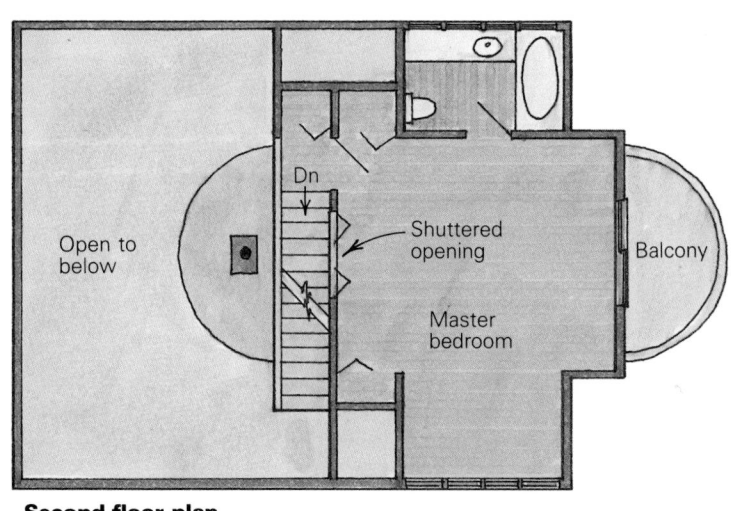

First-floor plan

Tile floor

Living/dining room

Kitchen

Main entry

Pocket doors

Guest room

Up

NORTH

0 2 4 8 ft.

Second-floor plan

Open to below

Dn

Shuttered opening

Balcony

Master bedroom

woodstove (photo below). The rest of the floors are ¾-in. T&G oak strip flooring finished with three coats of satin urethane finish.

I lobbied for the installation of a ¾-in. plywood subfloor beneath the tile and a ⅝-in. plywood subfloor beneath the oak to achieve a level transition between the two flooring materials, but Cyrek wouldn't do it. Instead, he tapered the edge of the oak slightly to ease the transition. You can't win them all.

The walls are ⅝-in. drywall for a little extra durability, while the ceilings are ½-in. drywall. Trim is spare throughout, consisting of simple stock baseboards and casings stained a natural color. To save money, we also specified flush hollow-core doors with the thought that they can easily be upgraded in the future.

The burning issue—Cyrek's typical spec houses include a zero-clearance fireplace to supplement the main heating system (which consists of hot-water radiant baseboards connected to a gas-fired boiler in the basement). He usually installs the fireplace at the outboard end of the living room. However, none of us wanted to obstruct the view with a fireplace, nor did I want to pitch water against the backside of a chimney. Though a properly installed cricket will divert water around a chimney, I prefer to work with gravity and place chimneys at the ridge whenever possible. Neal, who had recently returned from many years in the Southwest with thinned blood (the placement of his wool cap is an annual event), proposed the installation of a woodstove for extra heat production on those cold Catskill nights. We felt comfortable having a stove exposed on three sides because Ken and Jackie don't have children. I also liked the idea of the stove as the centerpiece of the house, using the tile hearth as an integrating feature.

We ordered what was supposed to be a readily available Vermont Castings stove (Vermont Castings, Inc., Prince St., Randolph, Vt. 05060; 802-728-3181), but it arrived late and was installed in the late spring after the clients moved in. By that time they were used to the room without it and thought it made the room look like "a factory." But when an unexpected spring snowstorm hit, they fired up the stove to keep warm and decided it didn't look so bad after all.

The only regret I have with the house is that to save money the heating contractor refused to offset the boiler flue in the ceiling as we specified so that it would terminate in the fireplace chimney. Instead, he ran the flue straight up, and the additional chimney required for it alongside one dormer still bothers me. Cyrek likes the completed house so much that he had us redesign the plans for his own new house, to be built just down the road from "the chapel," his nickname for the Haas-Costello house. As for Ken and Jackie, they fled Manhattan altogether, and now occupy the house year around. □

Jeffrey Dale Bianco is an architect in Middletown, Connecticut.

Two gable dormers in the master-bedroom suite make space for a bath on one side of the room and a sleeping alcove on the other. The bedroom is further enlarged by the semicircular porch out front.

Surrounded by oak strip flooring, a sea of quarry tile underlies the woodstove in the living room and continues down the hall into the kitchen and bathroom. Upstairs, the master-bedroom suite peeks into the living room through an opening fitted with bifold shutters.

A Little Place in the City

Even though a house is small, it doesn't have to feel that way

by Chuck Miller

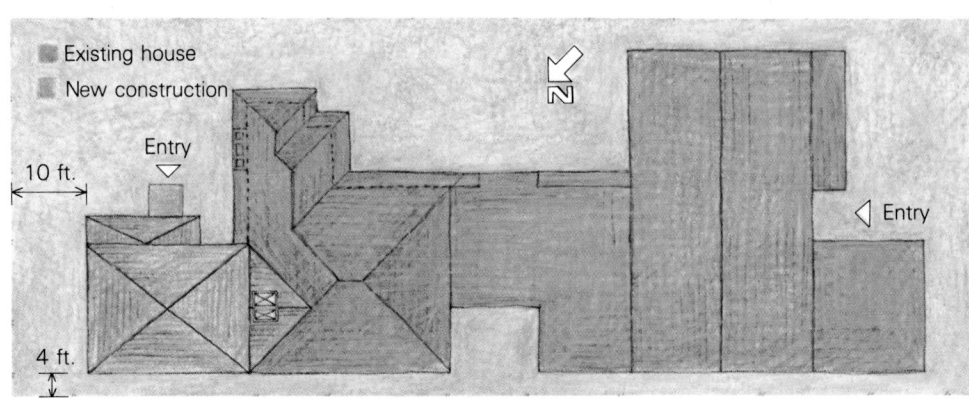

Existing house
New construction

Entry

10 ft.

4 ft.

Entry

Last winter, a front-page story in San Francisco's morning newspaper told about a British developer's plan to make housing affordable again. The project, a condominium development in Fremont, Calif., offered two compact floor plans—one of 440 sq. ft. and the other, 490 sq. ft. Completed, they will cost between $50,000 and $60,000, and be among the smallest homes ever offered for sale in the United States. Patterned after the studio-solo spaces common throughout Europe, the tiny condos are aimed at single, first-time home buyers who can't afford to spend more than $500 to $600 per month on housing.

A few hours after the affordable-housing article appeared on Bay area breakfast tables, the topic was being batted around on the local call-in radio station. For two hours a surprisingly polarized succession of callers argued the benefits and drawbacks of the small house. Toward the end of the talk show, a Berkeley architect named Thomas Lee Turman called in to tell about a 580-sq. ft. house he and his partner had designed. Its description generated so much interest that Turman was invited to give his phone number in case anybody wanted to find out more about it. Turman had to take the rest of the day off to answer the calls.

Design factors—Turman's building started out on the drawing board as a guest-bedroom addition to a 1950s ranch-style house. The owners needed room for their grown children's families to stay during visits. Turman and his associate, Steve Buhler, suggested a more independent kind of addition—one with its own entrance, living area, bath and tiny kitchen—to lessen the burden on the main house. The owners agreed, and gave the go-ahead.

Like many structures in the city, this little house was largely shaped by building-code requirements, site conditions and local style. The trick was to juggle the restrictions to create a design that worked. Setbacks whittled possible dimensions down to 15 ft. on a side, so the owners sought a variance to narrow the setbacks. They won their case by demonstrating with drawings that a larger addition wouldn't

Seen from the south, the hipped roof of the addition and its entry echo the roofline of the original house. The floor plan (drawing, facing page) takes advantage of a change in grade to isolate areas of activity and gain headroom under the sleeping loft.

be out of keeping with the character of the neighborhood or block any views. The buildable area grew to 20 ft. by 21 ft.

Drawings showed that a simple two-story building with a second-floor sleeping loft would fit in nicely with the existing house when topped with a matching shake-covered hip roof (drawing, facing page). Using production-framed walls and standard-dimension materials kept costs down, and an insulated slab-on-grade did double duty as a heat sink and as a first-level finish floor. The architects saw a 2-ft. rise in grade as an opportunity to vary the ground-floor elevations, rather than a reason to call in the excavators to flatten the lot. Within the basic box, Turman and Buhler devised an open plan around a central living area (drawing, right).

A step inside—The exterior siding, with its muted greyish-green finish (photo facing page), doesn't hint at the interior's variety of shapes and colors. Just past the 8-ft. entry ceiling, the space opens to expose the entire roof structure. Visible from nearly every point in the house, the ceiling pulls the eyes up and emphasizes the generous vertical dimension. It's a well-played trick that makes the space feel twice its size. The heavy rafters, careful joinery and western red-cedar decking are a pleasure to look at, and can be faulted only for the neckstrain they may cause (photo next page).

The sleeping loft takes a diagonal jog across the second-floor beamwork, creating a low ceiling below that seems to add an extra space to the living area. Instead of a busy row of tightly spaced balustrades, the designers combined a railing-height gypboard wall for privacy (drawing p. 27, bottom right) near the dressing area, and a tempered glass panel adjacent to the passageway. The glass allows a view of the ceiling from below, and a glimpse of the pine-tree garden from the bed in the loft.

Consistent and uncluttered detailing is another element in the success of this little place. Rather than play down the square nature of the building, Turman and Buhler chose to elaborate on it as a unifying theme. Square wooden windows were custom-made in various sizes to use either in clusters or individually to frame a special view. Square low-fired tiles from Italy, tinted reddish brown with water-base pigments, cover the downstairs slab floor. Smaller tiles on the kitchen and bathroom counters repeat the grid-like pattern, but in different colors and scale.

Kitchen—Locating the kitchen on the lower ground-floor level had two advantages. For one, plumbing runs were kept to a minimum because the new pipes could be tied into the existing lines in the adjacent house. More important, the change in level created a conversation zone that puts people sitting at the counter in the living room and someone working in the kitchen, at eye level. In a sense, this design borrows space from two separate areas to create a third (photo top of p. 27).

The U-shaped kitchen counter gives the cook access to work stations and appliances without any wasted steps, and the hallway, required be-

Illustrations: Christopher Clapp

East elevation

Storage
Loft
Soaking pool
Loft closet
Entry to original house
Bathroom
Refrigerator
Hall
Living area
Kitchen
Oak counter
W.H.
Closet

Floor plan

Bath
Hall
Kitchen
W.H.
Living
Entry
Bedroom loft
Loft closet

Because the hip roof comes to a point and covers a rectangle rather than a square, the rafter/king-post junction (photo facing page and drawing, below) gave builder Ed Kelly plenty to scratch his head over. Instead of doing all the work on scaffolds 16 ft. above the ground, Kelly made a mockup king post and cut the two pairs of common rafters before the walls were framed. He used the mudsills as substitutes for the wall plates while temporarily assembling the rafters a few feet above the slab to check for accuracy. Once the walls were up, Kelly planted the real king post at the desired height and assembled the precut pieces. Each rafter is lag-bolted to the king post from above, and further bound by let-in steel straps across the tops of opposing rafters. Collar ties were added after the jack rafters were bolted in place.

The sloping site was worked into a two-level ground floor with the kitchen on the lower level. A pass-through to the living area includes a chair-high counter for eating or for chatting with the cook (photos, right). Red cedar walls, fir posts and rafters and the red oak countertop establish the dominant warm colors carried throughout the house.

The bathroom (far right) takes up only 50 sq. ft. but its two-level ceiling and carefully chosen appliances keep it from feeling tiny. A 40-in. deep soaking tub (here reflected in the vanity mirror) occupies only a small corner. And there's much needed storage above the vanity and below the drying bench.

cause codes do not allow bathrooms to open onto a kitchen, feels like part of the workspace.

A 20-gallon Hoyt water heater (Hoyt Heater Co., P.O. Box 60129, Reno, Nev. 89506) is tucked under the counter to the right of the sink. Measuring a mere 25½ in. high by 22 in. in diameter, including its thermal blanket, the heater runs on 110 volts, needs its own 20-amp circuit, and has to be used judiciously—it doesn't reheat very fast.

Bathroom—Instead of an ordinary tub or shower, the bathroom (photo center right) has a fiberglass soaking pool with a telephone-style shower head on a hose. Made by American Standard (P.O. Box 2003, New Brunswick, N.J. 08903), the pool is 40 in. deep by 40 in. in diameter, and has a built-in seat. These fixtures eliminate the need for a cramped shower stall in a small room. The bathroom's two ceiling heights draw attention away from its scant 50 sq. ft. and play a practical role—the lower ceiling is the bottom of a 50-cu. ft. overhead storage space accessible from the kitchen. Three-lap teardrop redwood siding, urethaned for the moist location, covers the wall behind the slat-topped drying bench.

Moving in—When the kids came visiting for the first time, they were in for a surprise. Mom and Dad had moved into the little house, leaving the main house for them. It's much brighter and sunnier than the original home, and its views of the garden recognize the outdoors in a way that the old house doesn't. With its centerpiece ceiling 20 ft. overhead and cozy loft space in the rafters, this little house offers a congenial variety of spaces. □

From *Fine Homebuilding* magazine (October 1982) 11:42-45

Plan of king post and rafters

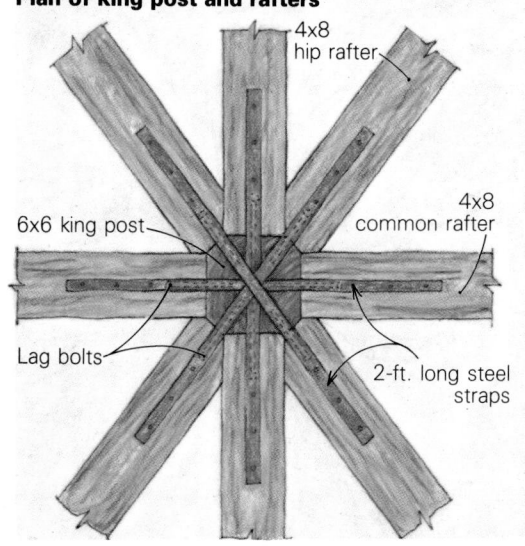

4x8 hip rafter

6x6 king post

4x8 common rafter

Lag bolts

2-ft. long steel straps

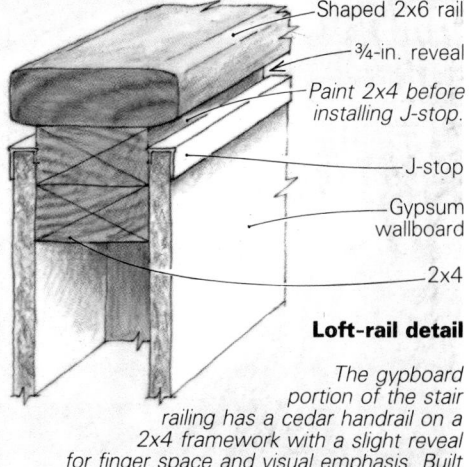

Shaped 2x6 rail

¾-in. reveal

Paint 2x4 before installing J-stop.

J-stop

Gypsum wallboard

2x4

Loft-rail detail

The gypboard portion of the stair railing has a cedar handrail on a 2x4 framework with a slight reveal for finger space and visual emphasis. Built with a J-stop for the finished edge, the detail (photo facing page) gives a finished look without tedious taping-knife work or moldings.

Main-floor plan

Dining room

Kitchen

Family room

Foyer

NORTH

Up

ENTRY

Mechanicals

Living room

Second-floor plan

Bedroom

Master bedroom

Dn

0 2 4   8 ft.

Laundry

Bedroom

Backyard Edwardian

An infill cottage inspired by Vancouver's architectural heritage

by Richard Fearn

I'm one of those people who has a soft spot for old, dilapidated buildings. In October of 1986, while driving through one of the older districts of Vancouver, British Columbia, a "cast-stone" Edwardian-era home that dates back to 1907 caught my eye. Back then, cast stones were a poor man's substitute for real stone masonry. Essentially concrete blocks, the stones were produced on site in portable molds. To give the blocks the faceted look of hand-tooling, the interior sides of the molds had undulating surfaces. Builders often used the blocks for ground-floor walls and as quoins at the corners of block buildings to add visual interest.

This home was in a very sad state of repair. Its spacious, high-ceilinged rooms had been divided into boarding-house bedrooms in the '40s. The original porches had long since rotted away and been replaced with expedient, utilitarian structures. But the elegant gable trim pieces and balcony rails were still intact. Their shapes could serve as guides to inform a restoration project, so I began to imagine the steps necessary to restore the old house to its former glory. And as I did, the soft spot started to tug on me. Within a month I'd signed a purchase agreement.

Financing—Vancouver is a very young and dynamic city known for its natural beauty. Unfortunately, the city has little respect for or appreciation of its architectural heritage. As a result, no tax incentives are offered to builders who want to refurbish buildings of merit. So my project had one strike against it before it even began. But to my benefit, the zoning of this property allowed the construction of another dwelling on the lot that could be "strata-titled," or sold off, to raise enough revenue to finance the restoration of the older house. Suddenly the project took on another dimension—in addition to putting the main house back in order, I had the task of designing and building some brand new living space that would be in keeping with the original building.

New space, old form—Because of the size of the old building, the zoning laws allowed the new structure to be no larger than 1,500 sq. ft. Faced with similar situations, most builders choose to add the new space to the existing building. I pondered that option, but decided against it because such an addition would have destroyed the symmetry of the original

building, and compromised the historical worth of the cast-stone exterior walls. Instead of an addition, I started thinking in terms of an entirely new house.

The front of the original house is fairly close to the northern extremity of a 50-ft. by 132-ft. lot. In the 20 feet between the building and the west property line, I had sufficient clearance for a driveway to service the three on-site parking spaces required for the main house. In addition to parking, this area could also serve as a buffer zone between the house and the back of the lot—a spot just big enough for a two-story house and a small patio (photo facing page).

I felt strongly that in order for the two buildings to co-exist on the same lot, the new dwelling had to be a diminutive of the existing building. This would require similar treatment of the exterior walls, soffits, windows, porches and rooflines.

With only 750 sq. ft. per floor, one must be judicious in the allocation of space. Yet, to achieve that "Edwardian feeling," I had to figure out a way to provide a spacious entrance foyer showing off a hand-crafted period-style staircase. As I struggled with this problem, it suddenly occurred to me that an L-shaped plan, with an entry in the middle, would satisfy these criteria (drawing facing page). The centrally located stair serves as a grand entry and a border that divides the living room from the dining room, kitchen and family room (top left photo, p. 31). Upstairs, three bedrooms would be located in each corner of the L. The master bedroom has its own bathroom. The other two bedrooms share a bath.

Cast-stone exterior walls—When I researched the possibility of having new molds made to reproduce the cast stone, it quickly became apparent that authenticity would have to be tempered by budget. The cheapest reproductions I could have manufactured were $30 per block. Exit that idea.

Solution number two was to modify split-faced concrete block with a diamond saw to give it the cut-stone look. Labor costs didn't make this alternative look much better. And besides, there were other drawbacks to block construction, such as how to insulate the blocks and where to run the wiring and plumbing. Also, the thick concrete-block walls would use up valuable floor space.

The third option, which became the solution, was a three-coat stucco finish with built-up stucco corner quoins over a conventional 2x4 platform frame structure. Our stucco finisher, Ralph Spyker, used screed boards to control the thickness of the added stucco at the corners. Once he had it built out and while the stucco was still soft, he used a trowel to cut away the excess stucco to give the illusion of interlocking blocks divided by mortar lines. Then he used a paint brush as though it were a small trowel to sculpt bumpy indentations that give the faux quoins their texture.

Initially, I was apprehensive about using stucco to duplicate the cast stone of the existing house. But then I considered that the existing house duplicated cut stone with molded blocks. And what about John Nash's marvelous successes in using stucco to duplicate cut stone on his developments around Regents Park in London? After all, if John Nash can do it, so can I.

Trim—While I wanted to build a house with an Edwardian feeling, I never kidded myself into thinking I could build an authentic reproduction of an Edwardian house. Time and limited funds just wouldn't allow it. Given that reality, we did our best with readily available materials and techniques.

A house that is supposed to look like it's made of stone never "feels" right with wooden steps, so we made the entry stair out of poured concrete (top right photo, p. 31). The steps are flanked by concrete plinths (with ovolo edges) and a pair of Ionic columns that we rescued from a nearby demolition. Our wood magician, Gary Fink, linked the tops of the columns with a shallow wooden arch and keystone assembly that matches the porch detail of the main house.

I decided to make the first floor a slab-on-grade because a slab costs a bit less from a schedule and labor standpoint than a joisted subfloor. But I think a wood floor is easier on the feet. Of course, you can always put down sleepers for a wood floor, but they take up valuable headroom and inevitably cause problems at stairs and doorways unless your planning is perfect. I got around this dilemma by using a prefinished hardwood floor called Kahrs Floors (25057 Viking St., Hayward, Calif. 94545). It comes in 8-in. by 96-in. T&G sheets that are later glued together at the edges. Rather than being fastened to the slab, the sheets rest on a thin foam pad. Expansion gaps at the walls allow the assembled floor to float freely, unattached to the structure; baseboards hide the gaps. This floor was a breeze to put down; it has held up well and with a material cost of about $5 per sq. ft. (depending on type of wood), I consider it worth the money.

Throughout the interior, the trim baseboards, crowns and casings have ogees, ovolos, coves and full and quarter-rounds to sustain a visual cohesiveness (drawing below). All the pieces were standard fare at the local lumberyard.

Old doors and windows—I think people underestimate the importance of doors and windows in the final appearance of a house. They are as crucial to maintaining consistency of style as moldings, and an inappropriate door or window will quickly thwart the success of an overall effect. Without knowing it, my penchant for collecting architectural antiques turned out to be critical to the harmonious detailing of this little house.

Years ago, at an open-air market of dubious repute on the east side of London, I had purchased some Edwardian-era doors and windows with no particular purpose in mind. One of the doors ended up at the entry of this house, where its leaded stained glass, semicircular arch and wood panels make the entrance both warm and inviting.

The windows worked their way into the three bathrooms (bottom left photo, facing page), the hallway and either side of the fireplace. But let me caution you that using old windows requires planning and patience. The initial problem is that of design—where should the antique go? Invariably, the door or window will need a new frame that has to fit into a rough opening, and that opening has to be conveyed to the framing crew. The implications are, obviously, that you've got to have the windows and doors well thought out early in the project. To complicate matters, leaded glass often needs repair before it can be sent out to the window makers.

Along with the doors and windows that I brought back from Europe, I included some architectural woodwork in the packing container. Among the pieces were several hundred feet of magnificent 8-in. wide mahogany handrail, along with a turned newel post. These parts became the starting points for the stairway. Using some of the 8x8 beams salvaged from the main-house basement, a local millworks turned three replicas of the newel posts (top left photo, facing page). The impact of the handrail and newel posts is so strong that people are unaware the spindles and steps are completely new.

As work progressed simultaneously on the main house, I collected a stack of old doors that didn't fit into my plans for that project. They were made of high-quality Douglas fir, with five panels each, and there were enough for the entire cottage. After removing the hardware, we stripped the endless layers of paint in a makeshift 4-ft. by 8-ft. by 16-in. tank lined

with plastic and filled with caustic solution for an overnight bath. The doors were then rinsed with water, dried, sanded, and given a wash coat of Pittsburgh Penetrating Oil Stain followed by two coats of varnish. Because older doors are invariably warped, we didn't apply their stops until they were hung in the pine jambs.

Pine, while relatively affordable in the lesser grades, is virtually impossible to stain. So our painter, Dave Romeo, used glazing techniques to transform the pine jambs and casings into turn-of-the-century stained and varnished fir. He began by brushing on a mixture of 1 part walnut stain, 1 part raw linseed oil and 2 parts Danish oil. This was allowed to dry for 48 hours in a heated house. The finish is two coats of Pittsburgh's sanding sealer. The results uncannily duplicate the rich depth of 80-year-old stained and varnished fir.

Cabinet work—With my cabinetry designs I sought to achieve the look of period furniture that was purposefully built for its location in the house. To that end, all the cabinets, shelving and valences are topped with a 3¾-in. crown molding (drawing below). This adds a unifying element that is obviously custom-made (bottom right photo, facing page). The doors close flush with the carcase, rather than overlaying the framework as is normally the case. This, too, emphasizes a furniture look

and requires a much higher degree of precision than overlay doors.

The door rails and stiles are made of 1x3 maple. They surround ¼-in. plywood panels. A ¼-in. thick maple bullnose bands all the doors, adding a slight reveal to each one. The cabinetmaker, Phillip Lipton, used a hand-mixed burgundy aniline dye (to match the exterior windows), topped with many coats of lacquer, to finish the cabinets.

The cornerstone ceremony—To celebrate the completion of the infill cottage and the restoration of the existing house, we held a cornerstone-placement ceremony on Halloween, 1987, with the Mayor of Vancouver presiding. Over 200 people attended, decked out, of course, in Edwardian garb.

The most memorable compliment I received was from an older gentleman who stopped his car in front of the main house and walked up the path toward the cottage. After a brief inspection and some head-scratching, he returned to his car. As he prepared to drive off, I overheard him exclaim to his wife, sitting quietly beside him, "For 60 years now I have been driving through this neighborhood and I can't ever remember seeing that old house in the back." I was elated. ☐

Richard Fearn is a builder and inventor from Vancouver, British Columbia.

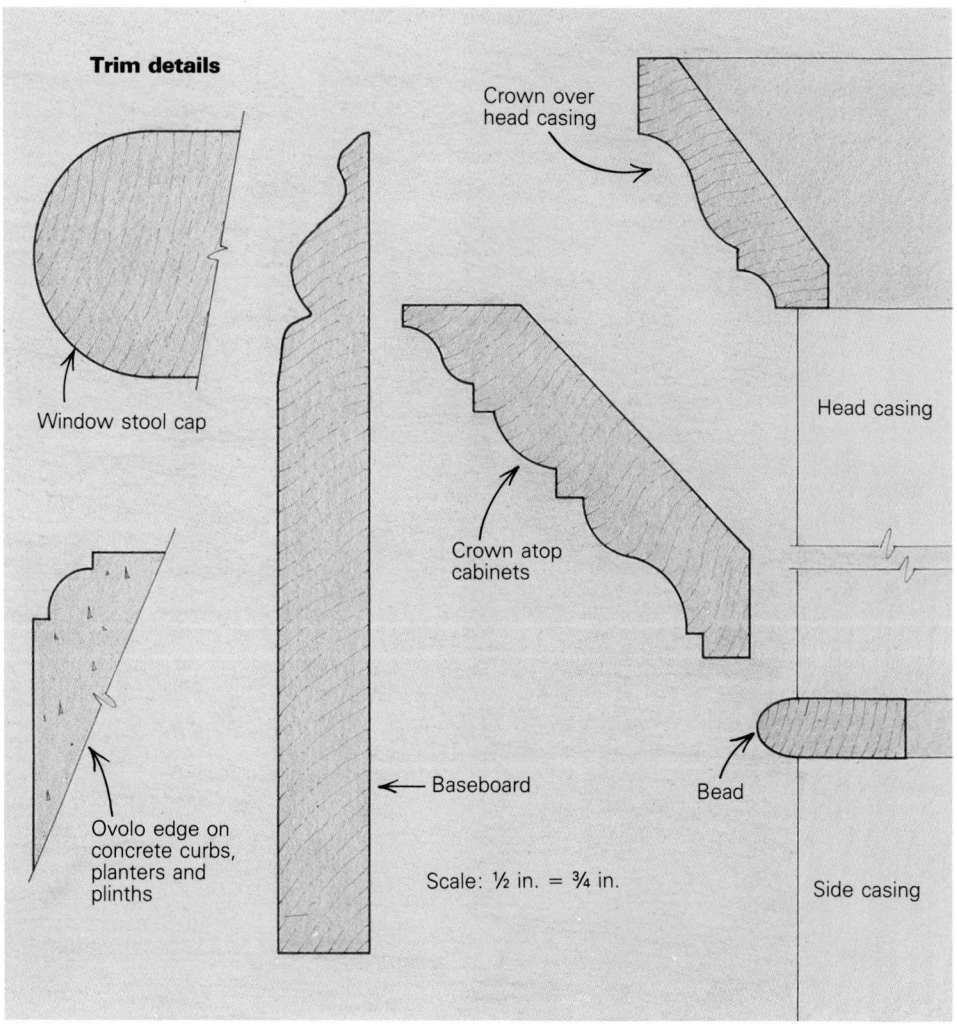

Trim details

Window stool cap

Ovolo edge on concrete curbs, planters and plinths

Crown over head casing

Crown atop cabinets

← Baseboard

Head casing

Bead

Side casing

Scale: ½ in. = ¾ in.

The downstairs living spaces are divided by an entry foyer located at the crotch of the L-shaped floor plan. To punctuate the historic presence of the house, Fearn strategically placed antique architectural components, such as the newel post, the front door and the light fixture, in the entry.

Leaded glass from a London flea market finds a new life in the upstairs bathrooms. The drywall ceiling follows the contour of the 12-in-12 roof framing, giving the viewer a geometry of roof planes to behold. At left in the photo you can see double doors that conceal the laundry center.

Poured-concrete steps and plinths project a weighty presence in keeping with the stone masonry look of the house. Note the ovolo edges on the plinths—they soften the hard lines of the plinth, and hint at the interior trim details.

Maple cabinets stained burgundy red with aniline dyes define the boundaries of the kitchen. The cabinets are connected across their tops with crown molding, emphasizing their furniture-like qualities and giving a custom-made look.

Victorian Log Studio

Basic carpentry techniques shape a unique workplace

by Peter Lauritzen

My wife's first office was a tiny third-floor cubicle with a perennially broken window through which came an intermittent stream of banging, curses and air-compressor blasts from the body shop on the street below. When her rent went up and the broken window went un-fixed, she moved to a new office on a quiet side street. This one was fine until the landla-dy raised the rent twice, almost doubling it in nine months. It was time to bow out of the Santa Fe rental market.

Site and shape—We decided to build a stu-dio on our land outside of town. There was a good spot on the lower part of our five acres, well away from our house. It was isolated, had good southern exposure and was surrounded by pinyon and juniper. It was also strangely barren; we wouldn't need to remove a blade of grass, much less a tree, to build there. The only drawback was its location on an elevated "island" between two large arroyos. Though

the site stayed dry when the arroyos ran, it was sure to be under water someday during a fifty- or one hundred-year flood. We would have to take that into account when we built.

My wife, a psychotherapist, had modest needs. She didn't want electricity; she would use kerosene lamps and a hand-wound clock. She wanted no plumbing; a water dispenser in the studio and a separate outhouse would work just fine. And she wasn't interested in the distraction of a phone; she would contin-ue to use her office phone in the main house.

What she did want was a warm and inti-mate space, open to the natural surroundings and just big enough for several chairs, end ta-bles and a desk (photo, facing page). We set-tled on a 12-ft. by 14-ft. floor plan. With no utilities, I figured it would be a simple project.

Adobe, the premier building material around here, is fine, but it is really a mason's medium, not a carpenter's. I wanted to play a bit in mak-ing this structure, so we decided to build the

studio out of logs (photo below). Like many people, we have always had a romantic associ-ation with log cabins. Also, I subscribe to my cousin's definition of a good house: one in which you can sink an axe anywhere and leave it, and it would look perfectly natural.

I've always been intrigued by Victorian ar-chitecture and ornamentation, but have had few opportunities to pursue it in my work. In stuccoed Santa Fe, anything more decorative than an occasional carved corbel raises a dis-approving eyebrow. This was my own project, however, and I could experiment with a few of the Victorian motifs that I had been photo-graphing and thinking about for years.

A log haul—I decided to go with milled logs to save time and hauled them down from Colorado at the beginning of the project. The logs are flat on the interior face and round on the exterior face, with two parallel ¾-in. wide by ½-in. deep tongues milled down the

Dovetailed logs and Victorian accents of this small studio create a counterpoint to the adobe and stucco buildings typical of the Santa Fe area.

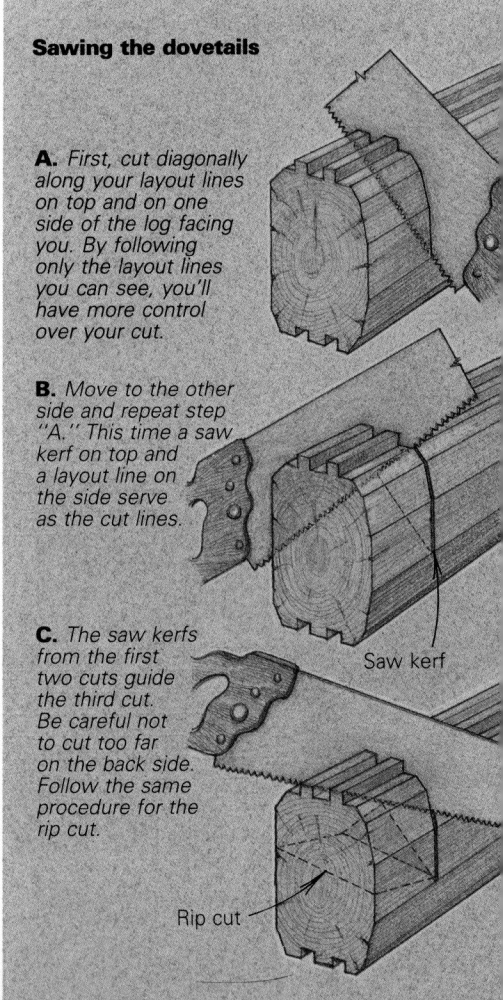

Sawing the dovetails

A. First, cut diagonally along your layout lines on top and on one side of the log facing you. By following only the layout lines you can see, you'll have more control over your cut.

B. Move to the other side and repeat step "A." This time a saw kerf on top and a layout line on the side serve as the cut lines.

C. The saw kerfs from the first two cuts guide the third cut. Be careful not to cut too far on the back side. Follow the same procedure for the rip cut.

Saw kerf

Rip cut

length of the top and matching grooves milled into the bottom. Because I wanted the curved face of the logs to project beyond the finished foundation, I kept them on site to allow me to measure the profile of the logs before doing the foundation layout. As a result, they sat around for several months before I used them. Though cut from standing dead spruce and perfectly dry, they distorted badly in the sun.

High and dry—The foundation was straightforward. I used eight piers—three on a side—around the perimeter of the building. I laid up the piers with 12-in. concrete blocks and mortar, reinforcing them with two vertical lengths of ½-in. rebar. A ½-in. anchor bolt embedded in the top of each pier secures the sills. The piers extend from footings 3 ft. below grade to about 2 ft. above grade for protection against the anticipated floods.

After laying a square piece of 15-lb. felt on top of each pier, we fastened the 4x8 pine sills to them with the wide face down. The logs we would be using for the walls measured 5½ in. wide by 7½ in. high, so there would be a 1½-in. ledge left on which to rest the floor joists. Before installing the sills, we treated them with a liberal coat of Woodlife (Roberts Consolidated Industries, Inc., 600 N. Baldwin Park Blvd., City of Industry, Calif. 91749).

The first course of logs served as rim joists for the floor system. After the first course and the 2x8 joists and blocking were in place, we put down a temporary plywood floor. We were now ready to lay up the walls.

Sprucing up the walls—I dovetailed the logs at the corners and cut them flush with the plane of the wall, avoiding over-shot corners. While attractive on structures built of unmilled logs, these overshot corners would not have looked right with milled logs. The dovetails were much harder to lay out and cut accurately than they would have been on unwarped logs and probably approached the same level of difficulty as working with unmilled logs (for more information on dovetail layout see *FHB* #13, pp. 54-59 and *FHB* #34, pp. 46-50).

Cutting the dovetails was primarily a handsaw operation. I used a circular saw only on flat areas of the log. Sawing heavy stock all the way through from one side with a handsaw seldom seems to work out. The cut tends to wander beyond the layout line on the back side, which is out of the line of vision. The trick is to make three cuts instead of one. With the first two cuts, I cut only the layout lines I could see. The third cut was then accurately guided by the sawkerfs from the first two cuts (drawing, facing page). After I roughed out each joint I cleaned it up with a 2-in. timber chisel, pairing each adjoining face slightly concave to encourage a tight fit.

I ran a bead of construction adhesive along the outside edge of the tongues on each log after it was in place, then spiked the next log to it with 12-in. spikes spaced on 3-ft. centers. I also spiked the corners, pre-drilling the dovetails to prevent them from splitting. When the logs reached window-sill height, I set the 4x6 pine window frames in place, leveled them and braced them to stakes outside. As succeeding courses of logs went up, I toenailed them to the frames with 6-in. pole-barn nails. I put three units of 1-in. patio glass into the south wall and a pair of homemade casement windows into the east wall.

Fitting the lid—To join the 4x8 rough-sawn rafter pairs at the ridge, I cut pegged bridle joints. Because the stock was slightly twisted, I offset the joints, which allowed me to use square cuts for the blocking.

To determine the amount of offset the bridle joint would require, I laid a combination square across both ends of each rafter (drawing, next page). I sighted down the rafter and then wedged up the closer square until the two blades were in perfect alignment. By measuring the resulting gap between the blade and rafter, I got the exact distance I'd need to offset the joint. Both rafters in a rafter pair needed to be adjusted this way. After the pairs were assembled, I used a 2-in. chisel to ease the joints, making the offsets less noticeable.

Every other rafter pair is joined by a 4x6 collar tie, mortised and tenoned to increase

The office is big enough for several chairs, end tables and the combination desk-cupboard-bookshelf unit that spans the rear wall. Pegged bridle joints link the rafters at the peak. Collar ties are mortised and tenoned into alternate rafter pairs.

Compensating for rafter twist

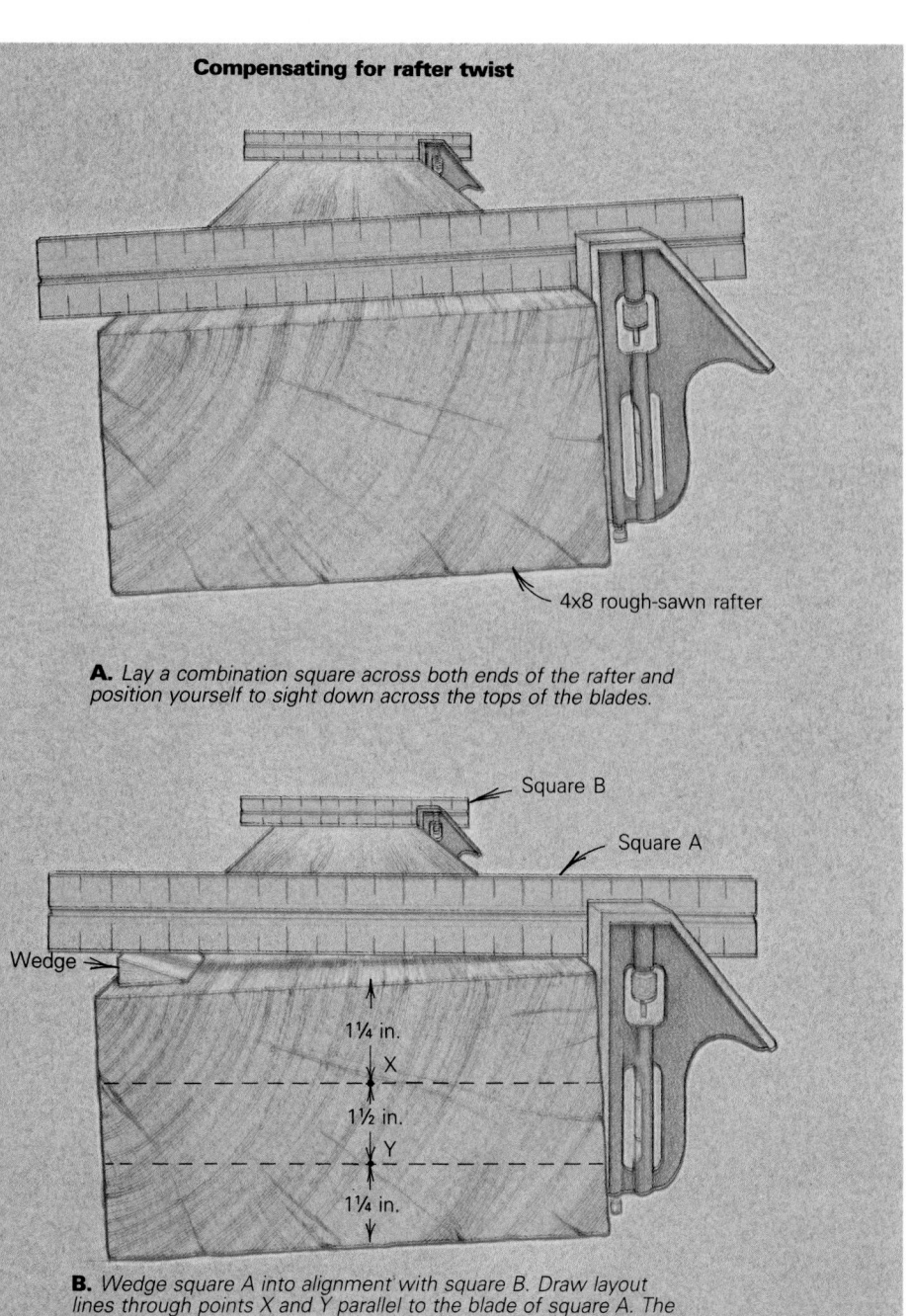

4x8 rough-sawn rafter

A. *Lay a combination square across both ends of the rafter and position yourself to sight down across the tops of the blades.*

Square B

Square A

Wedge

1¼ in.

X

1½ in.

Y

1¼ in.

B. *Wedge square A into alignment with square B. Draw layout lines through points X and Y parallel to the blade of square A. The bridle joint will now be in same plane as the plate end of the rafter. Adjust the layout this way for both rafters in a pair.*

Rafter assembly

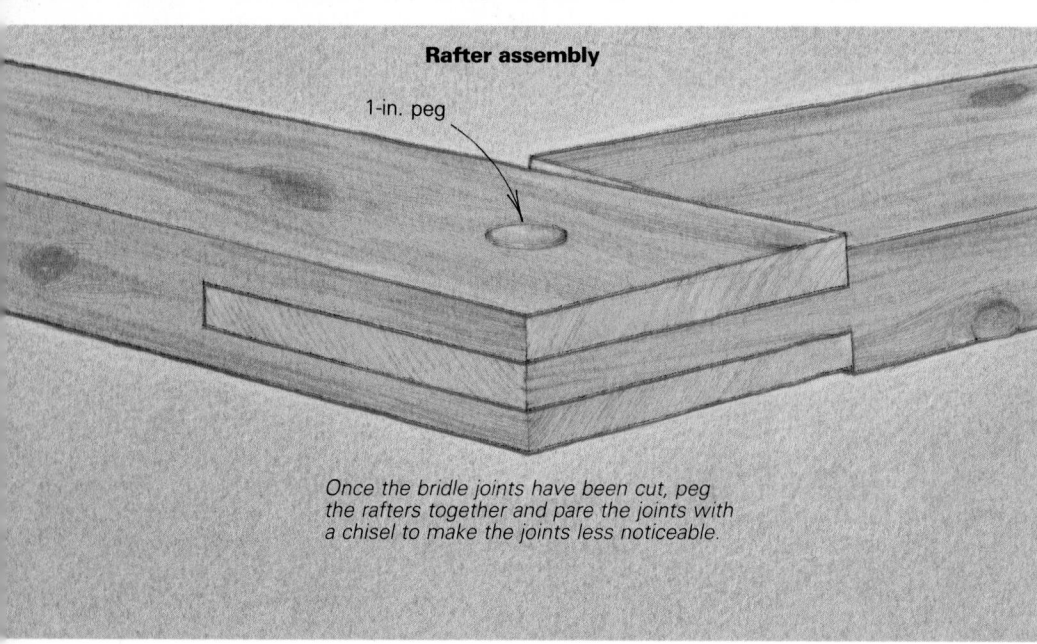

1-in. peg

Once the bridle joints have been cut, peg the rafters together and pare the joints with a chisel to make the joints less noticeable.

stiffness. Scrolled brackets support the barge rafters. I cut the brackets with a bandsaw, beaded the edges with a router and turned the pendants on a lathe (for more on scrolled brackets, see *FHB #35*, pp. 72-73).

Between the exposed rafters in the ceiling, we used a heavy-textured wallpaper called "Wall Sculpture" (Renovator's Supply, Renovator's Old Mill, Millers Falls, Mass. 01349) over fire-rated drywall. After installing the wallpaper, we rolled on a coat of light lavender grey paint, then painted the raised areas of the wallpaper a slightly darker shade with a foam brush. This gave it the look of an old-fashioned tin ceiling. In the context of the log cabin, the effect was one of wearing a silk shirt with jeans. Three inches of rigid urethane insulate the ceiling, and cedar shakes cap off the roof.

After stick-framing and insulating the gable ends, we covered them with fish-scale shingles cut from 1x5 rough-sawn pine boards 16-in. long. My bandsaw was a big help here. I started by putting my widest, most aggressive blade on the saw. Then I clamped two boards at least ¾ in. thick and 4½ in. high, onto the bandsaw table—one on either side of the blade and ⅝ in. away from it. This created a chute to guide each board through the blade. By using a push stick and skewing the board so the front and back edges rode against opposite sides of the chute, I was able to cut two tapered shingles out of each board. (drawing above right, facing page).

The door of the studio incorporates a sliding screened sash in lieu of a separate screen door. A spring-loaded locking-pin is installed in the sash and engages any one of eight holes drilled down the center of the door. Sliding the sash up or down adjusts levels of ventilation. *Photo by author.*

From *Fine Homebuilding* magazine (August 1988) 48:70-73

Once the walls and roof were finished, I could put down a proper floor. I nailed 1x2 cleats around the perimeter of each joist bay near the bottom. Then I dropped in ¼-in. thick sheets of masonite and filled the cavities with 5½-in. of fiberglass insulation. We used 2x6 pine T&G for the finished floor, with the V-groove side facing down.

A hybrid door—The door was an involved project. I did not want a separate screen door because I think they're generally ugly, flimsy and one more thing to open and shut. Instead, I combined the two doors into one. The four-panel pine door, with a screen replacing the two upper panels, is fitted with a sliding sash on the inside that can cover the screen to various extents (photo, facing page).

I joined stiles and rails with pegged mortise and tenon joints. The top and bottom rails and the lock and hinge stiles are 2½ in. thick, with a ¾-in. rabbet around the inside perimeter on the interior side of the door. The middle rail and stiles are 1¾-in. thick. Combined with the ¾-in. rabbet, this reduced thickness creates a recess for the sliding sash.

By screwing a rabbeted frame over the recess, I created a channel to contain and guide the sliding sash. The design calls for close tolerances and clean stock for the sash so that it will seal well and slide freely. Spring-action copper weatherstripping fastened to the edges of the sash on the top and sides enhances the seal.

I installed a spring-loaded sash-locking pin into the bottom of the sliding sash. This engages any one of eight holes I drilled down the center of the door. Next time, I would bush the sash pin holes with brass or hardwood to prevent their edges from becoming worn. Otherwise, the siding sash works very well. I'll never install screen doors again if I can avoid it.

Decking it out—Once the door was hung, my wife was in and working. But the cabin wasn't quite right. The piers gave the cabin the appearance of an overweight stork. We resolved to fill in between them. I did this by building a 2x4 frame between each pier. Then I stretched metal lath over the piers and frames, nailed it in place and finished up with a 3-coat stucco job. The result looks like a continuous foundation and not only gives the cabin a solid appearance but also keeps out the wind.

After this treatment, the studio still looked stork-like, and the transition between inside and outside was too abrupt. Also, it needed a place outdoors for one to sit when the weather was good. It needed a porch.

I prefabricated a porch frame out of 4x6s and fixed them to 12-in. by 12-in. concrete block piers. I blind-doweled the posts to the frame. Then I decked the frame with rough-sawn 2x6s. Urns turned from kiln-dried 6x6 Douglas fir cap the posts.

I cut the balusters that support the deck railing out of rough-sawn pine 2x8s using a bandsaw. I drilled four 1-in. holes for quatrefoils, and two 1-in. holes for both the top and the bottom cutouts on each baluster, finishing up the cuts with a sabre saw. Then I used a router to chamfer all the edges and cleaned up the inside corners with a knife and chisel.

The balusters have ¾-in. long by 1¼-in. thick tenons on both ends which slide into grooves in the 3x5 railings. I cut the tenons with a dado blade on my table saw. Since the rough-sawn balusters varied widely in thickness, I used an auxiliary fence to ensure that all the tenons would be the same size (bottom drawing, right). A heavy set of steps with one railing completed the porch.

Shading the entry—Because the late afternoon sun coming through the door was intense, and a driving rain could probably work through the sliding sash, we decided to add a small roof over the door. I didn't have any pictures of rain hoods, so I took my inspiration from overhangs on old railroad stations, adding some Victorian spoolwork to blend in.

Before cutting the parts for the sides, I sized them out on a full-scale drawing. After I cut them, I blind-doweled the pieces together. I turned the spools in one piece and let them into the rails top and bottom, then blind-doweled this unit to the sides. Though the pieces of the rain-hood frame were planed to thickness, I made a point of keeping the remaining rough-sawn faces to the outside.

Finishing up—I allowed the cabin to season for a few months, then sealed the outside with two coats of clear NWF #92 (Behr Process Corp., 3400 W. Segerstrom Ave., Santa Ana, Calif. 92704), which I put on with a garden sprayer. The walls on the inside received two coats of boiled linseed oil, and the floor two coats of Wellborn gym floor sealer (Wellborn Paint, 215 Rossmoor Rd. S.W., Albuquerque, N. M. 87105).

Not short, but sweet—The cabin has gone through two winters and has performed very well. We put in a small woodstove and have used about a fifth of a cord of wood each year, mostly for small, quick fires in the morning. The studio stays cool in the summer due to the mass of the logs, heavy insulation, good cross-ventilation and enough overhang at the eaves to keep the sun out.

My wife loves the studio, and it has been one of the few places I've built about which I've had almost no regrets. However, as I was starting the project, a friend asked how long it would take to complete it. I replied, "Oh, working weekends, I should have this thing done by September, no problem." It was done by September all right, but two and a half years later. □

Peter Lauritzen is a carpenter and woodworker in Tesuque, New Mexico.

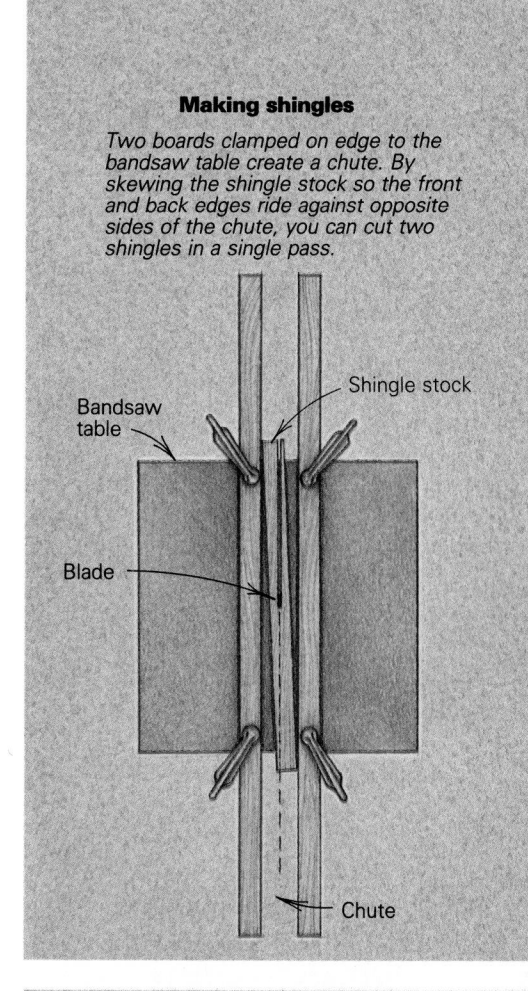

Making shingles

Two boards clamped on edge to the bandsaw table create a chute. By skewing the shingle stock so the front and back edges ride against opposite sides of the chute, you can cut two shingles in a single pass.

Shingle stock

Bandsaw table

Blade

Chute

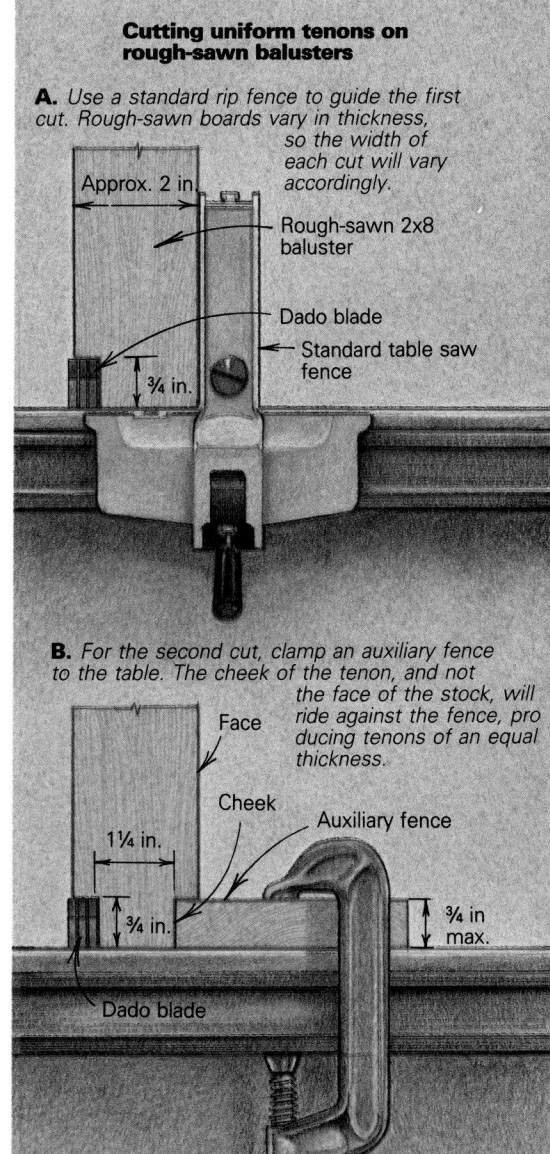

Cutting uniform tenons on rough-sawn balusters

A. *Use a standard rip fence to guide the first cut. Rough-sawn boards vary in thickness, so the width of each cut will vary accordingly.*

Approx. 2 in.

Rough-sawn 2x8 baluster

Dado blade

Standard table saw fence

¾ in.

B. *For the second cut, clamp an auxiliary fence to the table. The cheek of the tenon, and not the face of the stock, will ride against the fence, producing tenons of an equal thickness.*

Face

Cheek

Auxiliary fence

1¼ in.

¾ in.

¾ in. max.

Dado blade

Canadian Retreat

A compact cabin that features site-built structural elements and simple energy detailing

by Kip Park

"Christopher Park?" the solemn voice asked on the telephone. My heart leapt to my throat: no one but police, doctors and bureaucrats use my legal name, so I expected bad news. I was right. The Ontario Provincial Police constable was unhappy to report that my wilderness cottage on Shoal Lake near Kenora, Ontario, had burned to the ground.

The next day a visit to the site, located about 120 miles east of my hometown of Winnipeg, Manitoba, confirmed that the cabin I'd built in 1969-70 was gone. As I surveyed the ashes and jumbled scrap tin that had been a delightful, if somewhat uncomfortable, year-round retreat, I grieved as if an old friend had passed away.

Shoal Lake is the source of Winnipeg's drinking water. The water is said to be so pure that it's fit for royalty to drink, as the King and Queen of England did throughout their cross-Canada tour of 1939. Although there are now about 150 cottages around the lake, there's still plenty of elbow room. In the winter my wife Sylvia Mouflier and I reach our property on cross-country skis or snowmobiles over a three-mile-long trail. The rest of the year calls for a brisk hike over the trail or a four-mile boat trip.

On the day I learned about the fire, I spoke with Stan Hutton, who had recently graduated from the Faculty of Architecture at the University of Manitoba. One thing led to another and he volunteered to design a new passive-solar cabin for us (photo right).

Hutton's design had to take a number of factors into account. For one thing, we weren't about to pack all the building materials on our backs to the job site. Our only alternative was to haul them over water, which meant the materials would have to be transportable in our 18-ft. aluminum boat. Also, we wanted a cabin that would be easy to heat in a climate with an average of 10,766 heating degree days. The more energy efficient the building was, the less wood we would have to cut and split, and it was mostly our own energy that we were looking to conserve. We also wanted the cabin to be relatively inexpensive and, given our inexperience as builders, easy to build.

The final design met all the criteria. The cabin has one room downstairs incorporating all the main living areas, plus a small sleeping loft upstairs (drawing, p. 38). It is only 325 sq. ft., and we built it for about $30 per sq. ft.

Of course, before we could build anything, we had to clear the site. Sylvia, her brother

This passive-solar cabin is topped with a tower fitted with an awning window up top. In the summer the window is left open to create a cooling thermosiphon effect inside. The rest of the year, it provides a convenient way to freshen up the interior. The second-story deck is supported with joists cantilevered out from the sleeping loft, and a 4-ft. sq. wall bolted to the end acts as a box beam to provide support.

Richard and I spent the remaining weekends that summer yanking deformed metal and charred timber from the rubble and hauling the stuff out with our boat. Before construction could get underway the next spring, we'd need to arrange for electricity at the job site. It would be too expensive to bring in power lines, and I didn't want to build this cabin solely with elbow grease like I did the first one. The solution was simple. We purchased a portable 5,000-watt generator, giving us enough power for all our portable power tools and a radial-arm saw.

As soon as winter was over, we began hauling the building materials to the lake in our half-ton pickup and boating them up to the site. We built an 8-ft. square tool shed, plus a framework of 2x4s and 6-mil polyethylene sheeting to protect our materials. Now we were ready to start on the cabin.

Foundation and floor framing—A continuous concrete or masonry foundation would have been both impractical and unnecessary. We opted instead for seven concrete pads, each 6 in. high by 18 in. square. Each pad was carefully leveled in a bed of sand in the bottom of a shallow excavation (about 6-in. deep). Because of the stable subsoils (the bedrock is just a few feet down), this is the foundation of choice for cottages in this area.

Four perimeter floor beams carry the floor joists and support the exterior walls of the cabin. But instead of specifying solid wood beams, which would have been a nuisance to transport to the site, Hutton designed a box beam to be built on site out of ½-in. plywood and 2x4s (drawing facing page). Each 1-ft. 4 in. high beam was framed like a stud wall, with a single top and bottom plate, studs spaced 24-in. o. c. and plenty of fiberglass insulation. A double layer of ½-in. plywood was glued (with construction adhesive) and nailed to one side of the frame, while a single layer of ½-in. plywood was applied to the opposite, or exterior, side. Except on the west wall, the exterior plywood extends ½ in. beyond the top of the beam, allowing us to slug nails through this lip into the bottom plates of the walls.

The beams on both the east and west walls extend beyond the floor platform to support what we call "wing walls" on the south end of the cabin. The wing walls are purely aesthetic; they make the cottage look larger and add variety to the facade. A third wing wall is attached to the northeast corner of the cabin. The posts supporting the box beams were made by gluing and nailing six 2x10s together, coating the ends with construction adhesive and capping both ends with ½-in. plywood to keep moisture from soaking into the end grain. All the posts except for one are well protected by the building, so we left them untreated. The exposed post to the southwest is protected with a galvanized-steel cap. Once again, the design saved us from having to lug hefty timbers to the job site.

Once the beams were fixed to the posts, we pulled the corners together with a pair of ½-in. by 8-in. lag bolts and reinforced the inside corners with angle iron bolted to the beams with 4-in. lag bolts.

To complete the floor framing, we nailed 2x6 ledgers to the bottoms of the east and

From *Fine Homebuilding* magazine (August 1989) 55:42-44

west beams to support 2x10 floor joists. We placed the ledgers so that the tops of the joists would be flush with the tops of the box beams. Then we installed the joists 24 in. o. c., blocked the ends and installed 2x2 bridging at the midspans to keep the joists from twisting. Next we stapled chicken wire to the underside of the floor joists and dropped R-30 fiberglass insulation into the joist cavities. Finally, we installed a 6-mil poly vapor barrier over the joists and finished off the floor with ¾-in. T&G fir plywood.

Variable-thickness walls—To create a sense of extra space inside what is, after all, a tiny building, and to add headroom for the sleeping loft, we decided on 10-ft. high walls downstairs. Also, Hutton suggested that we vary the thickness of the walls. Except for the 4-in. thick south wall, walls were built 6-in. thick, with wall sections around windows reduced to 4-in. in thickness. This added visual interest to the facade without badly compromising the energy-efficiency of the building (photo next page). It also cut the cost of the windows by about 5% by avoiding the need for jamb extensions. Finally, it created recesses that could later house insulated shutters for increased energy efficiency and better security.

The north, east and south walls were easy to build and erect, but the long west wall was complicated and a bit awkward to get up. It's really a 2x4 wall inset into the 2x6 wall. The 2x4 wall houses a door and three windows, including one built into a triangular niche that projects into the interior. A site-built box beam serves as a continuous header. The 2x6 wall is almost 24 ft. long and incorporates yet another box-beam header. To reduce weight, we left the interior sides of the beams open until after we raised the walls. The headers are of a slightly different design than the site-built floor beams, but the concept is the same (drawing right). We filled the cavities in both box beams with fiberglass insulation. The exterior of each beam is faced with ⅜-in. plywood, and the interior is covered with a sheet of plywood screwed and glued over both beams to tie them together.

The floor joists supporting the loft, which we installed diagonally for visual interest, cantilever to support a 4-ft. by 8-ft. exterior balcony. The balcony is stiffened on one end by a 4-ft. square wall that's anchored to the building. The wall, which is braced internally with a diagonal 2x4 and sheathed with ⅜-in. plywood on both sides, works like a box beam to support the outer edge of the balcony (photo facing page).

The roof—Once we built the upstairs walls and hoisted them into place, it was time to fabricate the central roof beam. This beam is actually a hip rafter which extends from the northeast corner of the cabin up to the west wall. We built the beam by butting two 2x12s together and laminating double layers of ½-

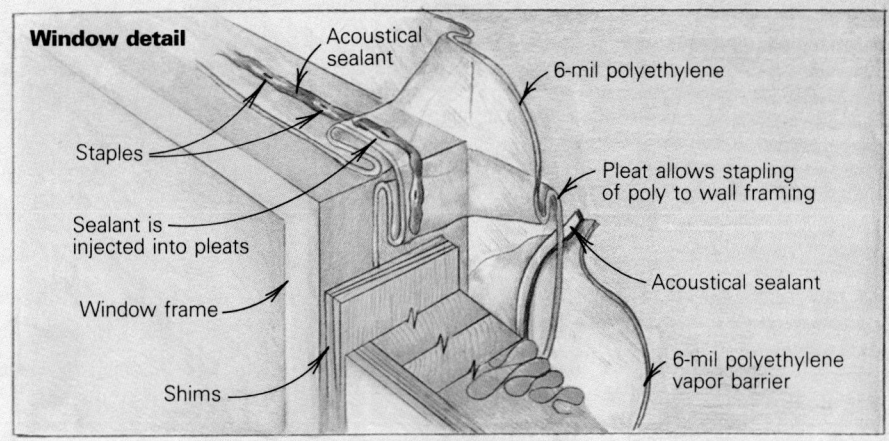

Window detail

Acoustical sealant
6-mil polyethylene
Staples
Pleat allows stapling of poly to wall framing
Sealant is injected into pleats
Acoustical sealant
Window frame
6-mil polyethylene vapor barrier
Shims

Information courtesy of R-2000 Program of the Canadian Homebuilders' Association

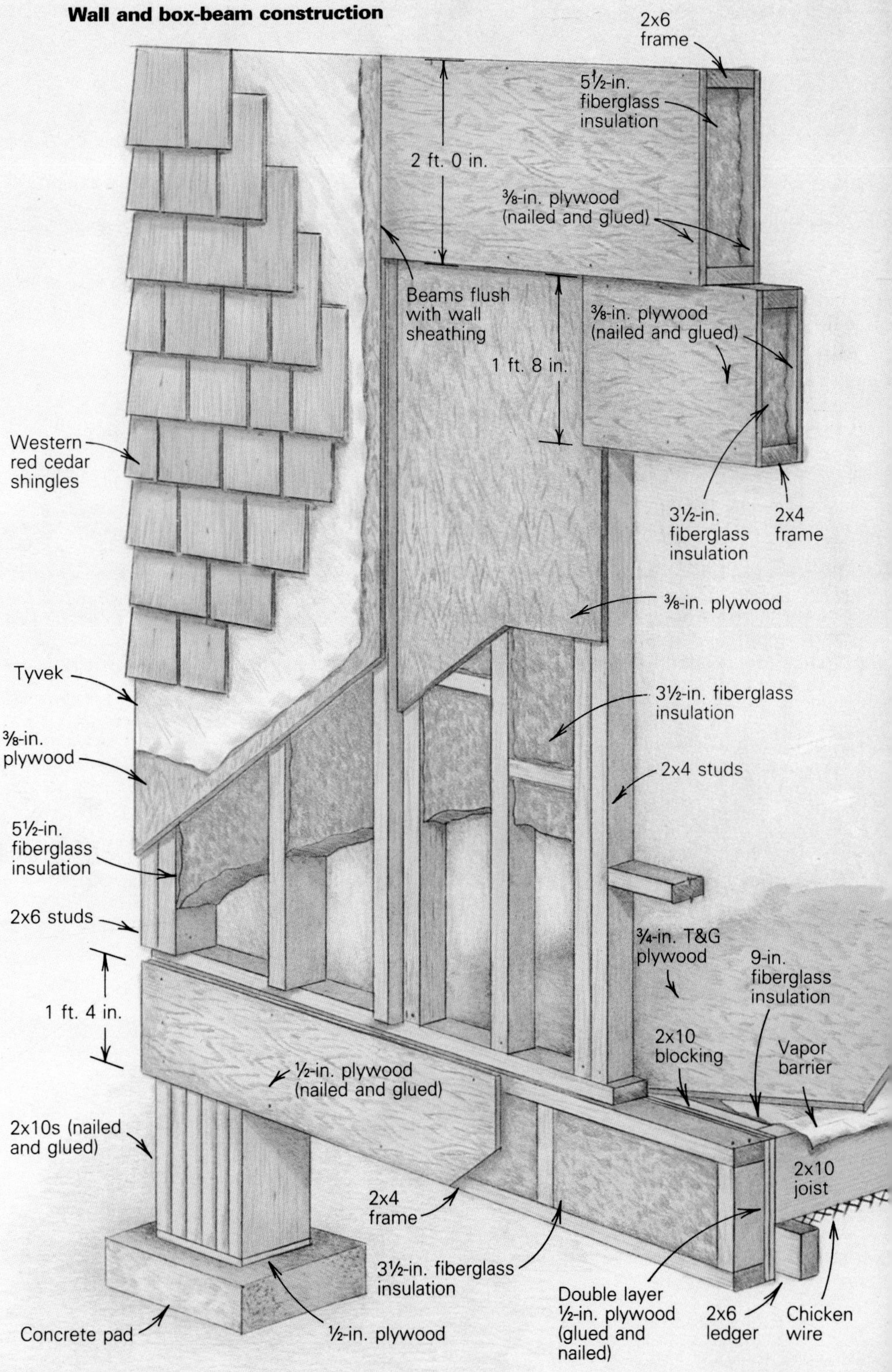

Wall and box-beam construction

2x6 frame
5½-in. fiberglass insulation
2 ft. 0 in.
⅜-in. plywood (nailed and glued)
Beams flush with wall sheathing
⅜-in. plywood (nailed and glued)
1 ft. 8 in.
Western red cedar shingles
3½-in. fiberglass insulation
2x4 frame
⅜-in. plywood
3½-in. fiberglass insulation
Tyvek
2x4 studs
⅜-in. plywood
5½-in. fiberglass insulation
2x6 studs
¾-in. T&G plywood
9-in. fiberglass insulation
1 ft. 4 in.
2x10 blocking
Vapor barrier
½-in. plywood (nailed and glued)
2x10s (nailed and glued)
2x10 joist
2x4 frame
Concrete pad
3½-in. fiberglass insulation
½-in. plywood
Double layer ½-in. plywood (glued and nailed)
2x6 ledger
Chicken wire

Drawings: Michael Mandarano

in. fir plywood to both sides. The finished beam weighed over 300 lb., yet we managed to coax it into place with a lot of muscle power and a little good luck.

While Sylvia and I sheathed the walls with ⅜-in. plywood, Richard framed the rest of the roof with 2x8 rafters 24 in. o. c. and nailed 2x4 purlins 24 in. o. c. on edge across the rafters. The roof was insulated with R-30 fiberglass, sheathed with ½-in. plywood and finished off with Western red cedar shakes. The purlins provided a 3½-in. air space between the top of the insulation and the sheathing. We also slid lengths of wood lath between the purlins and the insulation to depress the insulation. That way, air could circulate freely across the top of the insulation to pick up moisture condensation and escape through the ridge vent on top of the hip beam. The air enters the roof cavity through a gap at the eaves between the siding and roof decking. We covered the gap with nylon screening to keep out insects, then with steel mesh to keep out animals and birds.

Wrapping the windows— By this time, cold weather was on the horizon. After wrapping the house with Tyvek, we hustled to get the windows into place. We wanted them to be as airtight as possible, so before we installed each one, we ran a bead of acoustical caulking all the way around the outside of the window frame (top drawing, preceding page). Then we pressed a 24-in. wide strip of 6-mil polyethylene into the caulking and stapled it to the frame through the caulking. At the corners, we pleated the polyethylene and caulked the folds. When we installed the windows, the pleats allowed us to fold the polyethylene back into the interior of the cabin, where we stapled it to the trimmer studs. After insulating the walls later on, the vapor barrier was stapled over these flanges and the joint caulked. This technique preserves the integrity of the air/vapor barrier.

Drywall is unusual in a wilderness cabin, I guess, but it's relatively easy to apply, even in a structure as oddly shaped as this one. Also, it's inexpensive. But more important, I recognized that ⅝-in. drywall is an effective fire-retarding material. After my previous experience with fire, I figured that this was the best reason of all to use it. After the drywall, we installed a Kozi II woodstove, which was the smallest airtight stove we could find (APR Industries, Ltd., 1354 Waverley St., Winnipeg, Manitoba, R3T 0P5).

Performance overview— We've now had the opportunity to check the performance of this structure both summer and winter. Just out of curiosity, we ran its specs through Canada's HOT-2000 computer program. We found out that the annual solar-heating contribution is 35%. On the last day of our Christmas holiday, we let the fire in the woodstove die out at about 10 a.m. As the early afternoon sun streamed through the windows, the cabin warmed to 80° inside, while the outside temperature was only 6°. By opening a window, we quickly lowered the temperature to the comfort zone.

In the summer the key to temperature control is the awning window in the tower, which acts as a thermosiphon. When the awning window is open, hot interior air escapes the house and cool air is drawn in through open ground-floor windows to replace it. We leave the window open all summer, and the cabin interior remains comfortable regardless of the heat outside.

More important, the thermosiphon effect contributes to indoor air quality. When the awning window is open, fumes from cigarettes, the propane refrigerator, the stove and the Coleman lanterns are exhausted from the house immediately.

Unfortunately, we didn't take the fall and spring into account when we oriented the cabin on its site—it will often heat up to over 90° inside in the afternoon. We'll soon be adding a trellis over the downstairs deck to shield the west wall from the sun. □

Wing walls extend from all but the northwest corner of the cabin, creating the illusion of a larger structure. The cabin was framed with 2x6s except around the windows, where 2x4s were used. The difference in thickness adds visual interest and reduced cost by eliminating the need for jamb extensions. The triangular niche in the wall houses a casement window and is oriented to capture both sunlight and the breezes off the lake.

Kip Park lives in Winnipeg and writes about housing construction and energy technology. Photos by the author.

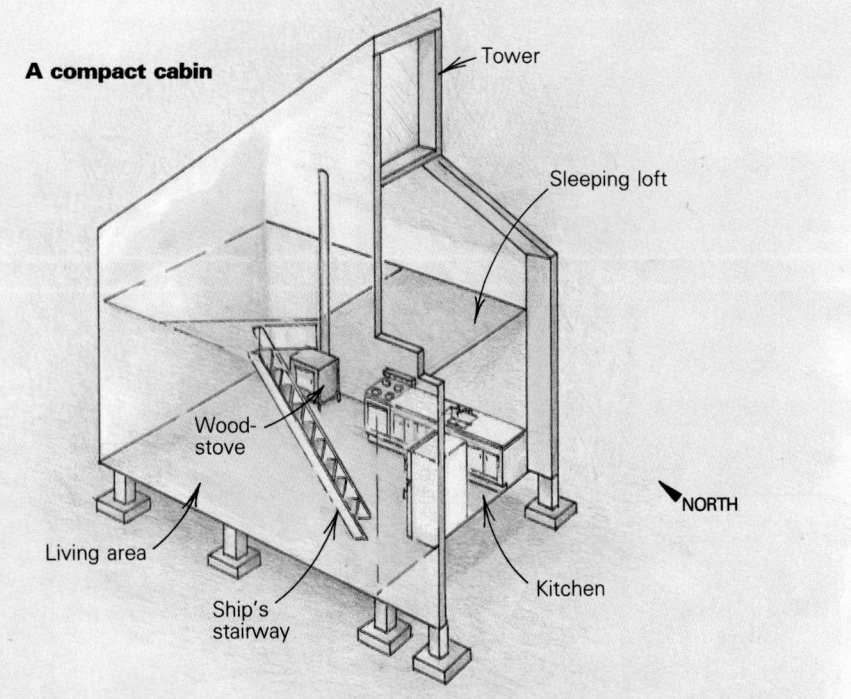

A compact cabin

Tower

Sleeping loft

Wood-stove

Living area

Ship's stairway

Kitchen

NORTH

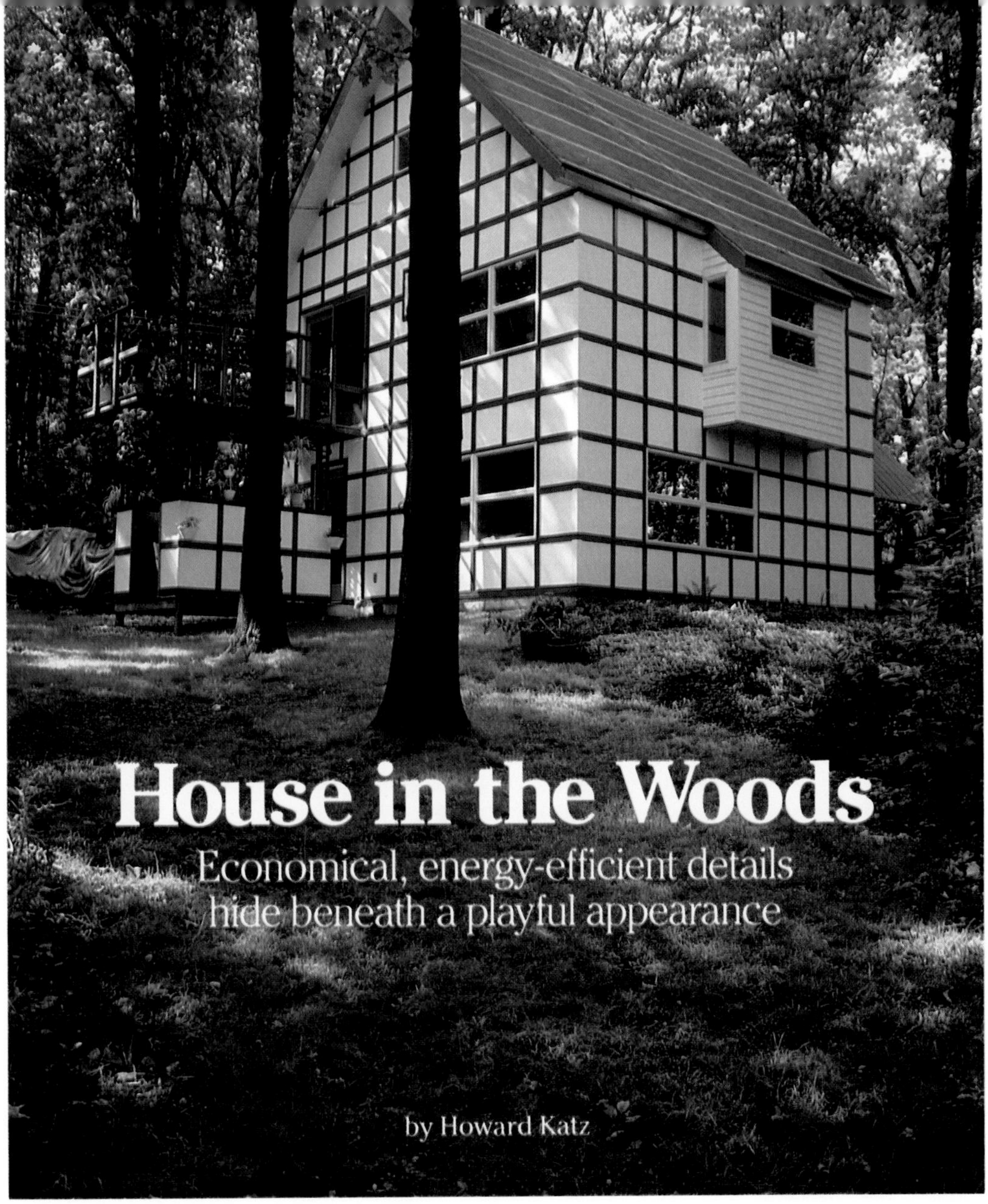

House in the Woods

Economical, energy-efficient details hide beneath a playful appearance

by Howard Katz

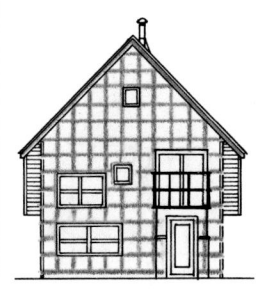

I can safely confess to a lifelong love of toys. On a few occasions I have tried to interest prospective clients in the idea of building a toy-like house, one that might have the coloring and implied modularity of a giant Lego or Lincoln-Log building. Technicians in the building industry spend untold hours trying to make plastic look like wood; why not make wood look like plastic? It would also be a challenge that would fulfill the frustrated toy designer in me. Needless to say, there were no takers.

When the time came to move out of my apartment, I decided to build the house I had been toying with all these years. The practical requirements were simple: The house would need to be large enough for my friend Ruth and me and for my two children, and we needed to keep the total budget under $80,000, including land.

Diverse inspiration—While I was designing, my two small daughters were busy with their own version of our new home. Their drawings showed the traditional two-story: a simple gable elevation with two windows, a door, a steep

Designer Howard Katz lives in Riegelsville, Pa.

roof and a crooked chimney with a snake of smoke running off the top of the page. Except for the crooked chimney, it looked like a pretty good design for a house in the woods. The cubic form and steep roof coincided with my penchant for cottage-style houses.

Cottages and bungalows are enjoying something of a revival. Quaint touches like porches, custom cabinetwork, bright colors and novel trim detail give these diminutive homes a charm that most large houses lack. My two-story design is a cottage that borrows its major proportions from my daughters' drawings. The plan (top drawing, p. 40) is a square with sides just over 22 ft. long, and the 12-in-12 roof pitch makes the building just slightly higher (28 ft.) than it is wide. The only breaks in the boxy form are two small, second-floor cantilevers—one in each bedroom (photo above). Including the attic, which we use for an office, an exercise

Green battens spaced on a 2-ft. grid, red trim and stripes of grey and green on the roof give this small Pennsylvania house the bright modularity of a large toy. Its cubic form is broken by 2-ft. cantilevers in both upstairs bedrooms.

room and storage space, the total living area is 1,350 sq. ft.

On the exterior of the house, green battens, caulked and nailed to white-painted plywood, define a 2-ft. grid that gives the house its modular appearance. Windows and doors are sized and placed to emphasize the grid. Red trim accents and stripes of green and grey on the roof are added toy-inspired touches.

We wanted to live in the country, and the house, with its scale and color, needed to be situated in dense woods, ideally on the edge of a meadow. In any other setting, my design would look like an Italian-Mexican restaurant. We found our site in August of 1984, in upper Bucks County, Pa. This five-acre parcel had the dense mix of hardwoods we were looking for, with an adjacent large meadow. The lot also had a moderate slope to the south, where the most sun and best views were. I made some minor floor-plan shifts based on the views, but otherwise there were few changes in the design.

Energy efficiency was a final design essential. In this small house with no basement, I didn't want to surrender the floor space (or spend the money) for a conventional heating system. If the house was tightly built and well insulated, it could be heated very inexpensively. A woodstove and a small electrical heater constitute the heating system.

The work begins—By October, a designer friend, Peter Quinn, had determined the details and drawn up the plans. It was time to find a builder. We chose a local general contractor, Dale Ahlum, whose own house indicated a high level of craftsmanship. Ahlum also had the dry sense of humor that would help him cope with my unconventional, if not capricious, design.

We gave Ahlum full responsibility for the excavation and foundation work, for all rough and trim carpentry, for plumbing and electrical hookup, roofing, septic system and for drilling the well. I was responsible for most of the interior finish, including painting, cabinetry, the woodstove and the masonry surround. Our combined estimate was $45,000. In the course of building, we made several upgrades: a marble vanity for the upstairs bathroom, mahogany and butcher-block countertops in the kitchen, stone instead of cement block for the hearth, and a finished attic. These changes raised the construction cost to $54,000. Including the attic space, this works out to $40 per sq. ft. (land cost excluded).

Foundations were dug in mid-October, and the slab was poured and scored on the 2-ft. grid that defines many aspects of the design. The slab would be the finished floor, so I wanted the grid to look like large square tiles. Unfortunately, the results look more like control joints in a concrete sidewalk. Had we planned more carefully, Ahlum could have used a different finishing sequence for a more realistic tile look. By the time we stained and sealed the floor and put down rugs and furniture, the sting was mostly gone.

To finish up the foundation, the perimeter concrete-block walls were insulated with 2 in. of expanded polystyrene foam. These rigid insulation boards were placed in a bed of bituminous foundation coating. Then the foam was covered with two coats of cement parging, followed by a final layer of foundation coating.

The wall framing I chose is based on Scandinavian techniques that combine balloon framing with horizontal strapping to achieve high R-values with few thermal bridges and a continuous vapor barrier. The principal framing members are 2x6 studs set on 24-in. centers. Except at the second-floor cantilevers, the 2x6s extend up to the rafters. Framing went quickly, except for the rough openings for windows and doors. The location of these openings had to be more precise than usual because the trim around the openings would also be part of the green grid that covers the siding.

Strapping, in the form of 2x3s, was nailed horizontally to the studs every 2 ft., with the vapor barrier placed between the 2x6s and 2x3s. The wall was filled out with 6-in. and 2-in. unfaced fiberglass-batt insulation (R-20). All wiring runs are in the space created by the 2x3 strapping, so the vapor barrier remains unpierced (drawing, right).

Once the framing was complete, Ahlum stapled Tyvek against the outside of the studs, wrapping the walls with an air-infiltration bar-

rier. Then we used hot-dipped 6d nails to put up the siding—½-in. A/C plywood (A side out) that had been primed.

The first and second floors of the house couldn't go any higher than 16 ft. I didn't want to use 2x10 joists to support the second floor because this would sacrifice too much headroom below. But to go with an 8-in. joist depth meant using either 3-in. by 8-in. joists (too expensive and heavy-looking) or manufactured steel joists (too expensive and too many problems attaching things—like the second floor). My alternative was making low-cost, built-up floor beams that look very nice overhead. Stained green and assembled with Tremont rose-head nails (Tremont Nail Co., Dept. FH-126, Elm St., Box 111, Wareham, Mass. 02571), the beams stand out against the 2x6 T&G planks used as the upstairs finish floor (top photo, facing page).

To make each floor beam, I sandwiched a 2x8 between a pair of 2x4s. In section, the top edge of the 2x8 sits ¼ in. below the top edges of the 2x4s, which are even with each other. At the ends of each beam, the 2x4s run 1½ in. beyond the angle-cut 2x8, creating a steel-joist-type connection. Along the exterior walls, the protruding 2x4s bear on a 2x6 ledger nailed against the studs, as shown in the drawing below.

Down the center of the house, the beams are supported by a box beam that also acts as a plumbing and wiring chase for the second floor. An open steel column fabricated from tubing sections is the midspan support for the box beam. Like the ceiling beams, the column is painted the same green as the exterior trim. The 3-in. dia. copper pipe that runs down the center of the column is actually the waste line from the upstairs bathroom and laundry. I could have hidden this plumbing by rerouting it through the

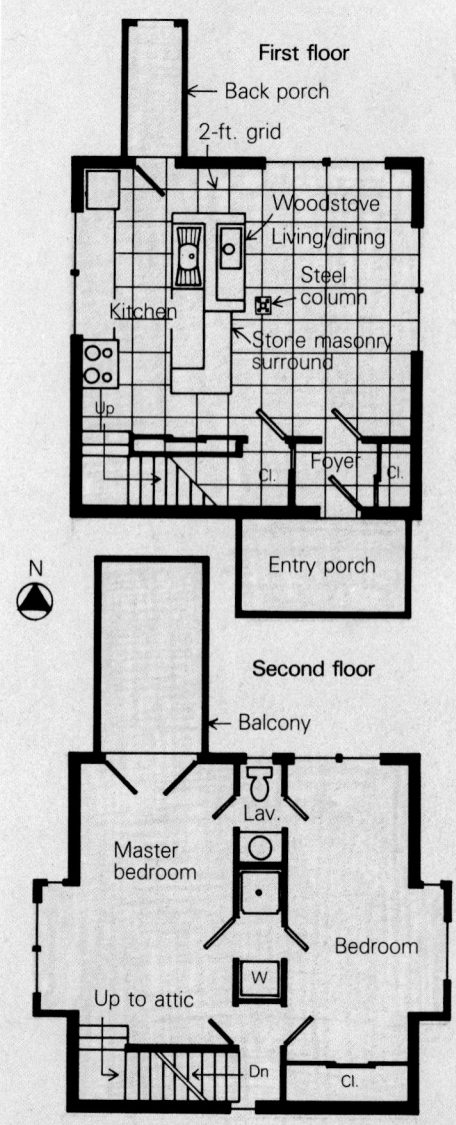

First floor

- Back porch
- 2-ft. grid
- Woodstove
- Living/dining
- Steel column
- Kitchen
- Stone masonry surround
- Up
- Cl.
- Foyer
- Cl.
- Entry porch

N

Second floor

- Balcony
- Lav.
- Master bedroom
- Bedroom
- W
- Up to attic
- Dn
- Cl.

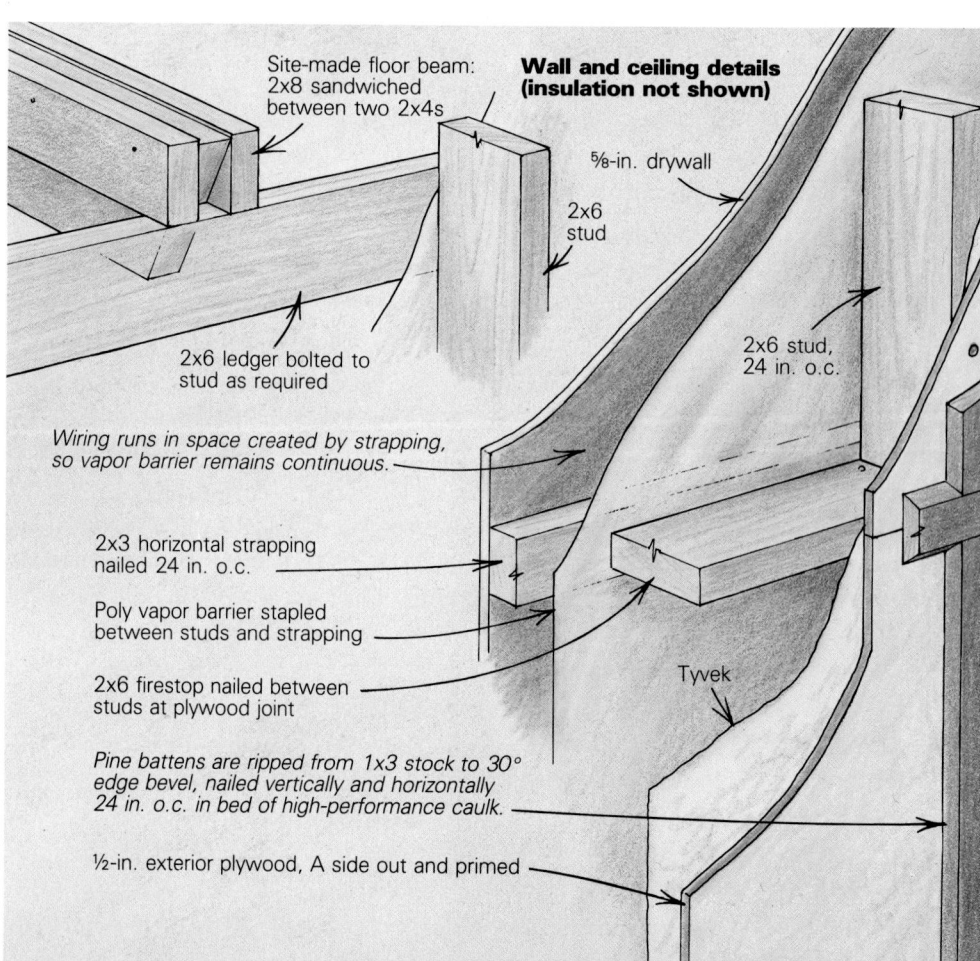

Site-made floor beam: 2x8 sandwiched between two 2x4s

Wall and ceiling details (insulation not shown)

- ⅝-in. drywall
- 2x6 stud
- 2x6 stud, 24 in. o.c.
- 2x6 ledger bolted to stud as required

Wiring runs in space created by strapping, so vapor barrier remains continuous.

2x3 horizontal strapping nailed 24 in. o.c.

Poly vapor barrier stapled between studs and strapping

2x6 firestop nailed between studs at plywood joint

Tyvek

Pine battens are ripped from 1x3 stock to 30° edge bevel, nailed vertically and horizontally 24 in. o.c. in bed of high-performance caulk.

½-in. exterior plywood, A side out and primed

Drawings: Chuck Lockhart

The first floor of the house is open, with a kitchen work island that doubles as dining area. Glass doors on the upper cabinets are recycled barn sash. A column built up from steel tubing supports a dark-stained box beam that is also the wiring and plumbing chase for the second floor. Green stain accents the site-built floor beams. A woodstove nestles in a stonemasonry surround. The insulated slab (which is the finished floor) repeats the 2-ft. grid pattern of the exterior siding.

Continuing to play with proportion, Katz built a tool shed at roughly one-third the scale of the house, using green-painted lattice to create an 8-in. grid. The birdhouse on the tree is a 1/24-scale replica. The main house (in the background) has an awning entryway supported by columns made from alternating layers of square concrete paving tile and cast chimney blocks.

utility room, or by boxing it in. But the visual and auditory properties of this centerpiece (photo top) were too interesting to pass up.

The grid—Andersen awning windows (Andersen Corp., Box 12, Bayport, Minn. 55003) are great 2-ft. grid fitters. Looking through their catalog, I was able to choose from a nice range of units with gross dimensions in even feet.

Though simple in conception, the grid was more labor intensive than we anticipated. The battens that make up the grid are 1x3 common pine, ripped down on both sides to a 30° bevel. The 24-in. spacing means that every joint in the plywood siding is covered by a batten. Ahlum started the grid at sill level and worked up. Each

batten is nailed (with hot-dipped galvanized 6d box nails) in a bed of white Geocel adhesive/caulk (Geocel Corp., P.O. Box 398, Elkhart, Ind. 46515), a paintable, copolymer-based caulk that can be applied in temperatures as low as 5°F. Nevertheless, Ahlum was constantly switching cold tubes for warm when he installed the battens during January and February.

We waited until spring to paint the exterior. Bob Bauder, the painter, cracked up when we told him what we wanted: green battens, red rake boards, fascias and doors. "Bob," I said, "We won't hold you responsible for our bad taste." Before he finished, Bauder got into it and was even taking pictures. The bill was $1,200.

The entry porch is another version of the play-

ful functionality I've tried to incorporate throughout the house. The walkway is 1x mahogany boards over a frame of pressure-treated pine, with a built-in foot scraper grate. The column bases are neo-Egyptian, made from alternating layers of cheap, pink-colored concrete paving tiles and chimney blocks. I glued these pieces together with construction adhesive, figuring it would better withstand the uplift of wind into the canvas awning. Painted green and bolted to the concrete bases, a Tinker-Toy-type framework of steel pipe forms the armature for the awning (photo below left).

Inside—As with the exterior, I wanted the inside of the house to be fun and well done, but I didn't want to spend a lot of money. Lauan plywood underlayment is great stuff. A 1/4-in. sheet costs about the same as 1/2-in. drywall, and with a little linseed oil, it looks terrific. I used lauan plywood for the second-floor ceiling, with 1x3 lauan boards as battens at the joints.

Downstairs, I hired stonemason Larry Hange to build the woodstove/counter surround from locally quarried stone. Tight joints and lots of shadows contribute to the cottage-style effect we wanted. The countertops are lauan and factory-made butcher block. Without a dishwasher, you need a double-drainboard sink. Ours is an old porcelain model that we bought at a nearby salvage place for $6—a real find. On the working side of the kitchen island, I built mahogony drawers beneath the countertop. The wall cabinets are simple lauan and pine carcases with barn window sash for doors.

The local utility was extremely helpful in providing not only heat-loss calculations, but also in recommending and sizing an off-peak storage heat system to take advantage of their cheaper rates. A single wall-mounted heater is filled with ceramic bricks, which are heated at night by electric resistance. An exterior sensor regulates the charge to the unit, depending on the temperature, and during the day a small fan blows across the bricks when the thermostat calls for heat. My alternate heat source is a Vermont Castings Resolute woodstove. Since the house is tightly built, I used the optional outside-air adaptor kit to bring fresh air in under the floor slab through plastic piping. Although this is the second smallest stove Vermont Castings makes, it's hard to keep the first floor below 75°F when we're burning wood. A few floor grates installed in the ceiling should help move the heat around.

Playing with scale—With the house nearly complete, I began my scale-down project—a design venture that could get me down closer to toy size and also populate the property with some interesting outbuildings. We needed a tool shed first. Its scale is about one-third that of the house; it's got an 8x8 floor plan and an 8-in. grid made of lattice that will eventually be entwined with ivy (photo above left). On a tree next to the shed you'll find our 1/24-scale example in the form of a birdhouse. Soon to be completed is a 1/2-scale screened pavilion on the southeast side of the house. And perhaps later we'll do a doghouse at 1/16 scale, or a Christmas ornament at 1/48 scale. □

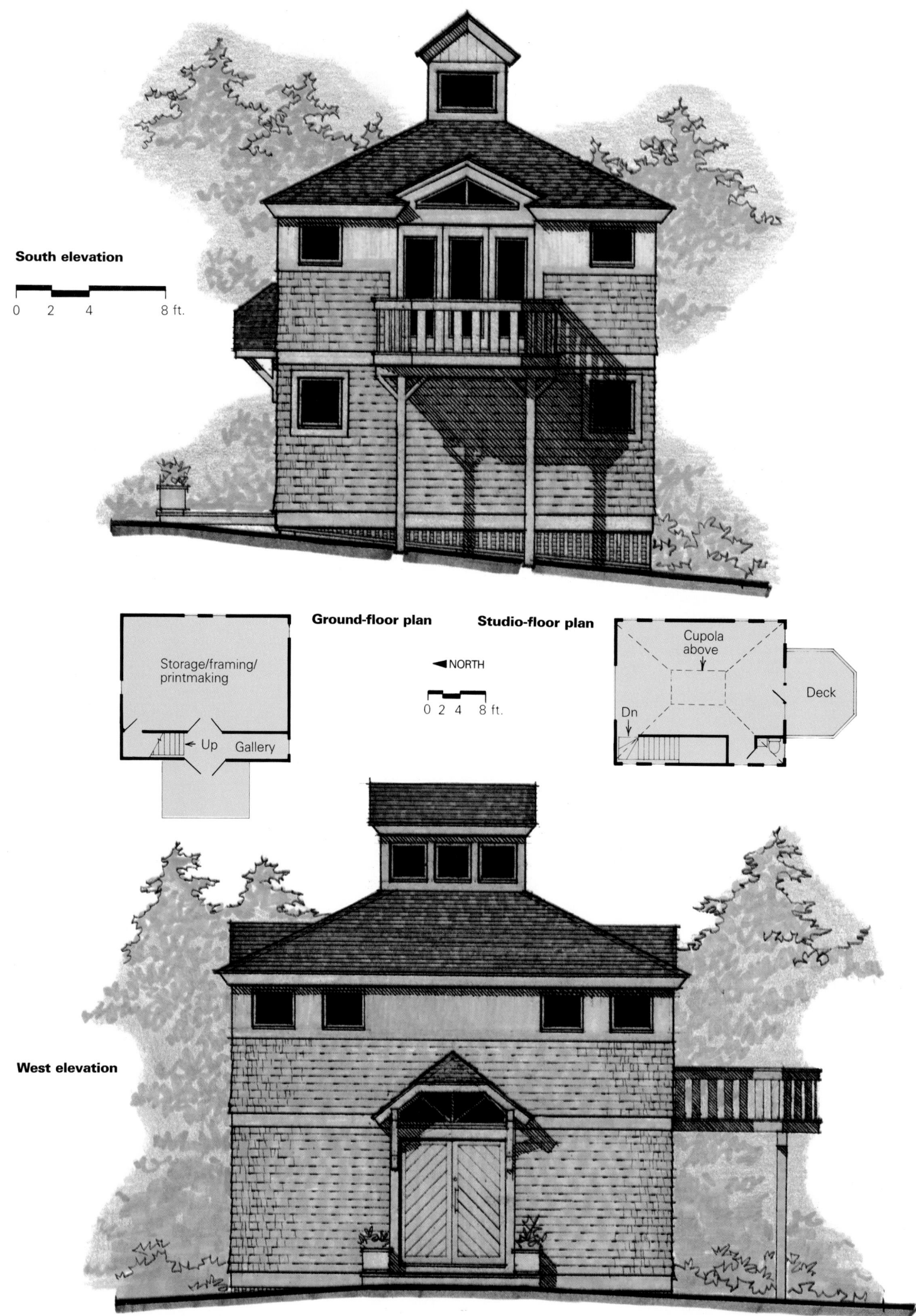

South elevation

0   2   4   8 ft.

Ground-floor plan

Studio-floor plan

Storage/framing/
printmaking

Up   Gallery

◄ NORTH

0 2 4   8 ft.

Cupola
above

Deck

Dn

West elevation

From *Fine Homebuilding* magazine (December 1988) 50:78-81

A Modest Studio on the Maine Coast

Its unusual wall-framing system battens down against the cold

by Jane Lamb

When architect John Silverio agreed to design a studio for Barbara Blanchard, her interest in Far East architecture struck a sympathetic chord in him. As he began designing the little studio for the spruce grove beside Blanchard's house, he thought of blue-and-white willowware, the familiar dinnerware that is decorated with scenes of streams, willows and tiny Oriental temples and houses. He is partial to the imagery of a small structure set alone in a romantic landscape. Silverio himself is a romantic who prefers to work with indigenous materials and colors that blend into the landscape.

The back-to-the-land movement in the 1970s brought to Maine an imagery of self-sufficiency, shed roofs and solar greenhouses. Silverio sees the work and lifestyle of those days as utilitarian to the point of being anti-art. "After living that way," he says, "people have softened a great deal. Now, we realize that it's essential for our freedom and our spirits to include play, beauty, rest—things we used to consider decadent. But, I think they can be recreated so that they don't grow out of luxury."

Working from his interest in the romantic and in tempered self-sufficiency, Silverio designed Blanchard's studio to be a modest, inexpensive building in a style he calls "oriental-shingle-romantic" (drawing, facing page). Although its primary use is not as a full-time dwelling, the studio is an example of Silverio's vision of the "hut of the future," an archetypal house that is simple in structure and responsive to nature and the human spirit.

A light post-and-beam frame—Blanchard and her husband Sumner moved to South Bristol in the spring of 1986. The house they purchased, a passive-solar envelope house, wasn't large enough to accommodate Blanchard's printmaking and painting activities. She wanted to build a detached studio that was not necessarily in the style of the main house. Because Blanchard paints largely from nature, she would use the studio for completing and framing watercolors and for printmaking. She requested two floors: the upper for a well-lighted work space and the lower for storage, framing and printmaking. And she wanted space up high to capture as much light as possible in a wooded setting. The resulting building, rising 25 ft. to the top of the cupola,

presents a vertical image that echoes the surrounding tall spruces. Its roof overhangs, sharply pointed at the corners, suggest a little Chinese temple.

Silverio designed Blanchard's studio to incorporate a framing and insulating system that he hasn't seen used elsewhere. Neither had Richard Lane, the project manager for builder Bruce Laukka, nor foreman John Frye. Silverio developed the method, which he calls "light

Drawing: Michael Mandarano

Wall assembly (at corner)

- 4x4 post, 4 ft. o. c.
- ½-in. drywall
- 2-in. rigid insulation
- 1½-in. rigid insulation
- Horizontal 2x4, 2 ft. o. c.
- Wiring in chase
- 1x3 base cap
- 1x6 base
- Electrical box
- 2x4 sill
- 2x8
- 1x4
- 2x8 joist 16 in. o. c.
- 2x6
- Double 2x4 top plate
- Tyvek over ½-in. plywood sheathing
- White cedar shingles

post-and-beam," from an old United States Department of Agriculture bulletin on farm buildings and first used it on his own barn and outbuildings. Unlike conventional post-and-beam construction, this system has no notched joinery. All framing members are simply lapped and spiked, economical of both materials and labor and demanding no unusual skills.

Silverio designed the entire building around a 4-ft. square module. The foundation is straightforward. Six-by-six pressure-treated posts were drilled to receive drift bolts, which were 12-in. long rebars cast into 4-ft. deep tapered concrete piers. The first-floor deck was framed with 2xs, decked with plywood and T&G pine and is well-insulated beneath with 2 in. of rigid foil-faced foam insulation. After the first-floor deck was built, the first-floor walls were framed and then raised into place like standard stud walls. But instead of 2x4 framing, Silverio used 4x4 rough-cut spruce posts at 4 ft. o. c. A conventional 2x4 double-top plate ties the posts together (drawing, left).

To stiffen the structure and provide space for rigid insulation, 2x4s were nailed horizontally to the outside of the 4x4 posts at 2 ft. o. c., and a 2x6 was nailed to the outside of each double plate to provide a stop for the edge of the interior layer of insulation. Windows were roughed in and 1½-in. rigid insulation was fit between the 2x4s and nailed to the posts. Before raising the walls, Frye and his crew added ½-in. CDX plywood sheathing and Tyvek wrap. After all the walls were in place, Frye installed a second layer of 2-in. thick insulation between the 4x4s, then hung drywall between the posts using extra-long drywall screws. Although Laukka originally was somewhat skeptical of the labor involved in Silverio's system, it turned out to take no longer than standard stud construction that uses batt insulation.

Keeping warm—The well-sealed walls resist the wind and cold of Maine's coastal winter. By using phenolic foam insulation (Koppers Co., Inc., 1900 Koppers Bldg., Pittsburgh, Pa. 15219), the walls achieve an insulation value of R-29, and 9-in. batt insulation over 1 in. of rigid insulation boosts the roof rating to R-35. Phenolic foam insulation is less flammable and toxic than urethane foam, and boasts a greater insulating value per inch than ure-

one atop the other. The collectors draw cold water from the lower tank and send heated water back to the upper tank. Cold replacement water enters the system at the bottom of the lower tank. Having two tanks reduces the mixing that occurs when cold water enters a single tank, thus increasing the amount of usable hot water. The upper tank also has a backup electric heating element (almost always turned off). The floor had to be engineered to carry the weight of the tank (more than 600 lb. when full). The system is entirely passive, supplies virtually all of our hot water, and cost only $1,500 installed.

Controlling air quality—I feel that mechanical ventilation should be present in all houses to assure indoor air quality. There is a lot of hand-waving occurring around this issue, with many people claiming to solve the problem by not building their houses "too tight." These houses, with no predictable ventilation, often turn out to have the worst indoor air quality. Common sense rejects the use of potentially hazardous building materials, but even the healthiest house needs a controllable means of eliminating odors and excess humidity.

I usually exhaust air from locations with the highest concentrations of odors and humidity—kitchens, baths, laundries and greenhouses. Once again, integrated design can improve the functioning of the ventilation system, as well as keep construction costs down. For example, my two bathrooms are stacked one above the other and share a common plumbing wall with the laundry room. A single, 6-in. PVC vent duct, which descends through this wall to the heat exchanger in the basement, serves both baths, the laundry and the adjacent kitchen. An additional inlet in the basement below the greenhouse helps to ventilate the greenhouse. The fresh-air inlet is at ceiling level in the basement hallway, where it won't cause anyone to feel a draft.

Many people confuse the need for ventilation with the need for a heat-recovery ventilator. The decision to ventilate is based on occupant health and building longevity. Adding heat recovery to the system is a decision that gets made on economic grounds—how much one can save in the future by investing now in a heat-recovery ventilator. In homes heated with fossil fuel, I almost always include heat recovery. In the houses I design that use wood heat, there is often no heat recovery, although I try to leave provisions for easy installation at some later date. When heat recovery *is* called for, the efficiency of the heat-recovery ventilator is important—it makes no sense to use 200 watts of fan power to save cheap wood heat.

Heat recovery at my house is provided by an AirChanger heat exchanger (distributed by Memphremagog Heat Exchangers, P. O. Box 490, Newport, Vt. 05855; 802-334-5412), which is both thermally and electrically efficient. It's controlled by an integral dehumidistat, which turns the unit on when humidity reaches a set level, and by 30-minute crank timers in each bathroom. Both of these controls bump the

A passive-solar thermosiphon water heater (top photo) works in parallel with a water-heater in the woodstove (photo above). Wood and solar are ideal complementary sources; the stove is typically on when the sun isn't.

The home's only backup heat is provided by an undersized 11,900 Btu/hour propane heater. But superinsulated houses, especially those that take advantage of solar gains, can function quite well with such units.

exchanger up to its maximum ventilation rate. It can also be run continually at a reduced airflow if desired.

Other energy savers—Water consumption is minimized by using low-flow showerheads and faucets, and by using 1-gal. flush toilets. Electric costs are held down by energy-efficient compact fluorescent lighting. One final area where I feel we saved energy is in the use of durable materials. Hardwood floors and stairs, ceramic tile, and cedar shingles are far more durable than their modern replacements.

Effects of a high time constant—Two years ago we had occasion to heat the house using only propane. I was apprehensive about relying on an 11,900 Btu/hour heater to heat a home that needs more like 16,000 Btu/hour at 20° below zero. But I discovered that houses like mine can get by with undersized heating units rather well. The key is what is called the "time constant."

The time constant is a building's thermal mass divided by its heat-loss coefficient. Any building, when its heat is cut off, will experience a continuous drop in temperature, the rate of which will slow as the building approachs the ambient outdoor temperature. The higher the time constant, however, the more slowly a building will cool down. High time constants can be achieved by using lots of masonry or heavy timber inside (increasing the thermal mass), or by adding insulation and sealing the building envelope (lowering the heat-loss coefficient). Mobile homes, being lightweight and poorly insulated, have very low time constants. Superinsulated homes like mine have large time constants. On a very cold night, when my heater is actually supplying less heat than the house requires, the house will cool so slowly that only a slight loss in temperature (2° F to 3° F) occurs. As soon as the sun comes up, however, the house begins to recover its lost heat. But beware: if a heater is undersized and the house cools substantially, it may take quite a long time for it to reach a comfortable temperature again.

Five years of experience—We've now been in the house for five years. From a conservation perspective, the house has been successful—our annual energy consumption is about 2,000 KWH of electricity and about 1⅓ cords of wood (or 210 gal. of propane). The energy-efficient features neither define nor intrude upon the house design. What has been most gratifying is the response of a wide range of visitors. The backhoe operator who worked on the site brought his wife over to see it, and the artist who lives in town cornered me at the store one day and asked if he could have a tour, "to see if the inside was as nice as the outside." □

Marc Rosenbaum, P. E., owns Energysmiths, a company that specializes in the design of low-energy use, environmentally sound housing. Photos by Charles Wardell.

The House Under the Garden
An owner-built house of salvaged materials cuts costs

by Charles Miller

Photos of the first house Charles Rand designed and built ended up in the Museum of Modern Art in New York. They're in a silk-screened box designed by Andy Warhol in the late 60s, which was crafted to mimic a container of laundry detergent. In dayglow colors, the box says *FAB* across its top, summing up a decade's worth of pop psychology research conducted in communes and Volkswagon buses all over the world. Inside the box is an issue of *Aspen* magazine, a coun-

ter-culture journal that documented the events of the times.

One of the magazine's contributors, Bob Chamberlain, crossed paths with Rand and his Parisian wife Lydia in Aspen in 1966. There he interviewed the young couple in their new A-frame chalet—a house style charged with alpine mysticism. Reaching skyward with its exaggerated roof, the A-frame embodied the spirit of the times, merging the rustic hand-hewn textures of the log cabin

with the purity of the Egyptian pyramids. "It was also one of the dumbest designs for a house ever conceived," remembers Rand. "All the heat rose to the ridge, where it escaped through the uninsulated sheathing."

Chamberlain recorded a dreamy conversation with the Rands about their house and their travels to Nepal. The transcribed conversation, bound into a pamphlet illustrated with black and white photos of the house, is but one of many artifacts from the 60s that ended

From *Fine Homebuilding* magazine (Spring 1989) 52:74-77

up in the *FAB* box. Rand, now a robust, fiftyish man who resembles Mark Twain just before his hair went to white, shudders to recall the disconnected dialogue. But he simultaneously flashes a sheepish grin about what was obviously a time of great fun, as he and Lydia discovered how not to build a house.

Twelve years later—As Aspen became an increasingly crowded playground for the rich, the Rands decided it was time to make a move toward a more egalitarian township. They picked Mendocino County, a piece of coastal Northern California known for its fog, redwood forests and craggy shoreline. The Rands joined up with another family to buy a 20-acre hunk of ridgetop land a few miles from the coast, in a ravine called Jack Peters canyon. Their share included a level spot on the northern edge of a small meadow, but most of it was on a south-facing slope of about 30°. For their house site, they chose a portion of the ridge just where it turns downhill.

Rand built a barn on the level portion of the site. It would serve as temporary shelter for the growing family, which now included daughters Tatayana and Arianne, and son Kyle. They all lived upstairs, while the ground level became a storage vault for recycled materials. Rand had begun to sell country real estate, and in his travels he kept his eyes open for buildings that were likely candidates for dismantling. A hodgepodge of old doors, windows, timbers, siding and sinks began to accumulate in the barn, along with piles of beach rocks and rusty steel implements that weren't exactly building materials, but were too interesting to pass up. Soon Charles and Lydia started sketching floor plans for the real house. For inspiration, they looked through books by the gurus of the back-to-the-land era: David Wright, Ken Kern, Rex Roberts and Calvin Rustrum.

Instead of a postage-stamp plan engulfed by a vast pointy gable, à la the A-frame, the Rand's new scheme laid the house down in a long string of rooms that follow the east/west contours of the site (drawing at right). The house is windowless on the north side, but makes up for this with an abundance of glass in the southern wall, opening the house to the view of the forested canyon. The one-story wings of the house are covered with leafy perennials that Lydia has nurtured into a luxurious mat (photo, facing page).

A bulge in the middle of this linear plan accommodates the great room. It's 32 ft. by 24 ft., with the southern corners lopped off at 45° angles. The kitchen counter is tucked along one of the lopped corners, and the window over the sink opens onto a greenhouse filled with tomato plants and herbs. An island built around one of the posts supporting the upstairs bedroom screens the kitchen from the sitting area in front of the masonry fireplace. At the southern end of the great room, a huge baronial table made of a solid slab of redwood is the center for entertaining, family dinners and homework (photo, following page).

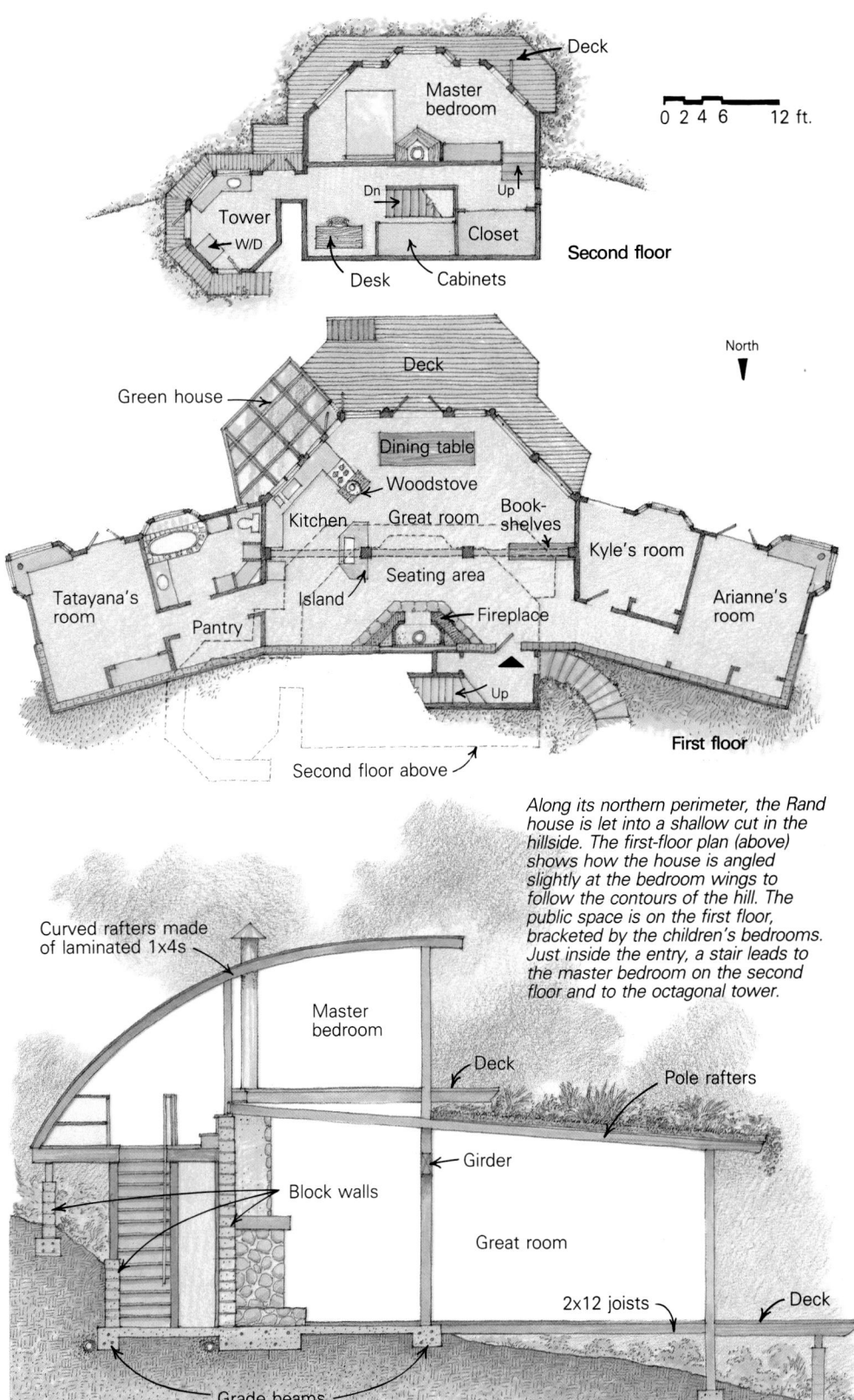

Along its northern perimeter, the Rand house is let into a shallow cut in the hillside. The first-floor plan (above) shows how the house is angled slightly at the bedroom wings to follow the contours of the hill. The public space is on the first floor, bracketed by the children's bedrooms. Just inside the entry, a stair leads to the master bedroom on the second floor and to the octagonal tower.

At opposite ends of the house are the girls' rooms—a move designed to promote harmony among teenage sisters. Kyle's room is just west of the entry. Giving each one of the children his or her own room was one of the compelling reasons for building the house, so Rand made the rooms large enough to contain the trappings of adolescence, with some room left over for play or an overnight guest. The girls' rooms are each about 150 sq. ft., and each room has a French-door outside entry and a window seat.

On a second level, centered above the living space, is the master bedroom (drawing above). From the side, its curving, shingled form resembles the arc of a wave about to break on the upstairs deck. A north/south section through the house shows how the curved rafters, which are made of four laminated 1x4s, spring from the north wall to form a canopy above the stair, the upstairs hallway and the bedroom (drawing above). The hall is wide enough to accommodate a

closet and some cabinets, along with a writing desk for Lydia.

Out of the ground, slowly—After the piles of salvaged materials had grown for several years, Rand finally felt as though he was ready to build the new house. A visit from the bulldozer took care of the cut needed to nest the house into the hillside. Then entropy hit. Speedy people move to Mendocino to slow their pace, and it works. Gripped by woodsy

Surplus meets serenity in the downstairs bathroom, where a used tub (photo left) is surrounded by a skirt of blemished culled tiles. At the heart of the house is the great room, a 600-sq. ft. space that encompasses the kitchen, living and dining areas. Shown in the center of the photo below, the window over the sink opens onto the greenhouse, where herbs grow at arm's reach.

torpor, Rand noodled around the site without accomplishing very much for a couple of weeks. Finally, his friend and co-landowner, John Knoebber, put it to him. "Are you going to build it or not?" The boot got Rand in gear. He rallied a group of friends to help with the concrete pour, and the project was on again.

The structural core of the house is the masonry wall that surrounds the fireplace. A fan-like array of redwood pole rafters bears on the wall, which is made of 8-in. concrete block reinforced with rebar in every other cavity.

Mendocino has a wet climate, and Rand knew that the masonry walls buried in the hillsides would get damp and stay that way unless he took the proper precautions. First he troweled a surface-bonding mix over the walls. This is a portland cement-based coating that is reinforced with chopped fiberglass. Next, he coated the below-grade portions of the exterior walls with asphalt emulsion, followed by a 2-in. layer of extruded polystyrene foam insulation. At the base of each block wall is a foundation drain that directs ground water around the wings of the house. And Rand is careful to keep the gutter at the base of the curved roof free of leaves, thereby preventing the roof runoff from collecting on the north side of the house.

Grade beams border the slab portion of the downstairs floor. Where the hill drops away, a grid of 2x12 joists picks up the living-room floor, and extends beyond the south wall to carry the deck (bottom photo, facing page). A couple of 12x12 bridge timbers bear on piers cast into the grade beam that traverses the living room. They carry a girder that in turn supports the southern wall of the master bedroom.

The southern wall of the main level is entirely post and beam. Log columns, pinned to a string of independent piers, support 4x8 headers over the many windows. Spanning 14 ft. over the downstairs bedrooms are 4x8s, 3 ft. o. c. The ceiling decking above them is 2x6 fir, followed by 3 in. of rigid foam insulation. A sod roof had to go over this assembly, and Rand was tempted to use as waterproofing inexpensive remnants available from a company that lines swimming pools with neoprene membranes. But the thought of a patchwork barrier between the sod and the ceiling didn't sit right with him, so he splurged on full sheets of 22-oz. vinyl-coated nylon waterproofing to cover the roof. So far it has paid off, and there have been no leaks.

For sod, the Rands laid down a 6-in. thick layer of a mixture known locally as "Albert's Best." It's a blend of redwood sawdust and composted fish waste. For the roof garden, Lydia chose plants that remain in leaf all year, while blooming at different times to ensure continual color. The plantings are very effective in concealing the house. The roof over Arianne's room is to the right of the entrance path, and is completely invisible as structure. One night she heard a heavy clump-clump up there. It was her horse, escaped from its corral and hunting for greener pastures.

For protection from the rain, the redwood poles and 4x8 rafters over the bedrooms extend beyond the southern walls to carry eaves that are about 2 ft. deep. Anything more would rob the interior of too much daylight, and in a climate that gets as much fog as Mendocino does, you want all the light you can get.

Keeping costs down—With the luxury of looking for building parts over a long period of time (and a place to store them), Rand was able to collect nearly every fixture type or material he needed. The big insulated windows on the south side of the house are patio door units, purchased at great savings because they are standard-sized pieces, which were bought in quantity without frames. And of course the house framing was designed to accept the windows, rather than vice versa. Some of the other windows and doors came from companies that install new aluminum-framed replacements. These companies often have a boneyard out back where they sell off for donut money what they take out of their clients' homes.

At salvage yards, Rand found used 2x6 decking, which he recycled into subfloors and roof decks, and 700 sq. ft. of strip maple. The maple came out of a high school gymnasium, and it now covers the living-room floor. Used plumbing fixtures are very cheap—if you don't need something an oddball size. In the downstairs bath, an old claw-foot tub has found a new home. It is surrounded by a border of bright tiles, some of which are hand-painted pieces brought back from Mexico (top photo, facing page). The other tiles are blemished culls bought from a local tile manufacturer.

Rand estimates that the house cost about $30,000 to build in 1981. At 1,700 sq. ft., that works out to just a little under $18 per sq. ft. Because Rand did about half the labor, he put most of the money into excavation and into essentials that couldn't be scrounged, such as concrete and septic and mechanical systems. But the used materials do more than cut costs. They have given the family freedom to live in a house that invites participation. Lydia can grow her flowery cape over the wings of the house, and if the roof springs a small leak, well, the ceiling decking already looks weathered. Kyle can pin a freshly collected sphynx moth to one of the old posts in the living room, and nobody complains about the hole.

Epilogue—Kyle is now twelve, and he made it known that he wouldn't mind having a room with its own entry, maybe a little farther from the center of the house. His dad planned to build the addition along the lines of a minaret, with an onion dome on top, until he realized that learning how to build the dome might de-

lay the project until Kyle was in college. So he compromised. Kyle's new rooms are on the second and third levels of a Victorianesque tower that rises from the northeast corner of the house (photo above). His bed is on the very top, where he has a view through an octagonal skylight. □

Charles Miller is senior editor with Fine Homebuilding.

The latest addition to the Rand house is Kyle's Victorianesque tower, rising from the northeast corner of the house. Its second floor starts just above the patterned shingles, shown in the photo above. From there, a ladder leads to a bed loft on the third floor tucked in among the rafters. The first level of the tower houses a lavatory, a shower and a stacked washer and dryer. In the foreground is the deck off the master bedroom, and to the right, yellow flowers grow atop Tatayana's room. The ground-floor framing extends beyond the dining area to support an intimate outdoor sitting area, which is surrounded by trees and potted plants (photo right). During their European travels, the Rands made it a point to visit flea markets, where they collected the pieces of leaded glass that are found throughout their house.

An Attic Studio Apartment

The necessities of home in about 350 square feet

by Robert Malone

Attic remodels are a favorite project for our construction company. As attics are transformed into living spaces, they almost always take on pleasingly quirky, angular volumes that reflect a challenging set of constraints, such as working with established ceiling heights and predetermined roof slopes.

One such project that gave us more than a typical share of problems to solve is this studio apartment (photo facing page). Our clients saw the dusty attic space over the garage of their mid-30's Tudor-style house as a potential bedroom for their teenage daughter. Shoehorning a bedroom into the space would have been pretty easy, but in addition to serving as a bedroom, they wanted the space to do occasional double duty as a guest apartment. Therefore, in addition to an alcove for a bed, a desk and some closet storage (top photo, next page), the new space needed its own bathroom and kitchenette. And to give it a focal point, our clients wanted the room to have a fireplace as well. Given that we had about 350 sq. ft. of floor space to work with, we knew we'd have to make use of every bit of it (drawing at right).

The dormer decision—It became apparent at the onset of my design work that we'd have to add some dormers to the garage roof to get enough space to accommodate everything. Because we wanted to keep exterior changes compatible with the style and proportions of the existing structure, we were concerned that the dormers would overwhelm the garage. Consequently, we placed the smallest dormer on the street side (photo above) and patterned it after a hip-roof dormer on the house. Two larger dormers with shed roofs round out the changes to the original roof over the garage (drawing next page). By adding the three dormers, we amassed 350 sq. ft. of floor area with ceilings high enough to legally qualify as living space.

The building code that most often constrains—or even dashes—our clients' grandest dreams of a new use for their neglected attic is the one that governs minimum ceiling heights. Fortunately, the building code (UBC in our region near San Francisco Bay) accepts the inclusion of sloped ceiling heights down to 5 ft. in the computation of required minimum floor area, and only 50% of the rooms with sloped ceilings are required to meet pre-

Only a small dormer on the street-side elevation of the garage hints at the changes inside.

Floor plan

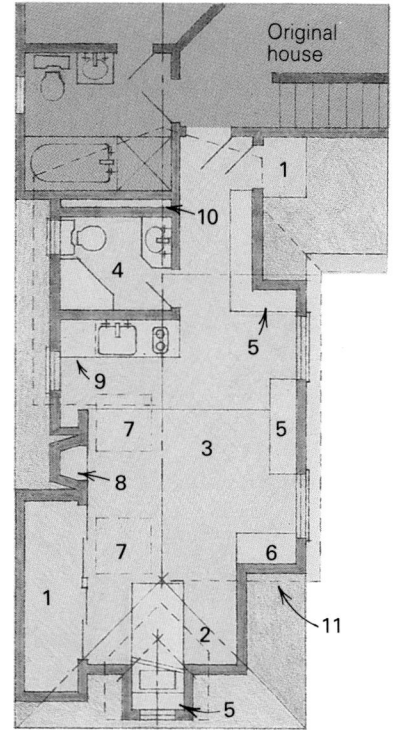

0 2 4   8 ft.

NORTH ▶

1. Closet
2. Bed alcove
3. Sitting area
4. Bath
5. Built-in shelving
6. Built-in desk
7. Skylight
8. Fireplace
9. Under-counter refrigerator
10. Plumbing and electrical chase
11. Line of dormer roofs

scribed minimum ceiling heights. Of course, these portions of the code can be subject to interpretation, so it helps when plan-checkers are flexible when looking over the drawings at the permit desk.

Pier and beam implants—The garage floor is a slab, and its walls are of standard stud construction. While all the components were in excellent condition, the depth of the perimeter slab foundation wasn't sufficient to support a second floor. To beef up the footings, we found a typical, and relatively inexpensive, solution. We poured new concrete piers, approximately 2 ft. 6 in. square by a minimum 2 ft. deep, on 6-ft. centers under the existing perimeter foundation. Each pier contains a steel-rebar grid anchored to rebar pins drilled into the original foundation.

Because we had substantially reduced the weight of the garage by removing much of the roof and the attic floor, we decided to go ahead and undermine the original foundation for all the new piers. That allowed us to pour all of the piers at once.

Attic floors from 30's-era houses in our area are typically framed with 2x4s, which are inadequate as floor framing. So we assume from the outset that a new floor system will be needed in most attic conversions. For this job we divided the lengthwise span of the garage (19 ft. 9 in.) into three bays by placing built-up 6x12 beams atop 4x8 posts bolted to the new piers and the original stud walls of the garage. In remodel work we always try to use beams that we can laminate in place because the individual 2x members are much more maneuverable in confined spaces. Site-built laminated beams aren't always as strong as timbers, however, and have to be overbuilt accordingly.

We set the beams as low as was practical to provide adequate headroom in the garage (residential garage ceilings aren't required to meet the height requirements of living spaces). Then we filled in the roughly 6-ft. spans between them with 2x6 joists 16 in. o. c., secured to the sides of the beams with joist hangers. Over the study at the rear of the garage we had to span 9 ft., so we tightened the spacing of the 2x6 joists to 12 in. o. c. Because we had to maintain the headroom in the downstairs study, we had to step up this section of the floor frame. This level change

The east side of the studio has an alcove for a bed and a corner for a built-in desk. Behind the low doors on the right, closets reach into the triangular space above the eave. The hinged door above the bed opens into a storage compartment for blankets and sheets.

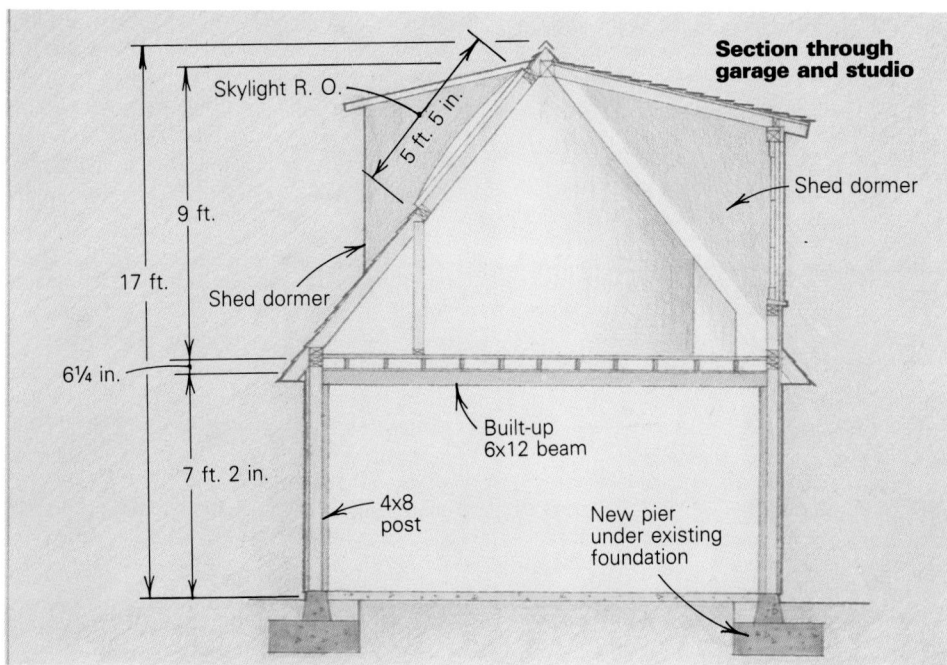

Section through garage and studio

Skylight R. O.

5 ft. 5 in.

9 ft.

17 ft.

Shed dormer

Shed dormer

6¼ in.

7 ft. 2 in.

4x8 post

Built-up 6x12 beam

New pier under existing foundation

---

occurs where the oak floor meets the tile at the kitchenette.

In a job like this, where every square foot is precious, the difference between 2x4 and 2x6 framing can be significant. If we had used 2x6s, the width of the building shell would have been 4 in. smaller, thereby trimming 30 sq. ft. (more than 50% of the bathroom) from the floor area. We used 2x4s.

The original 2x4 rafters were on 32-in. centers. We filled in the spaces between them with additional 2x4s to get 16-in. spacing for

our drywall. The exterior walls are also 2x4s, while the interior partition studs are 2x3s. To reach the required R-30 insulation in the ceiling we added ½-in. furring strips to the interior edges of the rafters. That gave us enough room for 4 in. of polyisocyanurate foam insulation (R-7.5 per inch).

Squeezing in the mechanicals—In addition to getting adequate headroom space, finding suitable places for a staircase to the main floor and for plumbing and electrical chases

creates the biggest dilemmas in attic remodel design. In this case, a linen closet off the second-floor hall provided a convenient connection between the new studio and the original house. We found our mechanical chase in a wall cavity between the new studio bathroom and the existing upstairs bathroom. This 1-ft. wide cavity had the advantage of being close to the new plumbing connections in the studio's bathroom and kitchenette on the upstairs side, while in the basement the chase opened up near the primary building drain and the electrical panel.

Still, we had to make some adjustments to allow for our plumbing within the shallow 2x6 joist bays. We solved the toilet problem with a rear-discharge toilet (large photo, facing page), which routes the waste line through the wall behind the toilet before heading for the drain. This kind of toilet allowed us to avoid having to squeeze a closet bend into a 2x6 joist space and around a lot of existing framing members that weren't going to be easy to move. To make room for the P-trap under the shower, we built a raised platform for the shower pan to rest on.

I think lighting is an important and often overlooked part of residential design. Consequently, I encourage our customers to look at the benefits of flexible lighting schemes that can provide a range of illumination for both area and task lighting.

In this job, the problem became the search for recessed fixtures that could fit in the meager 4-in. deep rafter bays. We ended up using a combination of compact low-voltage recessed cans (Alesco, a division of Sylvan Designs, Inc., 8921 Quartz Ave., Northridge, Calif. 91324) and surface-mounted cylinder fixtures (CSL Lighting, Inc., 25070 Ave. Tibbetts, Valencia, Calif. 91355-3447) as well as standard 110-volt mini-cans (Juno Lighting, Inc., 2001 S. Mount Prospect Rd., Des Plaines, Il. 60017-5065). Even the heat-fire detector (Chemetron Fire Systems, Inc., 1000 Governors Highway, University Park, Il. 60466) is a compact 2-in. diameter by 1 in. deep. Just below the ridge of the main room, a 13-ft. long site-built light fixture suspended from the ceiling can softly illuminate the entire space.

The main room is heated with unobtrusive Intertherm electric resistance, fan-assisted heaters (Nordyne, Inc., 10820 Sunset Office Dr., St. Louis, Mo. 63127) that fit into the toe spaces of the built-in cabinets. A thermostat controls the temperature in the main room, while another heater in the bathroom is on a separate switch.

Walls and shelves—As we finished the drywall walls, we worked to match the original rounded-corner and lightly textured plaster finish of the house, but with modern materials. Years ago, before we discovered bullnose metal drywall corner bead (Beadex Corp., 1325 El Pinal Dr., Stockton, Calif. 95205), our crew labored through a multi-step process using fabric joint tape and multiple layers of carefully applied joint compound over sealed three-quarter-round wood molding at outside cor-

From *Fine Homebuilding* magazine (April 1990) 60:42-45

A half-round molding hides the joint between baseboard and drywall.

ners. Now we can get the same look in a fraction of the time using the metal bullnose. By trimming about 1 in. from the flange on one side of the bullnose, we can also use it to wrap openings that have inside corners, such as those for windows, doors and skylights. Followed with a heavy skip-trowelling of joint compound over all the drywall surfaces, the new walls are quite compatible with the old ones.

At the baseboards, we started the bottom edge of the drywall 3½ in. above the finished floor height. After the flooring was complete, we filled the resulting gap at the bottom of the wall with ½-in. thick wood, followed by a strip of half-round molding to conceal the joint between the two (photo above). Painted the same color as the wall, the base is an unobtrusive detail that can take the wear from mopheads and vacuum-cleaner nozzles. And the base trim rides above the oak flooring, allowing the oak an expansion gap for seasonal movement.

In keeping with the bullnose look of the plaster corners, we built concealed-mount fixed shelves with rounded edges (photo facing page). The shelves are a 1½-in. thick sandwich of ½-in. birch plywood, separated by ½-in. thick plywood spacers on 6-in. to 8-in. centers. We affixed solid 1½-in. wide wood strips to the exposed edges of the shelves, and shaped them with a router and a round-over bit. These shelf units were then mounted to the walls on ½-in. dia. steel rods that extend from the cavities in the shelves into holes drilled into the wall studs.

Kitchen appliances and cabinets—Diminutive kitchen appliances proved to be harder to find than we anticipated. We finally located a two-burner gas cooktop from Modern-Maid (403 N. Main, Topton, Pa. 19562-1499). We ran into the same problem with an under-counter refrigerator, eventually discovering one made by Gerald Industries (16390 N. W. 52nd

Because the floor is supported by 2x6 joists, a standard toilet would have to rest on a built-up platform in order to accommodate the closet bend. Instead, a rear-discharge toilet hung from the wall allows the plumbing to exit through the wall. A laundry hamper hidden in the wall takes advantage of some available space. The towel bar is the handle to its hinged door.

Ave., Miami Lakes, Fla. 33014). As another frustration, the fridge only came with a door hinged on the right side—just wrong for our floor plan, but an inconveniece that could be tolerated. A toaster-oven mounted below one of the over-counter cabinets rounds out the appliance lineup. Because of space constraints we had custom cabinets, in plastic laminate with radiused edges, built to standard kitchen cabinet heights (34½ in.) but to shallower depths (18 in. to 21 in.).

Out the door—One of several tight clearance problems we encountered and solved was in fitting a full-size door into the passageway to the main house. At the ceiling the sloping roof of the dormer required that we slice about 2 in. off the corner of the door. Our solution was to cut an arched piece off the top rail of the door and affix the offcut to the corresponding part of the head jamb. By rabbeting the edges of the arched rail, both fixed and on the door, we were able to prevent a "daylight gap" at the top of the door. When viewed from the main hall in the house, the closed door deceptively appears to match the existing adjacent doors. □

Robert Malone runs Baywood Building and Design Company in Berkeley, California.

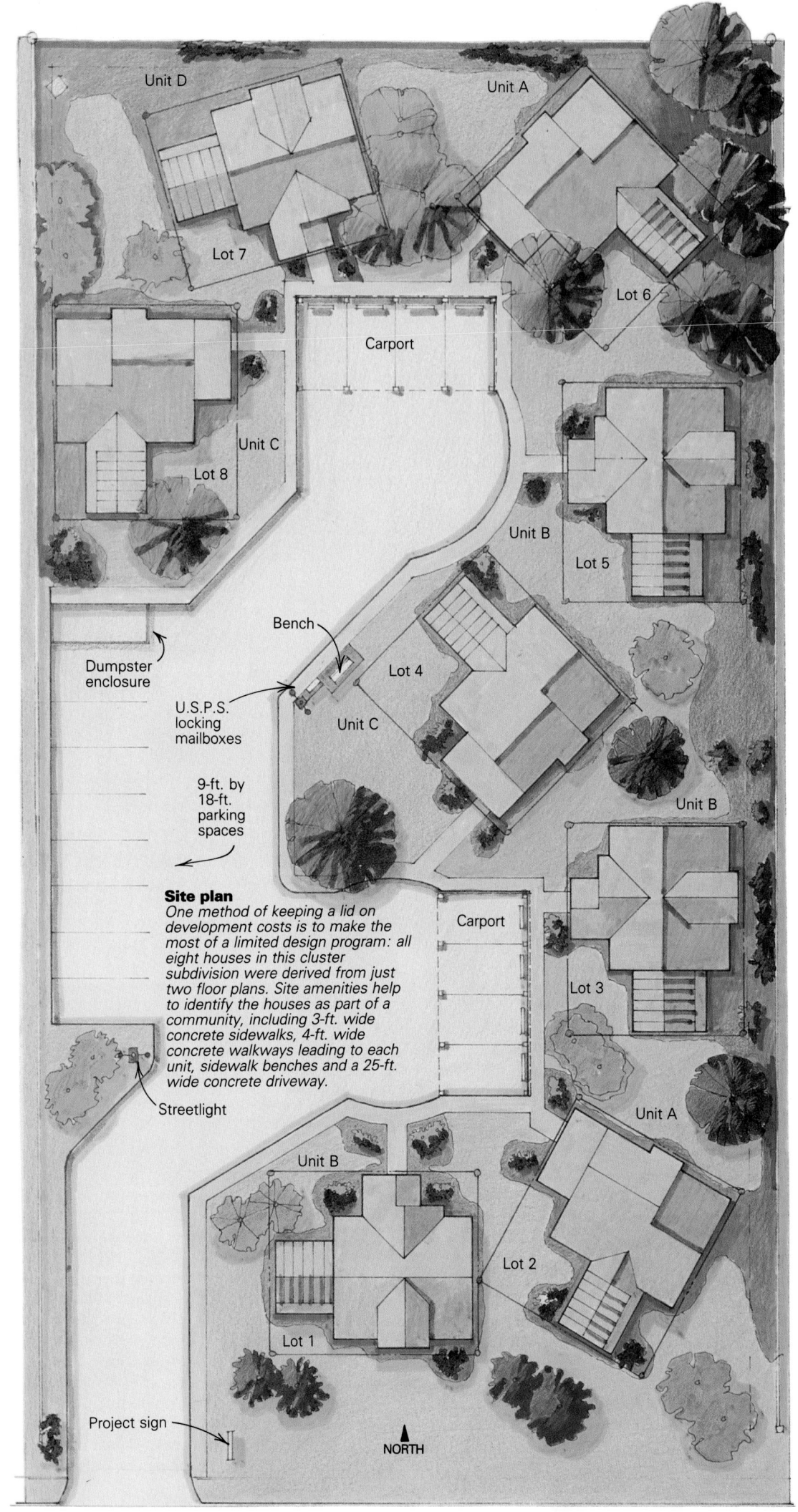

Unit D

Unit A

Lot 7

Lot 6

Carport

Unit C

Lot 8

Unit B

Lot 5

Bench

Lot 4

Dumpster
enclosure

U.S.P.S.
locking
mailboxes

Unit C

Unit B

9-ft. by
18-ft.
parking
spaces

Site plan
One method of keeping a lid on development costs is to make the most of a limited design program: all eight houses in this cluster subdivision were derived from just two floor plans. Site amenities help to identify the houses as part of a community, including 3-ft. wide concrete sidewalks, 4-ft. wide concrete walkways leading to each unit, sidewalk benches and a 25-ft. wide concrete driveway.

Carport

Lot 3

Unit A

Streetlight

Unit B

Lot 2

Lot 1

Project sign

▲
NORTH

A Cluster of Cottages

Eight small, cost-efficient houses make the most of an urban lot

by Daniel Milton Hill

Like many small cities, Eugene, Oregon, has relatively new neighborhoods that sometimes include several old, rundown houses. Usually such houses sit on an unusually large piece of property. Carl and Arlene Ihle purchased just such a property in 1979, along with the old rental house on it, in anticipation of doing something unique with it someday. When that time came, they called on me and my partner, Bill Randall, to handle the design work. We named the project "The Arbors," and the result was a community of eight small houses built for just $55 per square foot each, excluding site development. Careful construction practices and conscientious design work helped to keep costs in line.

A new development tool—Carl and I started talking about what to do with the .94-acre lot in late 1986. We first thought to build four large homes for independent living of the elderly. It seemed like a viable option, considering the fact that Eugene's older population was growing in number. At the same time, the local economy was beginning to strengthen after suffering some hard times, and the housing market looked healthy both for home buyers and renters. When we examined this possibility with Eugene city planners, they told us about another, newer way to develop small pieces of property such as this one—they called it a "cluster subdivision." Its chief advantage was that it allowed greater density than a standard residential subdivision without looking out of place in an existing neighborhood. Like a planned unit development (PUD), a cluster subdivision encourages a comprehensive design; everything from roads and storm drains to closets and carpets are considered as part of the whole. The cluster concept also offers flexibility in the placement of individual units. Each homeowner owns the land immediately under his or her house, along with a foot-wide strip of land immediately surrounding the house—each lot in The Arbors is 1,596 sq. ft. Everything else is owned and maintained by a homeowner's association.

After studying this option with the planners, we decided that we would try to create a small community of affordable, quality homes using the cluster concept. Market information indicated that there was a demand for relatively small houses for single parents, young professionals, widows and widowers.

Setting up the team—We used a team approach to structuring the design process. The members included Carl and Arlene as the owners and developers, real estate agent Pat Albertson, and my partner Bill Randall and myself as project architects. Carl's thrust throughout the project was to do a quality job from site planning to wallpaper, and yet make each house affordable. His job was to keep a close eye on operating expenses as the project progressed. He also set up the financing, interviewed and selected the building contractor, and even did some of the landscaping. Pat's job was to provide information about what kinds of houses were selling in the Eugene market and to find out what "hot buttons" buyers had. As architects, our job was to make the project a design and construction success. We used a standard AIA contract to structure our involvement; in that sense this project was just like one for a single house.

Determining density—The site itself did not have many amenities. There was the rundown rental house, of course, and a separate garage. The ground was flat and swampy, with scrub oaks scattered here and there. To the west was (and still is) a small rundown mobile home on two acres of swampy ground punctuated by a large stand of marginally healthy oak trees. To the north and east is a neighborhood of 15- to 20-year-old tract housing. On the plus side, though, there's a small shopping center nearby, a high school, a junior high and several established churches. Across the street is a well-established neighborhood of nice 15- to 20-year-old homes, and a stop for the city bus is within easy walking distance.

Our first task was to do a thorough site analysis of the property. Using a checklist Bill and I devised, we evaluated soil and subsoil conditions, natural drainage, solar orientation, noise levels and a number of other factors that could affect the design of the project. Given the constraints posed by all those factors, our first problem became that of deciding on the optimum density. The allowable density in this particular zone is approximately 9.6 units per acre. Our rectangular site is 150 ft. by 312 ft., or about .94 acres. That meant we could fit 9.1 units on the site. From a developer's point of view, the more units on the property, the more profitable the project. So after establishing some square footage and unit-shape pa-

rameters (based on information about what our market would want), we worked at fitting nine units on the property. No computer simulations here; we simply used paper cutouts and jockeyed them around a site plan until finding an arrangement that looked suitable.

It was important to all of us to keep the project from feeling like condominiums—to give it some character and make it unique, we wanted single-family detached homes. We felt our layout concept should be random, rather than linear like row houses, in order to include open pockets between the houses that would vary in size and appearance. We also wanted to provide at least two parking spaces for each unit: one covered and one uncovered. But after trying to fit in nine units, the site plan looked too crowded. Eight units became the target when Carl conceded that nine would make the project feel too cramped.

Because of the density of the project, each unit would have to be two stories to minimize the ground coverage. And because of the lack of views and the proximity of the busy street bordering the project, we figured we'd have to turn the front of each house to the center of the project; attractive rear and side elevations would carry the burden of relating to the street and the neighbors.

Plotting the layout—Access to the project from the main street was decided upon easily. The potential of later expanding the property to the west with as many as 16 more units determined that the location of the main entrance should be on the southwest corner of the property. We wanted our small street to have a meandering layout to break up as much as possible the "parking lot" image some developments have (site plan, facing page).

A civil engineer works up the actual specifications and design of the road, working from a conceptual plan provided by the architects or developer. But before he can get started, a decision has to be made by the developer: will the road be a public one or private? If public, the city will build and maintain it; if private, those tasks fall to the developer. The developer, however, pays for the road either way. If the city builds the road, it will be built to reduce maintenance costs, and that will mean relatively high costs up front. A developer can save as much as 30% by building the road to minimum standards, but someone—probably

The Arbors (photo above) is a community of eight small, affordable detached houses. To complete each one for approximately $55 per sq. ft., careful control had to be maintained over design and construction features. Though some of the exterior detailing varies, the interiors were based on just two different floor plans.

the homeowner's association—will pay for this later on in increased maintenance costs. For The Arbors, we decided on a concrete road for its durability and appearance.

The next challenge was to create a structure for the covered parking that would allow good visibility of the houses and blend with them architecturally. Bill and I came up with four 12-ft. wide gables with latticework in the ends; large rough-sawn beams and posts help define each space (photo above).

Solar access was also a design concern in the layout of the houses. Though there are various ways to figure solar layouts, the method we used is a straightforward graphic technique that's actually incorporated into the Eugene zoning codes. We were determined in all units to provide good natural light with the potential of some direct-gain heating, while protecting the neighbors' solar access (required by a city solar code). The project's density and non-linear layout made this a challenge, but our elimination of the ninth unit really helped. Some of the units have more windows facing to the south and east, and they're better able to take advantage of solar gain.

Finding a style—With the density and layout problems solved, we had to figure out what the houses would actually look like. Questions about architectural style, materials, street views, landscaping and automobile access were carefully studied. Most Eugene neighborhoods are fairly conservative in style, but we felt our target market would appreciate something a little more progressive. So we decided to base the designs on traditional cottage shingle styles and add contemporary details—that seemed like a safe, solid approach. We wanted the houses to be consistent with each other in style, color, materials and landscaping so that people passing by would see a small community of homes, not a subdivision. That meant that the houses would be vari-

ations on a common theme, not eight distinctly different designs (photos facing page).

The houses were designed around several basic ideas: energy-efficient construction; the use of great rooms and vaulted areas to make small spaces seem larger; simple architectural details; and conservative, yet pleasing interior finishes. And because the houses would be small—less than 1,200 sq. ft. each—they had to use space as efficiently as possible.

In development projects, the design of each house is often affected as much by economics as by aesthetics. Things were no different here. In line with the need to keep costs down, we decided to build only two different floor plans for the entire project. That meant we'd reproduce each design four times, rather than spend the time and money to design eight entirely different houses. By flip-flopping the floor plans we created different elevations for the exterior and different orientations for the interiors. Aside from savings in design time and expense, however, we also hoped for substantial savings in construction costs.

There was the obvious benefit of ordering in quantity, of course. But there were cost savings, too, in reducing the number of different materials required for the project. Also, materials not used on one house (sheets left over from a unit of plywood, for example) could be used on the next house, making the most of every order. By building essentially the same house eight times, we reduced overall construction costs by 10% to 15%. Some of the savings came from efficient use of labor, while others came from volume discounts on materials. We got a great deal, for example, on woodstoves because we bought eight at once; kitchen cabinets are also cheaper in quantity.

Two floor plans for efficiency—Both plans have two bedrooms, two full baths and laundry facilities, along with a protected, fenced-in patio/storage area. Unit C (and reversed ver-

sion Unit A) is a modified saltbox with 1,105 sq. ft. (drawing facing page). The main living areas are linear, with the living room, dining area and kitchen all on one side of the plan. The dining area cantilevers two feet over the foundation wall to create definition between it and the living room. Both the dining and living areas have a sweeping vault that leads the eye up toward a semi-open master bedroom; a dropped, flat ceiling clearly defines the kitchen. Also downstairs is a full bath, a 9-ft. by 10-ft. bedroom, and two storage closets. A woodstove backs up against a pantry that screens the bathroom from the living room (bottom photo, p. 62).

Upstairs in Unit C there's a master bedroom with a 10-ft. high ceiling and a study/sewing room/office. This room visually extends the master bedroom. The woodstove flue creates and alcove that can be used for a sitting area, a dresser or possible a desk. In the bathroom (top photo, p. 62), a closet contains the washer and dryer. It's a little unusual to have the laundry upstairs, but Pat's market information indicated that many people prefer to have the laundry near the master bedroom because that's where they dress and undress.

Unit B (and reversed version Unit D) is the cottage plan, and it's a bit smaller at 1,056 sq. ft. (drawing facing page). Here the great room has an L-shaped layout, with the kitchen as the short leg (top photo, p. 63). The pantry screens the kitchen-sink area from the living room. In this plan, the vaults are more dramatic: the underside of the 12-in-12-pitch roofs and valley are exposed to the interior (bottom photo, p. 63).

As in Unit C, the master bedroom is upstairs, along with a bathroom. The walls start at six feet and vault up to eleven feet at the ridge. A short hallway with a small walk-in closet on each side creates a dressing area. The upstairs is partially open to the living spaces below, making both the upstairs and

Drawings: Frances B. Ashforth

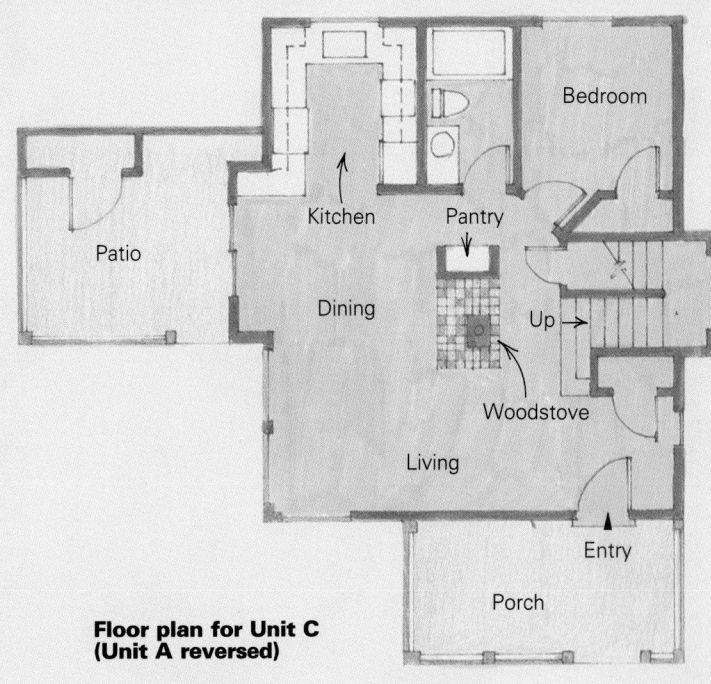

Floor plan for Unit C (Unit A reversed)

Bedroom
Patio
Kitchen
Pantry
Dining
Up
Woodstove
Living
Entry
Porch

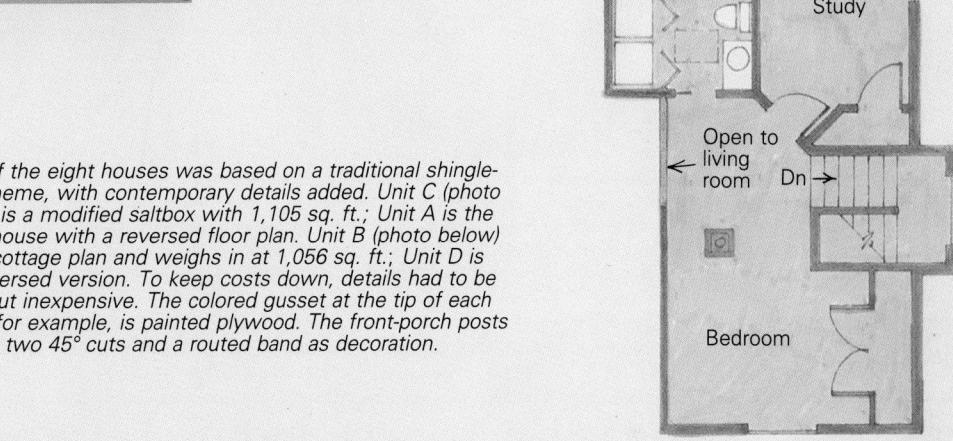

Study
Open to living room
Dn
Bedroom

Each of the eight houses was based on a traditional shingle-style theme, with contemporary details added. Unit C (photo above) is a modified saltbox with 1,105 sq. ft.; Unit A is the same house with a reversed floor plan. Unit B (photo below) is the cottage plan and weighs in at 1,056 sq. ft.; Unit D is the reversed version. To keep costs down, details had to be lively but inexpensive. The colored gusset at the tip of each gable, for example, is painted plywood. The front-porch posts feature two 45° cuts and a routed band as decoration.

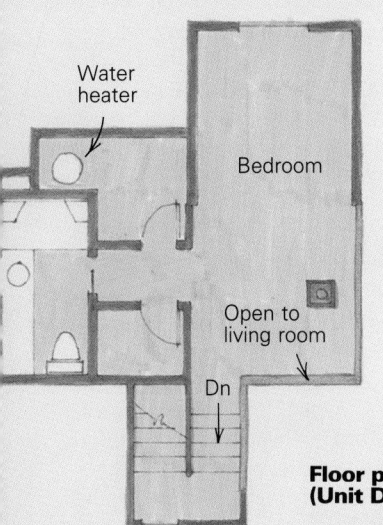

Water heater
Bedroom
Open to living room
Dn

Floor plan for Unit B (Unit D reversed)

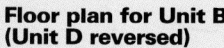

Bedroom
Kitchen
Pantry
Dining
Woodstove
Up
Living
Patio
Entry
Porch

Units A and C feature upstairs bathrooms that include laundry facilities (behind the bi-fold doors in the photo above). Light colors, a small skylight and a vaulted ceiling keep the room from feeling dark and cramped. In houses as small as these, it was important to screen out unwanted views. In units A and C (photo below), a pantry behind the woodstove screens the bathroom door from the living room. Small houses have small bathrooms, too, but the spaces can work hard.

downstairs feel larger. A scheme like this reduces auditory privacy somewhat (visual privacy is still good), but the loss, I think, is far outweighed by the improvement in openness, crucial for a small house.

The density of the project made it important to consider the view each unit would have from the main living areas. Our goal was to have the windows overlook open landscaped areas, not the main living areas of another house. We achieved this by reversing and alternating the plans, and by setting up landscape screens (site plan, p. 58). The patio areas are private outdoor spaces, unlike the public front porches.

Energy-efficiency on a budget—Bill and I wanted all the houses to represent responsible architecture, and to us that's synonymous with energy efficiency. But the fact that energy-efficient houses are also quite marketable wasn't lost on the developer. It also helped to know that the Bonneville Power Administration (the regional utility) and the Eugene Water and Electric Board (the local utility) subscribe to a program called "Super Good Cents." Builders who use energy-efficient construction methods to build new homes can receive a $1,000 incentive to offset the costs of making the homes energy efficient. All of the homes we design meet or exceed these standards, and The Arbors was no exception.

We used a variety of techniques to make houses in The Arbors hold heat in; all of them are cost-effective for this region. Advanced framing techniques dictated the structure. The houses feature 2x6 studs spaced 24 in. o. c.; walls and floors are insulated to R-19 and R-30 respectively. To beef up ceiling insulation, 1-in. rigid insulation was nailed to the underside of the 2x12 rafters, bringing the ceiling to R-38 overall. To reduce infiltration, we installed air/vapor barriers, caulked all sole plates, and used spray foam or caulk elsewhere as needed.

Windows and doors can play a significant role in making a house energy efficient, so I specified insulated vinyl windows (Northwest Aluminum, 1015 E. Lincoln Ave., Yakima, Wash. 98901). We balanced the amount of

glazing area with the floor area of each house and oriented windows wherever possible to maximize solar gain. We called for insulated weatherstripped doors at exterior openings.

Utility rates are relatively cheap here in the northwest—a kilowatt hour of electricity costs 3¢, compared to 8.5¢ cents in New England. So each house uses a zoned heating system that relies on an inexpensive fan-forced electric wall heater in each room (Cadet, 2500 West 4th Plain Blvd., P. O. Box 1675, Vancouver, Wash. 98668). Each heater, which looks like a small return-air grille, is a 240-volt unit. Heaters are controlled by a wall-mounted thermostat and have a squirrel-cage fan that is much quieter than an axial fan.

The efficiency in this type of a system is in its zonal control. Unlike a forced-air system that heats the entire house, our zonal system heats only the rooms that are occupied. Of course, the efficiency of this system depends on user control. If all the heaters are on but people are gathered in just the living room, the system isn't so efficient. But if you've learned to turn out a light switch when you leave a room, you can get used to turning off the heat, too. Because of the high insulation levels in the house, rooms stay reasonably warm once heated, so users don't feel as if they're continually walking into cold rooms.

In the spatial design of each house we tried to incorporate a thermal circulation loop. Heat generated downstairs rises up the vaults and stairwells to the master bedroom. Because each house is so small, chills caused by convection are eliminated, though this could be a problem in a larger house. Based on a 4,700 heating degree-day climate, I expect the space heating bill for each house will be less than $100 a year.

Cutting construction costs—A project like this not only has to pencil out for the developer, but it also has to pencil out for prospective buyers, so construction techniques were carefully tuned to keep construction costs in line. The foundation is a cost-effective footing/stem wall system with crawl space—no basement. The decking is 1⅛-in. thick T&G plywood that spans 4x6 beams 4 ft. o. c. Most builders in this area use 2x8 T&G decking, but thick plywood decking is quicker (and therefore cheaper) to install, and it also eliminates the need for particleboard or plywood underlayment as a base for finish flooring. Most of the siding is ⅝-in. rough-sawn cedar plywood with 1x3 cedar battens 24 in. o. c. (plywood goes up quickly and the battens give it character). Areas that have shingle siding were first sheathed with ½-in. CDX plywood and wrapped with 15-lb. felt before the shingles were installed. The roof was framed conventionally.

The exterior details had to be simple to keep costs down, but we didn't want them to be boring, either. The posts at the front porches are 6x6s with two 45° cuts and a routed band to decorate the surface (photos, p. 61). Window trim and cornerboards were cut from 2x4 stock instead of from 1x4 stock to make them look more substantial; the resulting shadow line is a nice accent. Layers of 2x8 and 1x4 cedar were used to break the lines where a change in siding material occurred at gable ends. We used simple plywood diamond-shaped gussets over bargeboard joints at the ridge, and painted the gussets for accent. We repeated this theme in the rain hoods for the chimneys and the front porch lights.

Interior finishes—As decisions were being made on interior finishes, we had to take a close look at our market. Pat Albertson, Arlene Ihle and Deb Johnston (our interior designer) grappled with the questions of how conservative or daring the interiors should be, how much wallpaper should be used and what colors would be pleasing to both men and women. They decided on four basic color schemes: blue, green, grey, and beige—timeless colors, not faddish ones. These schemes were conservative, but they'd allow prospective owners a great deal of latitude in adding interior furnishings.

In small houses it's important not to overwhelm the spaces with too much wallpaper, so we reserved it for the bathrooms and kitchens. Walls and woodwork, including cabinetry, are the same color. Door and window casing is paint-grade hemlock or birch—painted woodwork seems to make a small house appear bigger. The raised-panel Masonite doors were painted as well.

For finish flooring, we used either wall-to-wall carpet or Tarkett prefinished hardwood flooring with a pickled finish (Tarkett, 114 Mayfield Ave., P. O. Box 3053, Edison, N. J. 08818). In four units the hardwood runs everywhere except the bedrooms; these are carpeted. In the other four units, we used carpet in all of the main living areas except the kitchens and baths—those had hardwood floors.

Working out the economics—Carl and Arlene's objective as developers was not to make a huge sum of money from this project, but to do a quality project that might lead to similar types of development. The cluster subdivision was a new concept, however, and thus a gamble. The goal was to build the units for about $45 per sq. ft., not including site development costs such as parking, sewers and landscaping. The actual costs ran about $55 per sq. ft., excluding site development. Site development costs added about $10 per sq. ft., which was slightly higher than anticipated and was due to problems in working with the swampy ground. Much of the expansive clay soil had to be replaced with a crushed-rock base.

The builder, Bruce Bergby of Goldenridge Construction, and a crew of three built the project over 12 months. We might have saved more money if a larger crew had come in and built all eight houses simultaneously, but we believed that quality might have been sacrificed with the loss of close, personal

attention. Instead, Bergby built two houses, then another two, then the remaining four. Interiors were completed two at a time, depending on the availability of subcontractors. We held an open house after the first two units were finished, but found that it was difficult for people to visualize the completed project. So we decided to complete all eight units before making them available to the public.

During the course of construction, the local rental market changed, and that led Carl to reexamine the economics of the project. The vacancy rate in Eugene was approaching zero and rents had almost doubled in the last 18 months. Carl had already sold one of the units, but decided to hold on to the remainder of the houses as a rental complex. His logic was to cover his debt service on the project with the rents, holding the property for a year or two before selling. That would give the local housing market time to gain steam. He could depreciate the project as investment property and allow the value of the houses to appreciate with the market. Financially, Carl feels that he will come out much better with this plan.

The results—It is always a guessing game to know what a buyer's "hot buttons" are, but it looks like we were on target. We thought our market was the single parent (most likely a woman), young professionals (single or mar-

Open plans help to make a small house feel spacious. Units B and D (photo above) open the kitchen to the great room. Painted woodwork and light-colored floors and walls help to spread light throughout the rooms, while a dropped ceiling over the kitchen defines the space. Laminate countertops and solid-wood edging make an inexpensive but effective combination. In the bedroom of Units B and D (photo below), the vaulted ceiling maximizes the volume of the room while an open wall steals light from the living room below. The column is actually a boxed-in path for the woodstove chimney.

ried), and the widow/widower population. And we figured that they wanted small, affordable, efficient housing. The project was completed early in 1989 and houses one law student, two single women (each with a child), one semi-retired couple, a couple with a teenage daughter, a couple with a young child, a young couple with no children and another couple with two young children. Several of the renters anticipate buying their homes someday. □

Daniel Milton Hill and William Randall are principals and owners of Arbor South Architecture, P. C., in Eugene, Oregon. All photos by Gary Tarleton.

Adapting Usonian
Blending Wright's ideas about the small house with today's construction techniques

by J. Stewart Roberts

During the Depression, Frank Lloyd Wright built very little, but he formulated a number of new ideas for small economical houses. His first opportunity to put these ideas into practice came in 1937, with a commission to design a 1,500-sq. ft. house on a $5,500 budget for Herbert Jacobs in Madison, Wisconsin. Designed when Wright was almost 70 years old, the Jacobs House was the first of more than 100 Usonian houses.

Wright's approach to these houses was to establish a flexible modular-construction system, which he used again and again in different ways for many houses, creating informal living spaces appropriate to the new social conditions of the times. He gave these designs the name "Usonian" (perhaps a modified acronym for United States of North America), and they have had a lasting impact on residential design in the United States. The ranch houses that proliferated in the 1950s and 1960s were watered-down versions of Wright's ideas. Slab-on-grade construction, patios and carports are some of the Usonian vestiges.

When I first met Pat and Marty Schwarz, they were living in a small apartment and were looking forward to building their first home. In the countryside west of Boston, they found a beautiful secluded clearing that had been overlooked by other builders because it was at the end of a long, steep, unpaved path through the woods. The Schwarzes wanted a simple, informal, three-bedroom house constructed of natural materials.

They also wanted to take maximum advantage of passive-solar heating and to use wood fuel to make up the balance of the heating requirements. Together, we analyzed the sun angles on the site and found that by siting a house on the north edge of the clearing, the sun would just clear the tops of the trees on the southern side. This allowed us to build without removing trees.

Because they wanted a home that would merge with its natural setting, I suggested to the Schwarzes that they read Wright's *The Natural House* (New American Library, 1970). It seemed to me that Wright's philosophy toward

Drawings: Frances B. Ashforth

the small house addressed very well the way they wanted to live. After reading the book and seeing photographs of his houses, the Schwarzes committed themselves to a house based on Usonian principles. It is a testament to the strength of Wright's ideas that half a century later, they could be successfully adapted to the design of a contemporary house.

Amended Usonian construction—Architecture can define and enclose spaces, or it can celebrate the drama created when the space escapes. Usonian houses definitely fall into the latter category, and Wright was a master at orchestrating the drama of spatial escape. His goal was to blur the distinction between inside and outside so "one could not tell where the house left off and the garden began."

My intention in designing the Schwarz house was not to copy a particular Usonian design, but to include the same spatial organizations and integrated building components that the Usonian houses enjoyed. Unlike Wright's houses, however, we wanted to build with conventional framing methods and to use the latest energy conservation and passive-solar techniques.

Wright's Usonian houses were constructed on a slab over a drained gravel bed, without footings or foundation walls. While he was able to convince most building officials that this structural system was sound, we opted for a traditional concrete foundation. We did, however, use Wright's technique of coloring the slab, scoring it with control joints to express the planning module and leaving it exposed.

Wright used brick to construct load-bearing exterior walls, as well as a central masonry core containing the kitchen and fireplace. Additional exterior and interior walls were constructed by covering 1-in. plywood with building paper and screwing board-and-batten siding to both sides. Using the same finish materials inside and out was one of the ways in which Wright blurred the line between interior and exterior space.

Rather than build with load-bearing brick walls, though, and uninsulated exterior walls, we used typical frame construction. Two-by-six walls are insulated with R-19 fiberglass

Although the hip roofs and broad overhangs are reminiscent of his prairie houses, the design of this 1,900-sq. ft. house (photo left) is actually based on Frank Lloyd Wright's Usonian ideas. The modular system of construction is reflected in the alternating 10-in. and 2-in. shingle courses, and in the way they coordinate with the window and door trim. Oriented for solar gain, the house also has fascia boards that angle inward to allow maximum sun penetration in the winter. The lack of windows on the north side of the house (photo facing page, below) is another aspect of the passive-solar design.

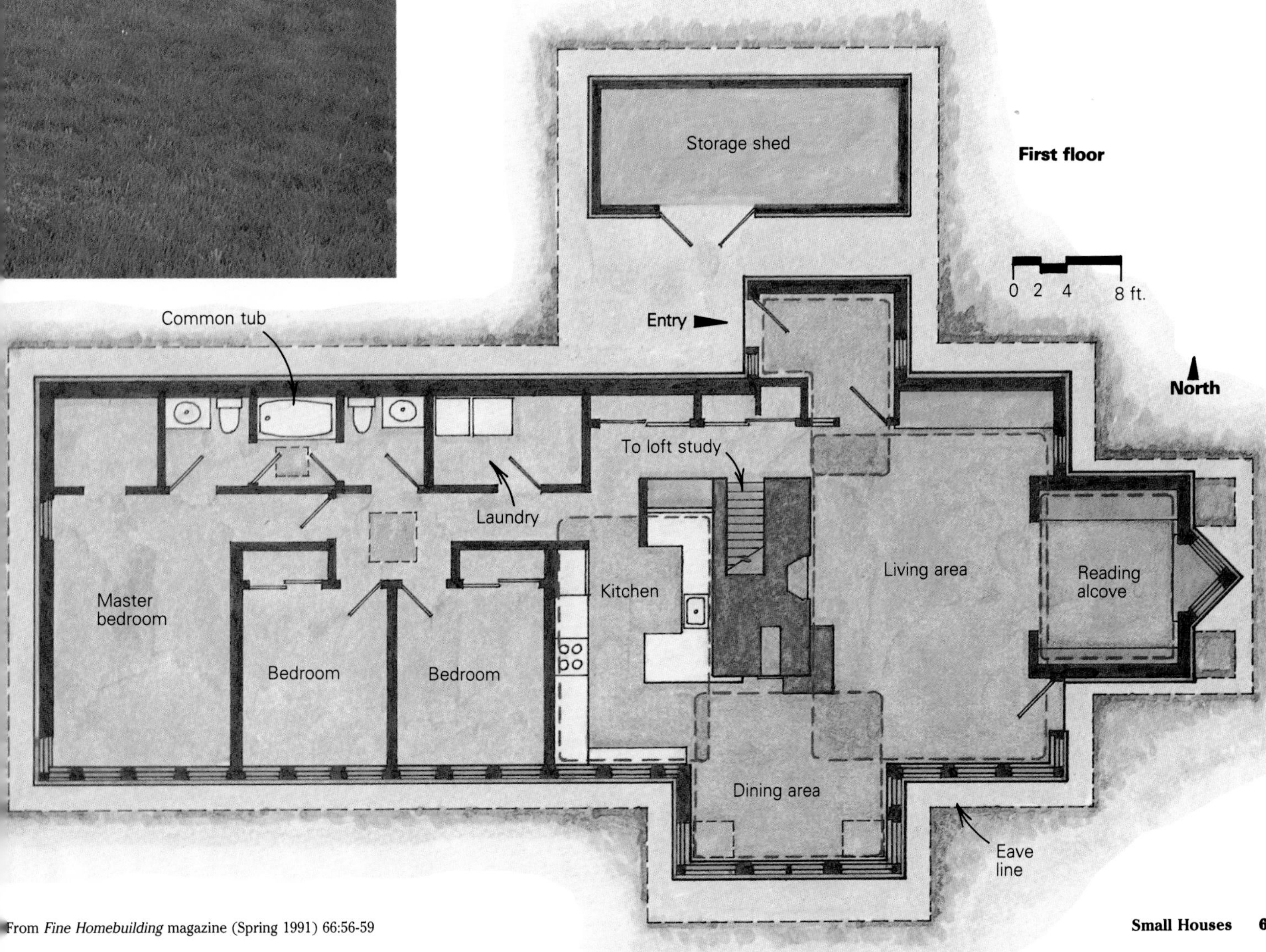

Storage shed

First floor

Entry ▶

0 2 4 8 ft.

▲ North

Common tub

To loft study

Laundry

Kitchen

Living area

Reading alcove

Master bedroom

Bedroom

Bedroom

Dining area

Eave line

batts and a layer of 1-in. thick foil-faced rigid insulation on the interior.

While the typical Usonian house was built with a flat roof, I felt that a flat roof was inappropriate for the New England climate. So I designed the Schwarz house with a hip roof and broad overhangs (large photo, p. 64) that are more reminiscent of Wright's prairie houses than the Usonians.

Overlapping corners—From the entry on the wooded north side of the house, one moves into the living area, where the view to the clearing is first revealed. In this sense the visitor enters the clearing by entering the house. The experience of moving through the house consists of a series of turns and shifting axes, requiring the visitor to change orientation, thereby revealing different aspects of the space. This approach is the antithesis of the symmetrical axial planning of the classical tradition.

The spaces are clearly defined—living room, dining room, kitchen—yet flow together at their corners. For instance, the corner of the living area overlaps the corner of the dining area (floor plan, p. 65). These overlapping corners, which belong to more than one space, provide diagonal views across the living area (top photo, facing page) and contribute a feeling of spaciousness to a 1,900-sq. ft. house.

The first floor is organized so all habitable rooms have southern exposure via a continuous band of operable windows. The entry, living area, dining area and kitchen all flow together around a masonry fireplace at the center of the house.

At the east end of the living room, a more private reading alcove provides a retreat from the openness in the rest of the living area. Down a short hallway off the kitchen, bedroom doorways are grouped together around a skylight alcove. Closets, bathrooms, laundry and storage line up along the north wall. No windows are located on the north side (bottom photo p. 64), so that cold-air infiltration and heat loss are minimized.

We built a small loft study on the second floor overlooking the clearing. This provides a place for Marty, a college professor and mathematician, to work quietly. Accessible by a ship's-ladder stair, the loft can be shut off from the rest of the house with a hatch door in the floor.

A portion of the ceiling around the perimeter of the house is lowered to align with the exterior soffit, thereby extending the feeling of the exterior to the interior of the house. Red

cedar clapboards cover these interior soffits and contain recessed light fixtures framed with cherry (bottom right photo, facing page).

A modular construction system—Like a flower's assembly of petals, this house grew from a modular system of repetitive elements. In the horizontal dimension, I laid out the plan on a 2-ft. by 4-ft. module to make efficient use of framing lumber and plywood. The control joints in the slab and the cherry-paneled ceiling in the main living area reflect this 2-ft. by 4-ft. module.

In the vertical dimension, elevations conform to a 1-ft. module, which is further subdivided into 10-in. and 2-in. modules. All window and door openings coordinate with this module. The exterior of the house is clad with 18-in. resawn and rebutted red cedar shingles, double-coursed with a 10-in. exposure and a 2-in. exposure to express the module and accentuate the horizontal lines of the house. Horizontal window trim is coordinated to align with the 2-in. shingle course. This double coursing uses the same number of shingles and provides the same triple coverage that a standard 6-in. exposure provides.

Interior walls of the living spaces are lined with horizontal cherry boards 10 in. wide, with 2-in. reverse battens between. Built-in cherry shelving, benches and casework coordinate with these modular dimensions and match the board-and-batten walls. Built-in shelves, for instance, have 2-in. nosings spaced 10 in. apart to align with the 2-in. battens of the walls.

A red slab floor—Wright's Usonian houses were built with exposed pigmented concrete floors, both for economy and because the floor contained the radiant-heat source for the house. We were interested in using exposed concrete as an inexpensive finish material and for the thermal mass it would provide.

Marty Schwarz contacted Taliesin West, one of the schools founded by Wright, to find out how Wright had finished his concrete floors. Kenneth Lockhart at Taliesin, who had worked on Wright's houses, explained the process. The procedure consisted of pouring the concrete, screeding it to the proper level and spreading a dry mixture of pigment (Master Builders Inc., 23700 Chagrin Blvd., Cleveland, Ohio 44122; 216-831-5500) into the wet concrete. About a pound of pigment was used per square foot.

The pigment was worked into the concrete with a power trowel, the control joints were then tooled, and the slab was finished with a hand trowel. After the concrete had set up, a sealer coat (also from Master Builders) was applied to give the concrete a slight sheen. Broadcasting the pigment on top of the slab yields an intense color that you can't match by mixing the pigment with the concrete beforehand. Rigid insulation was installed on the exterior of the foundation wall. This insulation was parged and capped with a wooden water table.

Heating systems—Wright disliked any mechanical equipment in the house that was not integrated into the architecture. He devised a system of underslab radiant heating, which he

based on a Korean system of circulating gas from a fire under a floor slab. We chose a masonry core that provides thermal mass and contains a pair of fireplaces. The living-room fireplace, a Rumford design, consists of a shallow firebox with angled sides that direct the maximum amount of radiant heat out into the room.

The bulk of the heating is provided by a Finnish fireplace built into the same masonry core as the Rumford, but facing the dining area (bottom left photo, facing page). Similar to a Russian fireplace, a Finnish fireplace stores heat for use over a longer period of time.

Both fireplaces are supplied with combustion air through ducts from the outside. Last winter less than two cords of wood were used to heat the house with the Finnish fireplace and to provide a cozy open fire in the Rumford. A small fan and ductwork distribute the heat from the living spaces to the bedrooms.

Dick Veatch, the mason who built the fireplaces in conjunction with the Maine Wood Heat Co. (R. F. D. #1, Box 640, Norridgewock, Me. 04957; 207-696-5442), was flown in from Chicago because of his experience restoring Wright buildings there. He laid the exposed masonry with Wright's characteristic flush head joints and raked bed joints to accentuate the horizontal shadow lines.

Backup heat is available from a radiant electric-heating system in the ceilings (ESWA, dist. in the U. S. by Sentinel Electric Heat, Inc., South Park, 1 Atlantis Way, P. O. Box 1563, Lewiston, Me. 04240; 800-321-3792). Installed behind paneling in some places and behind drywall in others, this system employs plastic sheets containing thermostatically controlled heating elements, and is simply stapled to the ceiling joists. Unfortunately, I can't report on its effectiveness: the Schwarzes have never had to turn it on.

An air-to-air heat exchanger, located in the attic, vents the bathrooms, providing humidity control and necessary fresh air with a minimum of heat loss. The house is kept comfortable on hot summer days by its natural cooling system. I designed the broad overhangs with a fascia that slopes back toward the windows to allow maximum winter sun into the house, while shading the entire house in the summer. Skylights on the north side of the house, and transoms above the bedroom doors, allow cross-ventilation in all rooms.

The inside temperatures can be kept several degrees cooler than outside by ventilating the house at night and early morning, then closing windows during the hottest period of the day.

Below-average costs—The economic success of the Schwarz house is due in large measure to the simplicity of its conception. We eliminated elaborate mechanical systems and expensive floor coverings, and we kept the massing and detailing simple. At a time when most custom homes built in this region cost over $100 per square foot, the Schwarz house was built for less than $75 per square foot. □

J. Stewart Roberts is an architect in Quincy, Massachusetts.

Diagonal views, like the one from the living room into the dining area shown in the top photo on the facing page, help make a small house feel big. As a way of blurring the distinction between indoors and out, the same 10-in. and 2-in. coursing used on the exterior shingles was repeated on the reverse board-and-batten cherry paneling inside (bottom right photo). Even the cherry shelving in the kitchen (bottom left photo), picks up on the same vertical spacing.

A Modest House in Bucks County

The dramatic roof shelters a simple plan with a hearth at its heart

by Jeremiah Eck

I met my clients Stephen and Nancy Bye through landscape architect A. E. Bye, whom I have known for years. Bye (Mr. Bye to his former students, like myself) has a subtle way of working his designs into the natural landscape. His blend of the existing and the new is why I feel so comfortable working with him: I carry the same intention with me in my own work. There is no greater compliment I can receive than to have someone ask about one of my house designs: "Is it new or a rehab?" Responding to the context, or setting, of a house is my greatest design concern today.

The Byes agreed that it was important to respect the context of their house. The land that they would build on in Holicong, Pennsylvania, is part of a larger tract deeded to the Bye ancestors by William Penn. Old Congress, the Bye homestead built in 1699, sits 500 yards from where the newest Bye house would sit. The new house would have to complement the architecture of Old Congress and other historic houses in the area, but not copy them. This, I thought, would not be easy because the best early residential architecture is constructed of stone, but Steve and Nancy's house must be wood to save costs. Despite this difference, the gabled roofs, the vertical massing, the well-proportioned and detailed windows and doors, and the handsome fireplaces of old Bucks County architecture influenced our final design.

This 1,750-sq. ft. country house takes its steep roofs and central chimney from its 18th- and 19th-century neighbors.

Both Stephen and Nancy Bye have been professional photographers and so had strong ideas of how their house should look. During our first meeting I showed them slides of my work, and in turn, they showed me images they liked, such as high ceilings and combined-use spaces. Most of the houses they showed me had prominent gables and steeply pitched roofs, including Gothic Revival houses by 19th-century architect A. J. Davis and landscape gardener/writer A. J. Downing.

A plan that ties new with old—While the exterior of the house needed a traditional look and had to blend in with its surroundings, its plan had to respond to the way people live to-day. It seems absurd to build a literal replica of a traditional floor plan today because it would have little to do with the way people live. Yet there are many aspects of the plans of early American houses that I try to recall. Ever since reading Wendell Berry's *The Unsettling of America*, I've kept in mind his concern about the lack of respect for place that the modern home has: "Once, households were producers and processors of food, centers of their own maintenance, adornment, and repair, places of instruction and amusement. People were born in these houses and lived and worked and died in them. Such houses were not generalizations. Similar to each other in materials and design as they might have been, they nevertheless looked, felt and smelled different from each other because they were articulations of particular responses to their places and circumstances."

Keeping in mind the history of the land and the fact that Nancy and Steve planned to stay in this house, I hoped to recapture some of the sense of home. For years I have talked with my clients about the American hearth—not simply a fireplace, but a space that expresses the true meaning of hearth as found in my dictionary: "the abode of comfort to its inhabitants and of hospitality to strangers." In Colonial houses, all rooms focused by necessity on the hearth. Frank Lloyd Wright's Prairie houses of the turn of the century and his Usonian houses of the

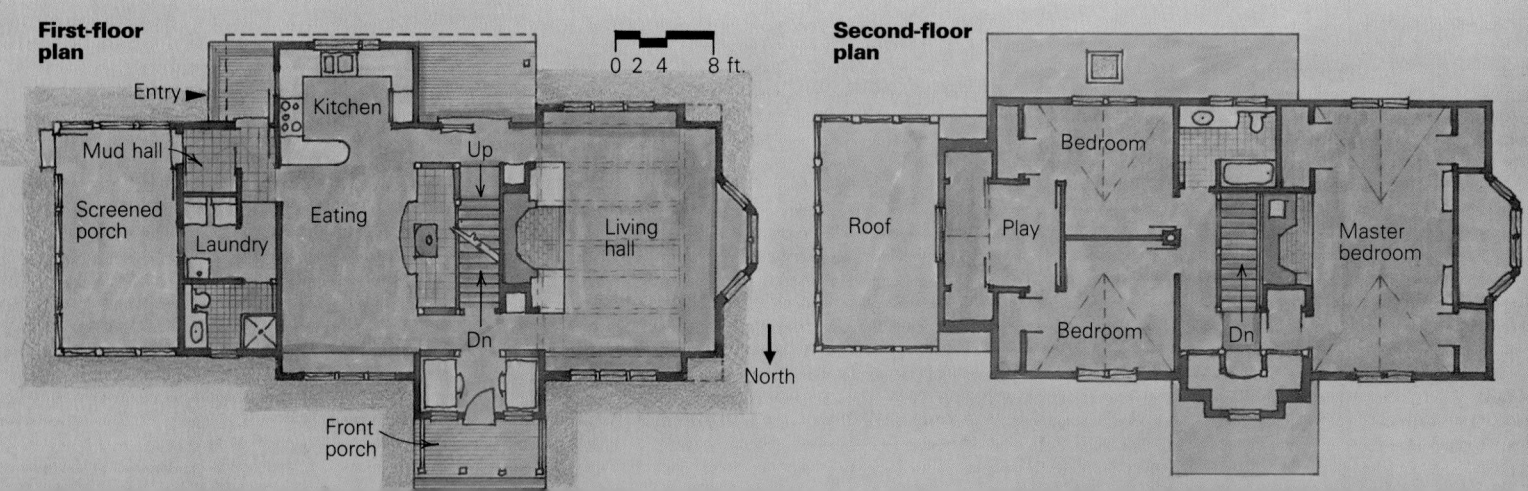

First-floor plan — Entry, Kitchen, Mud hall, Screened porch, Laundry, Eating, Up, Living hall, Dn, Front porch, North — 0 2 4 8 ft.

Second-floor plan — Roof, Bedroom, Play, Bedroom, Master bedroom, Dn

The house is entirely stick-built except for the fir post-and-beam living hall (photo above), one of the two large first-floor rooms that has a hearth as a focus. Built-in bookcases and benches are centered on the Count Rumford fireplace. Flooring is pegged 8-in. Southern yellow pine, and the ceiling is the exposed 2x8 T&G fir decking of the master bedroom above.

1930s centered around the hearth, less for actual warmth than for emotional comfort and hospitality. If the hearth is the focus of a house design, a contemporary plan can capture the essential character of 18th- and 19th-century American houses without copying them line for line.

Two other ingredients, restraint and necessity, were also essential elements in those early American houses. The restraint imposed by a limited budget can still lead to the efficient and beautiful use of materials. Necessity often breeds design solutions; many older homes are elegant simply because every design decision required discipline of thought, use and material.

With a young child and another child on the way, Steve and Nancy had a limited budget and wanted a house no larger than 1,800 sq. ft. Considering this need in addition to their requests about style and programming, I left our first meeting convinced that their new house should be cottage-like with a dominant hearth and a distinctive sense of place on the family property. A small house is harder to design than a large one, but keeping the plan simple and focused on the hearth gave us a good start.

Two hearth rooms — The house as built responded to the informal way that the Byes live. They spend most of their time in the informal kitchen and eating area (drawing, facing page). The other large space on the first floor is what I call the living hall, which is more formal than the kitchen and which has broader views of the surrounding landscape. This is where the Byes retire after dinner, lie down to take a nap or read the Sunday paper. Each of these spaces revolves around the hearth — a large fireplace in the living hall (photo above) and a woodstove in the eating/cooking area.

Off the kitchen are a mud hall, laundry and bathroom. A small entrance off the front porch contains work desks for each parent. The path from the driveway leads only to the side door and screen porch on the east, so the front door is really a symbolic entry. Upstairs are a master bedroom, two children's bedrooms with an adjacent play area and one bathroom. By combining spaces and keeping the massing fairly simple, we were able to give the Byes the spaces they wanted in 1,750 sq. ft. — the size they could afford.

Keeping the structure simple — Consistent with the need for economy, the concrete-block basement foundation is a rectangle with the least number of jogs possible. Several wall projections — the two-story bay off the living hall and master bedroom, the front porch and decks on each side of the kitchen — were appended to the floor framing and provided with separate cast-in-place concrete Sonotube foundations.

Most of the house was stick-built, using 2x6 studs with fiberglass batt insulation. A framing technique that I've been using for a number of years is to use a full 8-ft. stud on the first floor; with the addition of sill and top plates, the finished ceiling height is close to 8 ft. 2 in. The extra ceiling height makes a small house seem larger. The baseboard covers the gap below the drywall.

Another technique I often use is the creation of as much spatial variety as possible. To give the living hall a higher ceiling than adjacent areas, we lowered its floor framing almost 1 ft. below the rest of the first floor. This expands the sense of space in a small house. We also added a double-height bay that joins

One trick to making a small house seem larger is to change ceiling or floor levels. The living-hall bay, stepped up from the living hall (itself stepped down a foot from the rest of the first floor), is a two-story space that connects the first floor with the master bedroom (photo left). Upstairs, ceilings follow the complex roof framing. In this view of the master bedroom (photo below) is one of the three gables that add variety and openness.

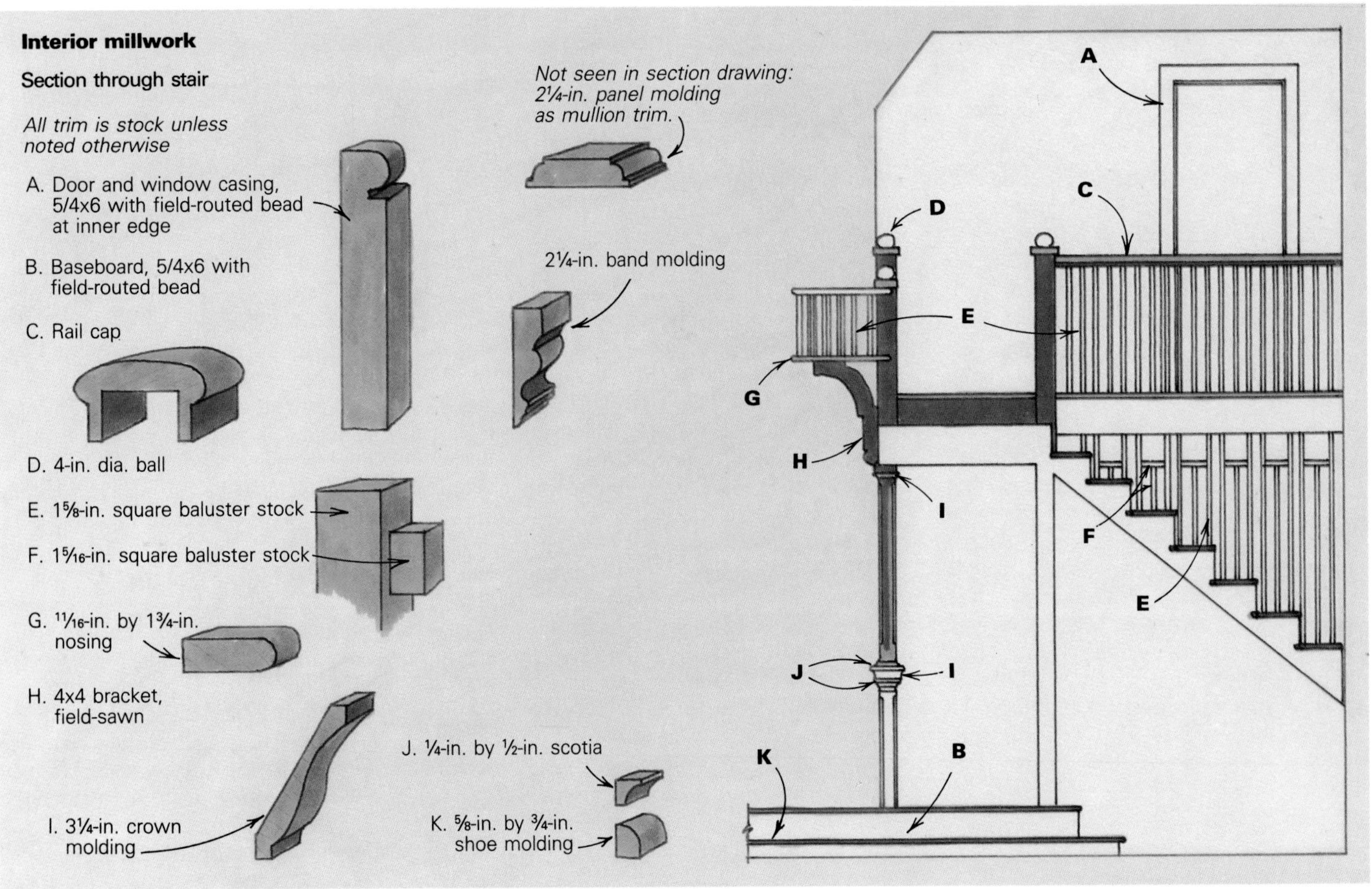

Interior millwork

Section through stair

All trim is stock unless noted otherwise

A. Door and window casing, 5/4x6 with field-routed bead at inner edge

B. Baseboard, 5/4x6 with field-routed bead

C. Rail cap

D. 4-in. dia. ball

E. 1⅝-in. square baluster stock

F. 1⁵⁄₁₆-in. square baluster stock

G. ¹¹⁄₁₆-in. by 1¾-in. nosing

H. 4x4 bracket, field-sawn

I. 3¼-in. crown molding

J. ¼-in. by ½-in. scotia

K. ⅝-in. by ¾-in. shoe molding

Not seen in section drawing: 2¼-in. panel molding as mullion trim.

2¼-in. band molding

Drawings: Frances B. Ashforth

the living hall with the master bedroom above (left photo, facing page).

The living hall has more than just a tall ceiling. We decided to frame the area using a modified post-and-beam technique in order to differentiate it from the rest of the house and to recall a cozy, traditional feeling around the fireplace (photo, p. 69). We used a Count Rumford fireplace, whose firebox is shallow but high and wide, to radiate plenty of warmth into the room. The firebox is painted with a white-colored fire-resistant mix that matches the white walls of the room, making the sides of the firebox seem more like part of the walls.

A steep roof kept low—Outside, the major feature of the house is the roof with its pair of large gable dormers that indicate the two major spaces on the first floor and the bedrooms on the second floor (photo, p. 68). By using a steep pitch (16-in-12 for the main roof and 22-in-12 for the dormers) and by springing the gabled dormers from a kneewall rather than from a full second-story wall, the house looks as if it has two full stories. The kneewall also saves on the cost of materials. Framing the roof was slow because of its multi-gabled configuration. Draining a steep roof is no problem, but we paid close attention to waterproofing the smaller, shallow

roofs and to the curved roof over the front porch. Bituthene Ice & Water Shield, a waterproofing sheet from W. R. Grace (62 Whittemore Ave., Cambridge, Mass. 02140), was applied to the sheathing of the shallow-pitch roofs, in valleys and on eave edges.

The roof is more than a mere covering: the family actually lives *within* it. Rooms below the roof take on the shape of the roof. Each of the children's bedrooms has a gabled wall with a window, and the master bedroom has three gabled walls (right photo, facing page). Rafters were carefully strapped to make a perfect surface for the drywall.

Millwork where it counts—Going with a simple plan allowed Stephen and Nancy to afford nice finishes and a moderate amount of millwork both inside and out. General contractors Tom Jarrett and Bryan Vaughn of Doylestown, Pennsylvania, also finished all interior and exterior details with precision and careful interpretation. We focused attention on the central stair hall, both upstairs and down (drawing, facing page). At first glance the staircase railing appears to be made of standard-size baluster stock (photo below right). In fact, there are two alternating sizes of standard stock: 1⁵⁄₁₆-in. and 1⁵⁄₈-in. The barely perceptible difference between the two gives the railing rhythm. By varying the rail-

ing sizes, we also avoided the alignment difficulties that occur when two identical-size pieces of stock must meet at right angles.

I've always thought that hallways and landings are wonderful places to pause, so we placed a curved bench at the landing upstairs (photo below left). Having only one bath upstairs means that waiting could be a possibility, but the view from the bench—either down to the entry area below or out the window to the neighboring horse farm—makes the wait tolerable. We used 5/4 clear fir with a bullnose edging for the bench seat and paint-grade fir for the 1⁵⁄₁₆-in. balusters (here, all balusters are the same dimensions). The bench is supported by a single bracket bandsawn from solid 4x4 stock (photo, next page). On both the stair and the bench, the 4-in. newel posts are clear fir with chamfered edges. Stephen, who is a professional house painter, finished the posts, bench and bracket with polyurethane and the balusters and decorative 4-in. balls with semi-gloss white paint.

We used similar details in the combination bookcase and inglenook in the living hall, where the decorative grid echoes the horizontal and vertical lines of the post-and-beam structure. The grid is repeated in the divided-light upper windows in the living hall and the dining area. Windows and doors

Up the stair. To give the stair rail a subtle rhythm, Eck used a smaller square stock for short balusters and larger stock for long balusters (photo right). From a bench at the landing (photo above) there's a view outside, as well as over the rail to the floor below.

Photo: Paul Ferrino

From *Fine Homebuilding* magazine (Spring 1990) 59:36-41

From the hall off the front porch there's a view up of the curved bench and gable over the stair.

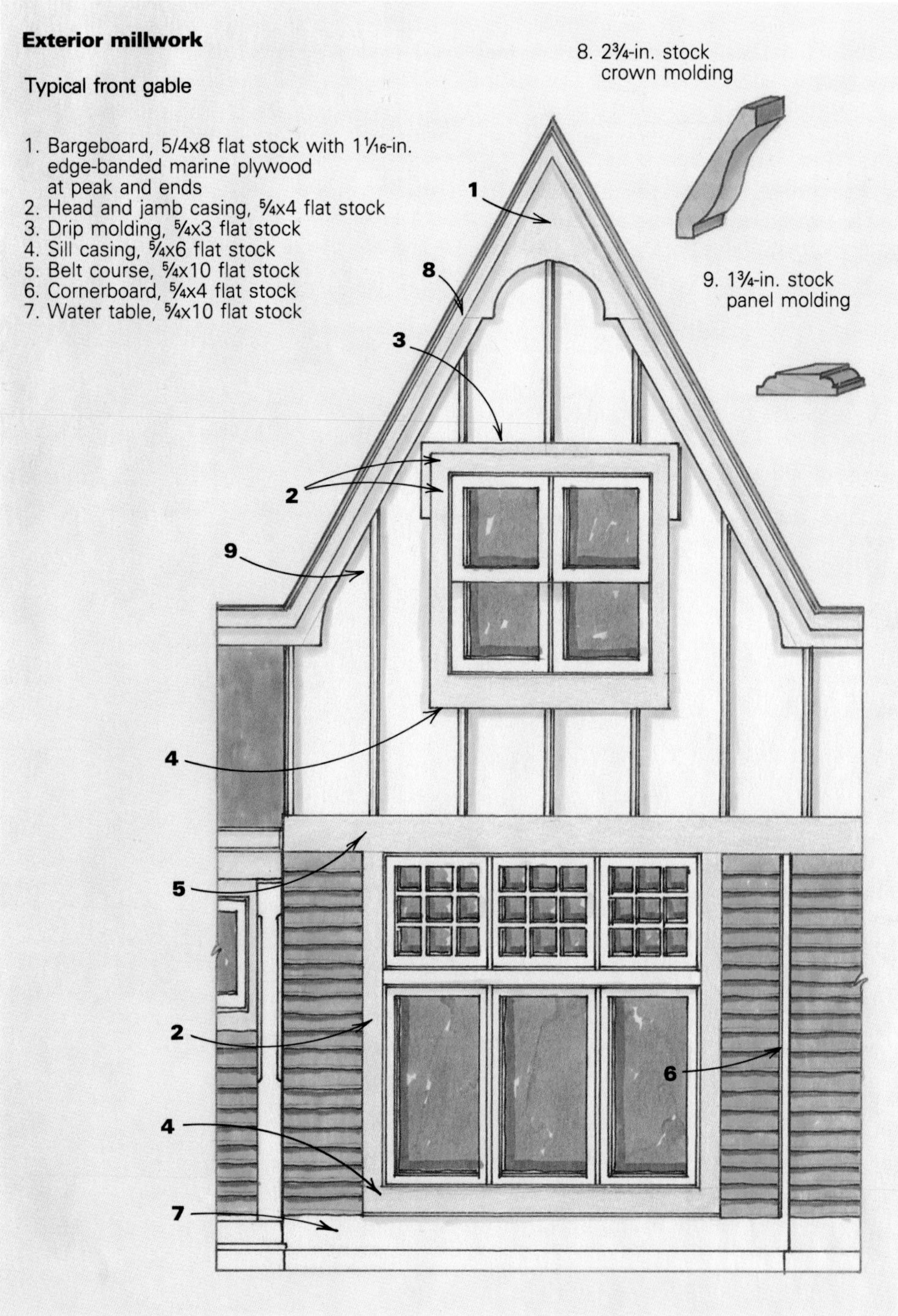

were cased with flat 5/4 stock that was given an edge bead in the field.

Finishing off the exterior—To emphasize the roof and the gables, the second-story kneewall and gable ends are sided with a different material than that on the first-floor walls. First-floor walls have 10-in. cedar clapboards with a 6-in. exposure. Clapboard edges were beaded in the field with a router to give a strong horizontal emphasis to the first story (photo, facing page). The clapboards were furred out from the Tyvek-covered plywood sheathing to allow them to breathe and prevent them from warping.

The second-floor walls are sided with medium-density overlay (MDO) plywood panels and stock panel molding. Battens are spaced at 2 ft. o. c. and are centered on window and roof configurations. Stephen painted the board-and-batten siding a light grey and stained the clapboards as close to natural as possible. He and Nancy have tested several other color schemes and still haven't settled on the final colors.

Trimming the exterior—Five major types of trim finish the exterior of the house: water table, belt coursing, corner boards, eave and rake trim and window casing. The first four types of trim tie the multi-gabled scheme together. They are lines of demarcation emphasizing the base, the second story and the roof edge. They also pull together auxiliary areas, such as the front porch and the screen porch.

The corners and edges of a building, such as the roof edge or water table, are important areas to detail carefully, both for weathertightness and looks. It is surprising how substantial a thick piece of flat stock or a piece of profiled trim can look compared with the standard thin stock that trims so many houses. The flat 5/4 stock (actually 1 1/16 in. thick) used as most of the exterior trim on this house makes a stronger shadow line than the more common 1x stock (actually 3/4 in. thick). It is more expensive initially, but withstands the effects of the weather better.

Profiled off-the-shelf trim is not much more expensive than flat stock. The challenge is in selecting the right trim from a large number of stock options. Here, the eave and rake trim is a standard clear pine factory-milled profile that I specified from Brockway-Smith Co., a northeastern millworks company (146 Dascomb Rd., Andover, Mass. 01810).

Over the history of American residential architecture, detailing the juncture of the rake and the eave at the corner of a house has always presented a challenge. The resolution of this detail depends very much on the roof pitch, the edge materials and the gutter if one exists. Here, we had intended to run a continuous length of crown molding from eave to rake, but the steep pitch of the roof (almost 60°) would not allow joining the moldings without great difficulty. Instead, Jarrett and Vaughn worked out the detail so that the eave crown is returned on the end wall and the rake crown dies into it from above. The

Exterior millwork

Typical front gable

1. Bargeboard, 5/4x8 flat stock with 1 1/16-in. edge-banded marine plywood at peak and ends
2. Head and jamb casing, 5/4x4 flat stock
3. Drip molding, 5/4x3 flat stock
4. Sill casing, 5/4x6 flat stock
5. Belt course, 5/4x10 flat stock
6. Cornerboard, 5/4x4 flat stock
7. Water table, 5/4x10 flat stock

8. 2 3/4-in. stock crown molding

9. 1 3/4-in. stock panel molding

To keep the shape of the basement foundation as simple as possible, a few first-floor projections, such as the front porch, are supported on independent concrete piers. First-floor siding is cedar clapboards with a wide exposure and site-routed beading; siding on the second-floor kneewall and gables is board-and-batten. Flat trim is 5/4 board; profiled molding is all off-the-shelf.

ends of the rake boards at this transition are curved to give a feeling of lightness to the roof edges (photo above). Bargeboards are 5/4 stock, but the curved portion at all gable peaks is edge-banded marine plywood.

Molding the land—A. E. Bye had owned this site for many years before Stephen and Nancy purchased it. Long ago he had planted many trees with the thought of starting a nursery. And 30 years later, we had an instant palette to work with.

Bye walked through what had become woods, marking trees to save or to cut down. Many trees were taken out to make the mead-

ow north of the house, but a few oaks and American beeches were left to mature to specimen size. A handsome grove of 20-year-old columnar-shaped Katsura trees was painstakenly whittled to open up the south yard. The two-story bay on the west side of the house was built close to a cluster of cedars that was left to act as a year-round curtain for the large bedroom windows.

The Katsura-tree grove and glorious European beech behind the house are results of Bye's farsighted planting, years of care and thoughtful selection during the building of the house. But his work on the front side was done in one day. One of Bye's trademarks is

to turn flat lawns to softly rolling berms by use of a bulldozer and a grader. He is careful to design these manmade swales so that they drain properly and can be mowed with ease. Throughout the day the undulations catch the shadows of trees and turn them to wavy lines (photo above). When the sun is low, the ridges themselves cast shadows. In winter, snow melts faster on the tops and slower in the valleys. Mist even forms in the valleys, making the lawn look like an aerial view of the Appalachian mountains. □

Jeremiah Eck is an architect in Boston, Massachusetts, and teaches at Harvard University.

Raven Hill

Canny planning makes this small New Mexico house feel big

by Baylor H. Trapnell

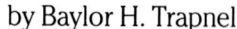

Four miles northeast of the plaza at Santa Fe, N. Mex., the foothills of the Sangre de Cristo Mountains begin to rise. At the 8,000-ft. level, piñon pines and low junipers cover the hills with a miniature forest. Higher up, vast stands of aspens look like great green meadows beneath the peaks, while far below and to the west, rose-red canyons merge into the immense Rio Grande Valley. Bordering the valley's distant edge is a row of ancient volcanic peaks that resemble pyramids. Beneath them at night, the lights of Los Alamos glow like a phosphorescent comet tail from 30 miles away.

I had purchased a piece of property on one of the foothills with a clear view of these absorbing sights. The only catch was that my upslope lot was on the chilly north side of the hill, and the view part of the site was 200 ft. from the nearest road. By building right next to the road I could save a lot of time and money, but it would mean missing out on the distant views. On the other hand, I could complicate the project by putting in a steep driveway to the uphill part of the lot, where a foundation would no doubt be more difficult to construct.

The views won. I picked the high part of the lot for the house, and consoled myself with the knowledge that many years before, horse-drawn wagons had removed limestone from an outcropping near the top of the hill. A crude trail still climbed diagonally across the land. If nothing else, a bit of the road grading had already been accomplished across this rugged terrain.

As I explored the land, contemplating potential building sites, I watched the ravens. Each morning they would glide past the site, sailing downhill toward Santa Fe. In the evening they beat their way back uphill, stopping sometimes to catch their breath before continuing on up the mountain to their rookeries. So commanding is their raucous presence that I took to calling the place Raven Hill.

Design development—I had a modest budget for this house, and to keep costs under control I knew from the beginning that it would have to

The fireplace and hearth, raised to be visible from the library as well as the living room, are the central focus of the downstairs spaces. Stacked windows afford views from both the library and living-room levels. At the far end, the semi-separate dining room is entered though a large portal. A deck at grade joins this space through sliding-glass doors.

Drawing: Gary Williamson

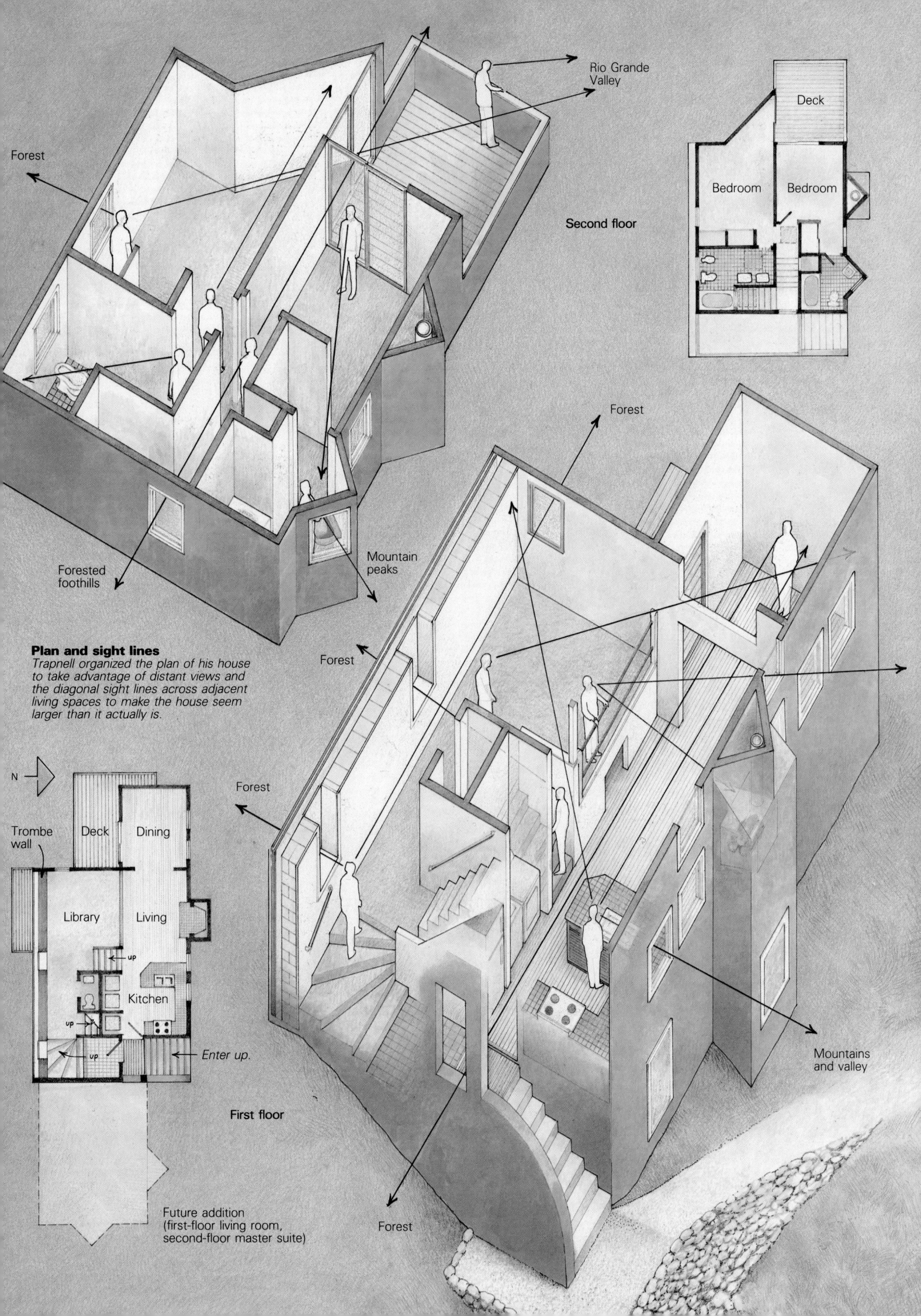

Forest

Rio Grande Valley

Second floor

Deck

Bedroom   Bedroom

Forest

Forested foothills

Forest

Mountain peaks

Plan and sight lines
Trapnell organized the plan of his house to take advantage of distant views and the diagonal sight lines across adjacent living spaces to make the house seem larger than it actually is.

Forest

N

Trombe wall

Deck   Dining

Library   Living

up

up   Kitchen

up

Enter up.

First floor

Future addition
(first-floor living room,
second-floor master suite)

Forest

Mountains
and valley

Forest

The library is 3½ ft. above the lower level. The resulting space between the two floors is a handy storage well for firewood.

Baylor H. Trapnell

Finished with an earth-colored layer of stucco, Trapnell's house on Raven Hill takes in the views by way of small windows in the north wall that are arranged in vertical and horizontal bands.

be a fairly small building. I set my sights on an energy-efficient, low-maintenance house of about 1,400 sq. ft. Within this envelope, I wanted two bedrooms, 2½ baths and distinct living, dining and library spaces. At some point I hope to add a large living room and a master bedroom to the house. My plan had to take these eventual modifications into consideration.

To get the best views and to minimize the foundation work, I decided to make the house two stories tall, with the kitchen and living spaces downstairs and bedrooms above (drawing, previous page). Trees do not grow quickly in New Mexico, and keeping the footprint of the house to a minimum would disturb as few of the surrounding piñons as possible. The soil conditions on the hill are a geological gumbo, with buried ledges and exposed outcroppings, hidden boulders, fractured rocks, and a combination of sandy soil and clay. Given the steepness of the site and the variety of subsurface conditions, my engineer recommended a pier-and-grade-beam foundation for the house. This was fine with me—the hand-digging required to excavate the pier holes was less likely to ravage the surrounding landscape than a backhoe digging trenches for perimeter footings.

Exploring space and highlighting views— As I began my designs for the house, I used several strategies to make the house feel larger than it really is. These are time-honored tricks that architects apply to every kind of building, and I put them to work in various ways in this house.

Since the hillside lot is fairly steep—about a 25° slope—I decided to build the lower floor on two levels (photos top left and facing page). This way the house could hug the hillside, and some ceiling height could be added to the main living space as well. The added ceiling height increases the sense of volume throughout the lower spaces, while the two floor levels stake out a clear boundary between the library and the living room.

To keep heat loss to a minimum and still see the sights, I framed specific vistas with small windows (photo bottom left) and I arranged them so that their effect has maximum impact. For instance, as you enter the house, a small window at the top of the winder stairs comes immediately into view. It looks out on the dwarf forest. A turn to the right looks into another window. It is on an axis with the hall to the library, and looks out on the forest as you approach the living area. People tend to move toward light, and when a window is placed at the farthest point from the viewer it emphasizes the distance between them.

Similarly, light sources not immediately revealed around a corner add unseen distance. I use this idea in the stairwell to the second floor. The treads are illuminated by a skylight that cannot be seen as you pass the stairs.

At the edge of the library, a diagonal sight line across the space looks into the dining room, about 30 ft. distant. When you enter a room at one corner and look diagonally to the opposite corner, the perceived distance is greater than if you entered at the middle of a room and gazed straight across it. If the diagonals of two adja-

From *Fine Homebuilding* magazine (October 1987) 42:50-53

cent rooms can be combined in a semi-open plan as in the library and dining room, the sense of space increases accordingly.

Another technique used to augment the spaciousness of a room is to let one wall of a hall continue on to become the long wall of the room it feeds. I used this concept for the south wall of the library, which is used to display artwork. The hall continues the display space, acting as a gallery and adding to the perceived size of the room.

Walls that are diagonal in plan can also expand the sense of interior space. I used one in the larger of the two upstairs bedrooms, where it directs the eye toward the distant view and frames a corridor to a tiny deck that is open to both bedrooms. Places like this little deck can function as rooms if they are comfortable places to be. A hall may be good for yoga practice—a carpeted landing a comfy place to read a book.

When you apply these concepts to designing a small house, it becomes very important to plan furniture layouts. I measure the pieces that I intend to use, and then I draw them on the floor plans to make sure there is enough room for people to circulate. There should be at least a 2½-ft. corridor to allow easy movement. It is equally important to consider the space required for doors to swing on their hinges, and don't forget the cabinets.

In a small house, little alcoves can be the solution to thorny problems brought on by lack of space, and they can also have an aesthetic impact. For example, adding a small bay to one of the upstairs bathrooms in this house accomplished several things. For one, the bay provides enough extra space for the pedestal sink. Second, it gave me a wall for a window that extends the diagonal sight-line in the bedroom. Third, it created an architectural element that is in keeping with the adjacent flue chase.

Style and finish—As the shape of the house emerged, I looked to some of the older homes in the area for inspiration. A thousand years ago, the Anasazi built cliff dwellings in New Mexico, Arizona and Colorado using dry-laid stone, plastered with clay. The walls of an Anasazi house were punctured with small windows and doors, often repeating an ordered pattern. Some Anasazi houses were built under rock ledges and tended to be linear in plan; others were freestanding circular, square or angled volumes. The edges of these buildings were crisp, and they were probably a uniform earth tone.

My updated cliff house pays homage to many of these ancient Southwestern forms. Its corners, parapets and angled bays are finished with clean, hard edges. It has small windows, arranged in both vertical and horizontal bands (bottom photo, facing page). And even though it has a wood frame, the dark brown stucco finish harkens back to the old mud-plaster walls.

I kept the interior finishes simple and utilitarian. The floor on the lower level of the first story is made of 2x T&G fir. I purposely left it unprotected as the house went together so that it would accumulate the scars of construction (I did cover it during drywall work and painting though). After a thorough sweeping, I finished it

The kitchen is an efficient U-shaped workspace with a broad counter that doubles as a place to prepare food or enjoy a meal while sitting atop one of the lunch-counter stools.

with a 50/50 mixture of clear and white shellac, which gives it a light, translucent appearance. Except for the tile floors in the entry and in the bathrooms, the rest of the living spaces in the house are carpeted with a light-colored, berberweave wool. Dark finishes in a small house will make it feel claustrophobic, so I painted the gypboard walls white. Most of the ceilings are the undersides of the T&G decking, which was lightly sanded to remove splinters and grade marks. In a few places, the ceilings are furred down with drywall to conceal the plumbing.

Heating—Although the site is on a north slope, the hill doesn't block the winter sun—even at the solstice. To take advantage of this good fortune, I built a concrete-block Trombe wall along the uphill side of the house. It is plastered on the inside and double glazed on the outside. The wall is one story tall, and it contributes heat to the house by radiating stored warmth into the library and hallway.

Raven Hill is without a natural gas line and winter access to the site can be difficult, so I ruled out using bottled gas. The operating cost of electric-resistance heating is prohibitively high, so I installed radiant baseboards that get their heat from hot water. A closed loop full of water circulates from a Monitron electric boiler (Slant/Fin Corp., 100 Forest Drive, Greenvale, N. Y. 11548) to all 10 radiators. So far this system has proved up to the task of heating the house. But if a long, chilly spell overloads it, the heat-circulating fireplace can step in as backup.

The domestic hot-water supply gets an assist from a pair of roof-mounted Grumman solar panels. They feed into an 80-gal. tank, which in turn supplies a 50-gal. electric water heater. This is necessary only during the winter. In the summer the water gets plenty hot enough to bypass the electric heater.

Monthly total electric bills, which include stove, lights, appliances, hot water and space heating, average $80 to $150 during the winter, and that is without any wood heat. The charges drop to $40 to $60 in summer. When I can afford it, insulating shutters will be my next energy-saving investment in the house. □

Baylor H. Trapnell consults nationally on residential land use planning, construction and design. He now lives in Blue Bell, Pa.

Vacation Cabin
A Rocky Mountain retreat combines pragmatic construction and rustic detailing

by Bill Phelps

Building a vacation house is about as close to a vacation as building a house can be. At least it usually means working in a pleasant location, and Andy Turner's site for his vacation cabin certainly fits that description. The lot sits on a ridge at 8,000 ft. in the Rocky Mountains of northwest Wyoming. From the top of the ridge, the views in all directions are spectacular.

When we first visited the site, we turned off the highway about five miles outside of Bondurant, Wyo., a two-gas-pump ranching community about 50 miles from the nearest grocery store or lumberyard, and then drove five more miles on a gravel road. The ridge is just inside the north boundary of a resort development. Houses are sparsely scattered among the sagebrush and timber over several thousand acres of land that is in turn surrounded by hundreds of square miles of National Forest. This would be a re-

mote but accessible building site, far enough from town to require careful planning and too far to commute every day. While Andy decided where to place the cabin, I decided where to pitch our tent.

Design and redesign—At 8,000 ft. in the Rockies, summer is short and sweet, so we had no time to waste. The road from the highway is open only from May through sometime in November, when the first major storm of winter closes it for the season.

Andy hired an architect, who designed an attractive little house, and I went to work preparing an estimate. Soon we arrived at that critical moment that occurs in many building projects. The house would cost more than Andy felt he could afford. We went over the estimate and eliminated what we could, but the house was

still too expensive so he decided to abando the project.

Two weeks later Andy called me again an asked how small a cabin could be and still b livable. We later did some sketches and decide that about 20 ft. by 20 ft. was the minimum. would cost less than half of what the origina house would have cost, and I promised him could build it from a drawing on a dinner nap kin. With the napkin in my pocket, I returned t the drawing board and the calculator.

The design we ended up with is about a compact as you can get (drawing, facing page The main floor includes a sitting area with woodstove, a dining area, kitchen, bath, an one bedroom with a closet, all in 440 sq. ft. Th cabin measures 20 ft. by 22 ft. in plan, and sleeping loft adds another 220 sq. ft. Since law yers tend to frown on dinner napkins as con

ract documents, I transferred the whole plan to one sheet of blueprint. I managed to fit elevations, a floor plan, electrical plan, foundation plan, section and a detail on the one sheet and still had room to spare. The cost of this little cabin was more in line with what Andy had in mind, and we were back in business.

Before the snow flies—Although I was happy to get started with the cabin, the new schedule was going to be tight. The summer slipped away as we made plans, and I found myself digging for the foundation on Labor Day. I had only about 60 days that I could count on before the gravel road to the site would be snowed shut. At the lumberyard, the clerks were amused when I told them how important it was to get all of the material to the site early. They told me stories about another contractor who once had to drag sheets of plywood behind a snowmobile to finish a house. Two nights later, I woke up in a cold sweat, convinced that all my profit from this job would be spent on snowmobiles while my tools and pickup truck would end up stranded by an early snowstorm.

After the size and floor plan of the cabin had been determined, the most important design decision was how to construct the walls. Andy favored a log cabin but he also knew about a problem his neighbors were having with their small log cabin. They spend several winter weekends there, and temperatures are frequently below zero when they arrive. The first thing they do is build a roaring fire in their woodstove. The air inside the cabin warms up quickly, but the logs do not, so they feel like they're sitting in an igloo. Because it takes so long for the logs to warm up, it takes a long time before the cabin feels comfortable. With this in mind, we decided to build with insulated frame walls instead of logs.

Achieving a rustic look—Once we had decided to go with 2x6 frame construction, we wanted to be sure the cabin would still have a rustic appearance. We decided to use exposed log purlins to support the roof structure, and we also included some log posts and a log beam to dress up a small 4-ft. deep front porch. Also, we used roughsawn pine for all of the exterior trim and for the board-and-batten siding, as well as for our finished ceiling. Finally, we finished all of the interior walls with #1 and #2 square-edge milled 1x6 pine boards laid horizontally with black 15-lb. felt behind them, so that the joints between the boards show as black lines. The strategy worked extremely well.

The roughsawn pine exterior resembles the siding that ranchers have been using on cabins in the mountains around here for years. The roughsawn boards on the ceiling inside are a nice contrast to the milled boards on the walls, and the combined effect of all of the wood surfaces gives the same warm feeling that you get with log walls. But it's the log purlins that make the most dramatic effect, partially by plan and partially by accident.

Although I am not a seasoned log builder, I live in a log house and I've done enough log work to appreciate that there is an art to working with hand-peeled logs. The log builder has to arrange the irregularities to end up with a symmetrically balanced structure.

When the time arrived to order the log purlins for this cabin, I consulted an experienced log builder in the area, and we decided that the heavy snow load at this site and the 22-ft. span justified some pretty hefty logs. We settled on a 12-in. dia. dimension. This would be adequate for the snow load but not too massive for such a small cabin. He agreed to hand-pick the logs for me and deliver them to the site. I was gone the day he delivered them, and when I arrived at work the next day, I was greeted with snickers from the crew. All of the logs were about 12 in. in diameter at the small end of the taper but they were more like 16 in. at the big end. They looked gigantic, but in the end, they worked out fine. We placed all of the small ends toward the front of the cabin (where fit was most important), and we placed the two biggest logs over the side walls, where they would be least conspicuous. Inside the cabin, the purlins look substantial but don't seem out of proportion to the space. In fact, they actually make the space feel bigger than it is.

Another feature that helps the cabin feel bigger is the size and the placement of its windows. Andy decided early that he wanted lots of windows so the cabin would be bright. The living/dining area has a large picture window in the south wall and large awning windows on each of the east and west walls. When you look in any of these directions, you have a reference point beyond the wall that helps to open up the actual space of the room. Similarly the small bedroom has a large picture window that takes up most of its north wall. The other windows in the cabin are smaller and positioned as much for ventilation as for light and view. Two small

windows in the loft are especially important for ventilation and have a spectacular view through the trees to a distant mountain range.

Insulation and mechanicals—The next critical decisions were how much insulation to add and how to install the water supply so that it would be easy to turn it on and drain it back during weekend visits in the winter. The insulation levels were selected to be adequate but economical for a vacation cabin. We filled the walls and joist spaces under the floor with R-19 fiberglass batts. We also insulated the foundation walls with 2 in. of extruded polystyrene in hopes that the crawl space would stay above freezing during as much of the winter as possible. Otherwise, when the water was turned on for a weekend, it would freeze in the pipes below the floor even though the cabin was heated.

Turning on the water and draining the water lines are the only real chores required to open and close the cabin, but they are very important ones. Andy gets his water from a supply that is shared by other houses nearby. We designed a system that is easy to use and that shuts off the pressurized supply below the frost line to prevent frozen pipes. To drain the pipes, he first turns off the valve located on the main supply line where it comes out of the ground in the crawl space. All the cold-water lines inside the house have enough slope to drain back to a valve located just above the main shutoff valve, and the hot-water lines drain back to a compact water heater that we installed below the floor.

Once all of the water lines and the water heater are drained, it is necessary to drain the main supply pipe below the main shutoff valve so the valve and the length of pipe just above the ground won't freeze. To accomplish this we installed a stop and waste valve on the main sup-

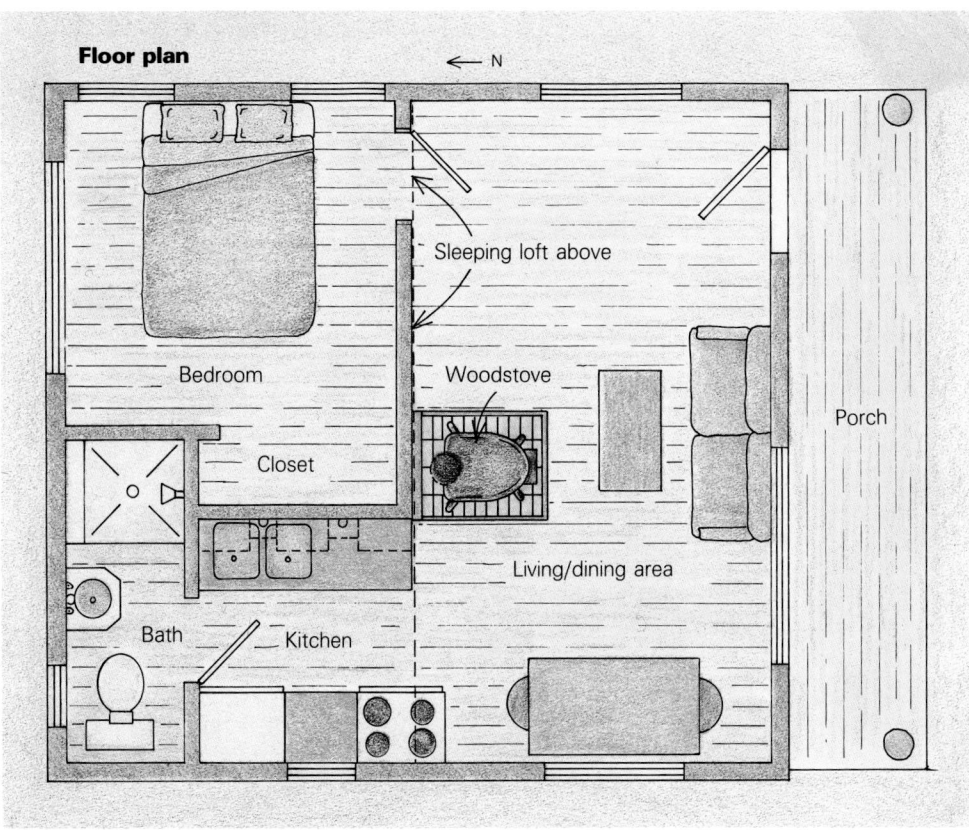

Floor plan ← N

Bedroom

Closet

Bath — Kitchen

Sleeping loft above

Woodstove

Living/dining area

Porch

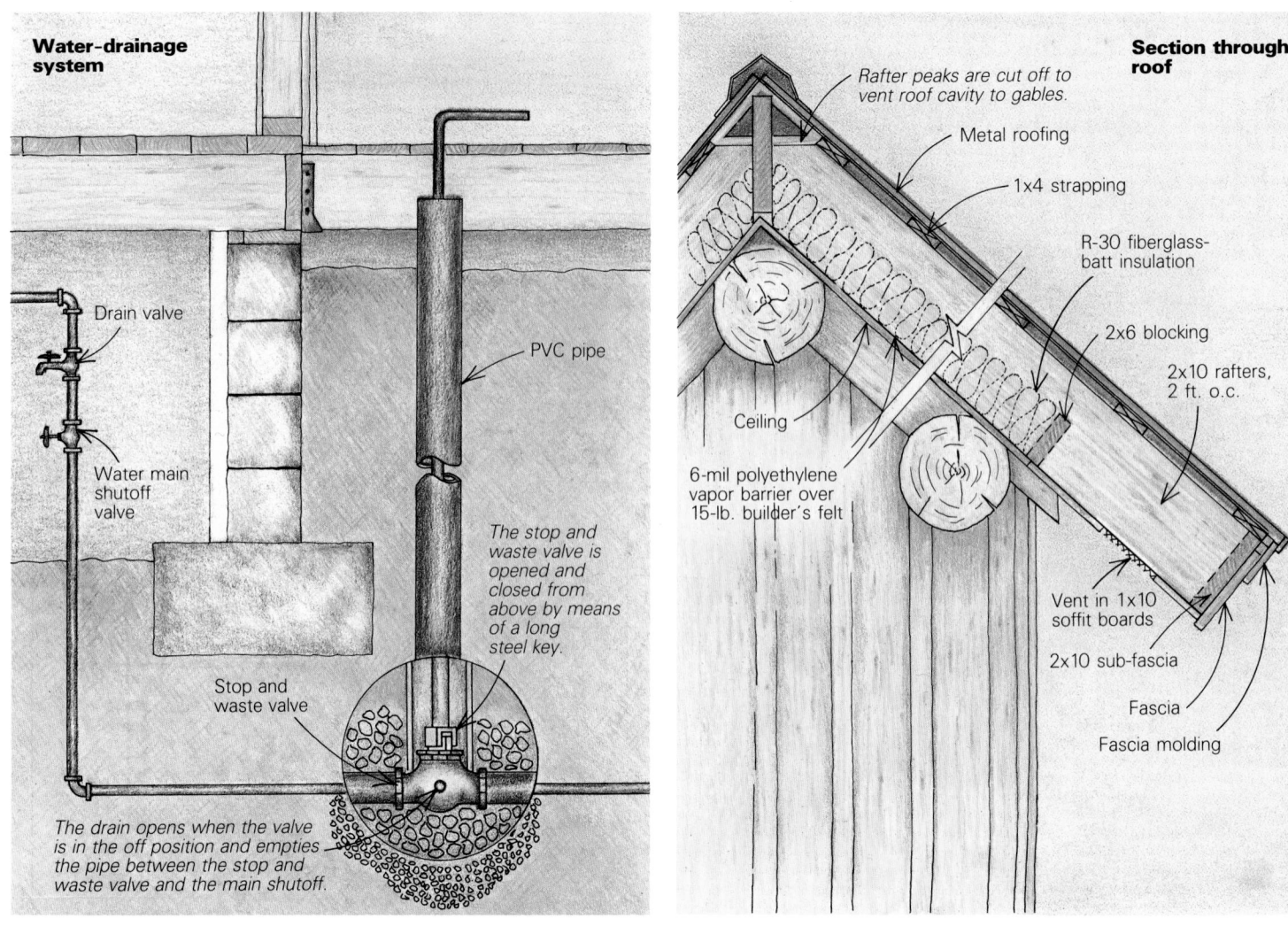

Water-drainage system

Drain valve

Water main shutoff valve

PVC pipe

The stop and waste valve is opened and closed from above by means of a long steel key.

Stop and waste valve

The drain opens when the valve is in the off position and empties the pipe between the stop and waste valve and the main shutoff.

Section through roof

Rafter peaks are cut off to vent roof cavity to gables.

Metal roofing

1x4 strapping

R-30 fiberglass-batt insulation

2x6 blocking

2x10 rafters, 2 ft. o.c.

Ceiling

6-mil polyethylene vapor barrier over 15-lb. builder's felt

Vent in 1x10 soffit boards

2x10 sub-fascia

Fascia

Fascia molding

---

ply line just outside the cabin. This valve is buried 6 ft. below grade and is turned on and off with a long steel key ending in a U-shaped sleeve (drawing, above left). When the valve is turned off, a drain port opens and drains any water left in the line into a small rock-filled pit beneath. This effectively drains all water to below the frost line.

Closing in—The 50-mile drive to the lumberyard and the threat of being snowbound in two months supplied some powerful motivation to keep the job moving along efficiently. We dug the hole one day, poured the footing the next, and the masons laid the foundation block on the third. The 2x6 T&G pine decking on the main-level floor would be cleaned up and sanded later for the finish floor.

The walls went up quickly although the gable ends, with three beam pockets apiece, required some serious grunts to lift into place. At the low side on the rake, we made the pockets 12 in. deep and 14 in. wide.

Getting the mammoth purlins into those pockets was our first real crisis. Setting them by hand was out of the question since one man could barely pick up one end. We were right on schedule when I called the log builder who had agreed to show up with his cherry picker and set the purlins. He was about to go hunting for a few days and said he could probably set them in a week or so. It was obvious that he didn't care about my predicament, so I started calling every

crane company I could find. About 20 calls later, I found a 60-ton crane that was not busy. Even though it would cost five times what I'd planned on, it seemed like a bargain compared to waiting one or two weeks for the cherry picker.

Once the purlins were set into the pockets, we shimmed them with plywood into a secure position and then spiked them through predrilled holes with lengths of ⅝-in. rebar from above and 8-in. nails from the side. Then we shaved off their high spots with a chainsaw so the 1x10 roughsawn ceiling boards would lie flat. We laid the boards perpendicular to the purlins and let the tails run wild. Later, we snapped a chalkline and cut them in place to form the soffit for our 2-ft. roof overhang.

The boards were air dried at the mill, and we nailed them as close to each other as we could. Even so, I knew that they would dry even more, and the resulting cracks between the boards could open up as much as ¼ in. With the black felt backing behind the boards, we wouldn't have to worry about insulation showing through. Over the felt we placed a 6-mil polyethylene vapor barrier and then set 2x10 rafters, 2 ft. o. c.

I had priced two different roof systems for the cabin. The method we chose *not* to use eliminates the need for rafters and is used frequently by some builders in our area. They place 4-in. foam panels over a 2x ceiling deck supported by purlins. On top of the foam panels they secure 1x4 strapping with long nails through the foam and into the 2x deck. A metal roof is then at-

tached to the strapping to finish what they feel is an adequate and inexpensive roof.

I found that method to be more expensive than using 2x10 rafters and insulating with 9-in. (R-30) fiberglass batts. As additional advantages, I was able to supply ventilation above the roof insulation, the 2x10 sub-fascia provided secure nailing for the tails of the 1x10 soffit boards, and we don't have hundreds of 6-in. nails holding the roof on and conducting heat past the insulation. The 2x10 rafters and 1x4 strapping do make for a thicker roof on top of the purlins and add extra weight to the roof structure, but with our beefy purlins the added weight isn't a problem. A thin roof profile would have looked skimpy and out of proportion.

We used a ridge-venting strategy for our cathedral ceiling that is adequate for a vacation cabin and virtually free compared to the cost of an add-on ridge vent. As shown in the drawing above right, air enters the roof cavity through screened slots that we cut in the soffit. It then travels over the 2x6 blocking between the rafters and continues between the insulation and the metal roof up to the ridge. On each side of the ridge board we provided a horizontal channel over the length of the cabin by simply cutting off the peak of each rafter to exhaust the air out the gable ends. We could feel the hot air pouring out of these little vent openings when we trimmed them out.

We used brown painted steel roofing for the cabin but even with a 10-in-12 pitch, snow does

The interior of the cabin features site-built woodwork and a woodstove with a copper heat shield (above). The door to the bedroom is at right, and near it a ladder leads to the sleeping loft. In the kitchen, there is built-in indirect lighting (left) between the shelves. Wall fixtures are three-sided wood shades lined on the inside with galvanized sheet metal.

not always slide off right away. If the first snow to fall on the roof is on the wet side and then the weather turns cold, the snow will freeze around the screw heads and additional snow will continue to pile up on top of it. This is especially true when the cabin is vacant and there is no heat loss through the ceiling to loosen the snow. When this much snow eventually does slide, it can take a plumbing vent and chimney with it. To avoid the use of crickets, we placed both of these projections right at the ridge.

Both the roughsawn board-and-batten siding and the 1x6 pine boards inside the cabin went on easily with a pneumatic nail gun until we reached the log purlins, where each piece had to be scribed and coped to fit around the logs. Boards that fit between two logs and had to be coped at both ends presented the trickiest cuts, and for those we resorted to strips of tarpaper. We scribed onto the paper and cut it with scissors until it fit perfectly. Then we used it as a pattern to trace the cut line onto the board.

A cozy interior—The finish details inside the cabin are simple, and we built everything on site. We made the interior doors with 1x6 T&G pine boards held together with Z-bracing on the back side. The doors were hung with half surface-mount hinges and fitted with old-fashioned thumblatches. We made the kitchen-cabinet doors the same way. For the small kitchen countertop, we used some vertical-grain 1x4 fir flooring I had left over from a previous job and then sealed it with a non-toxic clear acrylic finish (Fabuloy, made by Pratt & Lambert, 75 Tonawanda St., Buffalo, N. Y. 14207).

Above the sink and kitchen counter, open shelves are combined with two built-in lights (photo above left). The lights are simple porcelain fixtures mounted on the wall between the three shelf sections. A board nailed in front of the light connects the shelf units and results in attractive, inexpensive indirect lighting. We used this same technique for all of the light fixtures in the cabin. We installed a standard white porcelain bulb fixture wherever we wanted a wall light, and then covered it with a simple three-sided wood shade made from 1x10 roughsawn boards. Inside the wood cover, a galvanized sheet-metal lining protects the wood from heat.

Another low-cost yet attractive finish detail was the heat shield behind the woodstove and flue pipe. Instead of rock, brick or asbestos, we mounted a piece of sheet copper on the wall behind the stove. We were careful to hold it 2 in. away from the wall and to leave an opening at the top and bottom. The copper sheet looks good and reflects most of the radiant heat from the stove back into the room. The heat that it absorbs is quickly dissipated.

In the nick of time—While we worked on all of these finish details, winter was literally knocking on the door. There were several inches of snow on the ground and the road was passable with four-wheel-drive only. I took every possible piece of equipment out as soon as we could do without it and kept my ear glued to the weather forecasts. Since the subcontractor who was scheduled to sand the floors didn't have a four-wheel-drive vehicle, I drove down to the highway to pick him up just in time to hear the forecast I had been dreading. A monster storm was heading our way.

The painters arrived early the next morning just as it started to snow. Our plan was to tape off everything that wasn't wood and spray the ceiling, walls and floor with two coats of clear urethane varnish. By the time the first coat was sprayed, the air was pretty thick with overspray. We knew that would slow down the drying time but we couldn't open the door or windows because of the storm. We retreated to my canvas wall tent and sat by the woodstove to wait for the first coat to dry. It was really snowing by mid-afternoon, and the urethane was not yet dry.

When it was almost dark, we chained up all four wheels on our trucks. After one more cup of coffee, we decided the urethane was dry enough for the second coat (even though it wasn't). It was a slow drive to the highway but when we reached it about eight that evening, I felt like I was walking on air when I got out of the truck to take the chains off the tires. It was Nov. 8, exactly two months from the day we dug the hole and the last day anyone would drive into that cabin for the next six months. □

Builder Bill Phelps lives in Jackson, Wyo.

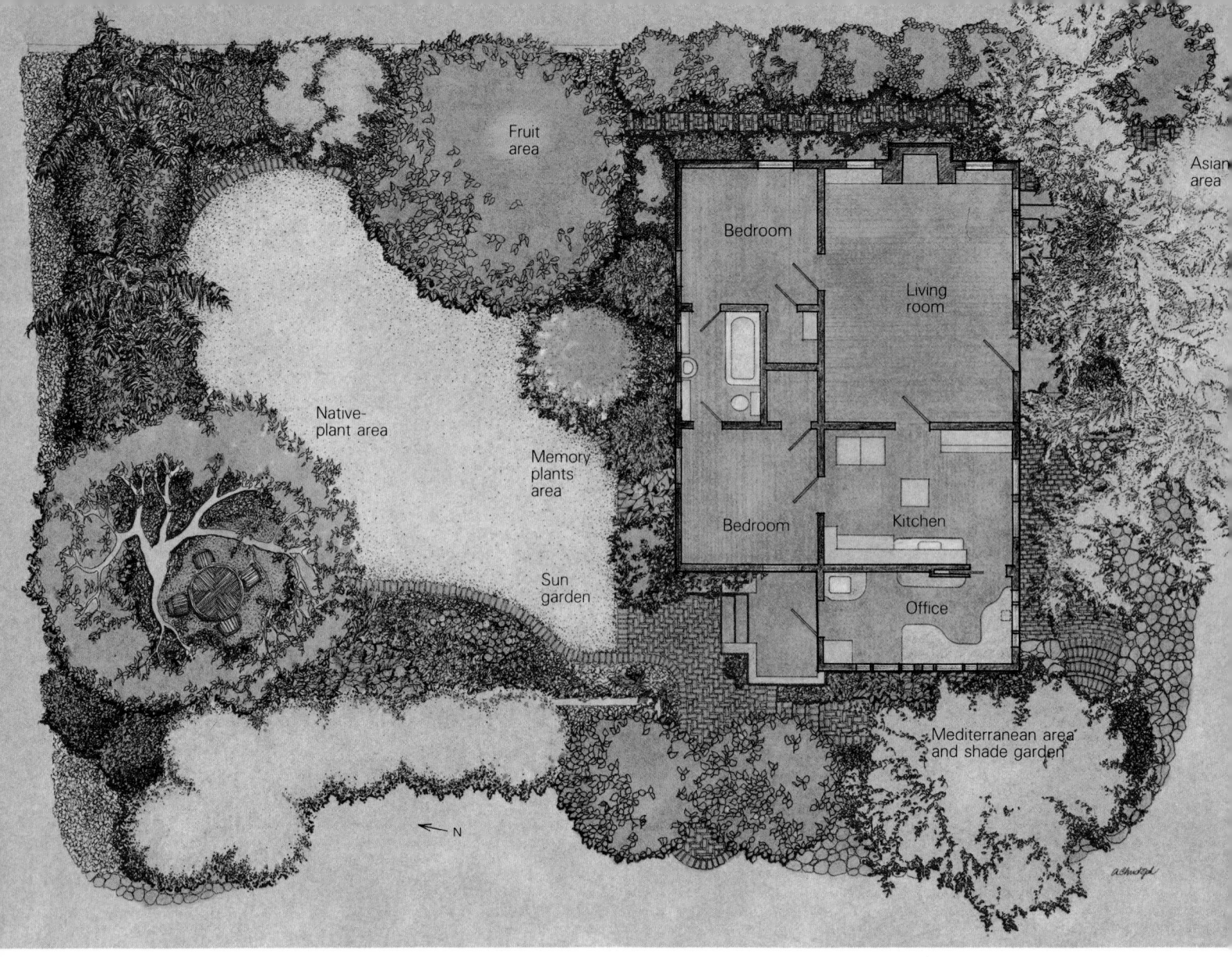

Fruit area

Asian area

Bedroom

Living room

Native-plant area

Memory plants area

Sun garden

Bedroom

Kitchen

Office

← N

Mediterranean area and shade garden

Better Home and Garden

A landscape architect designs inside and out to make the most of a small house

by Ann Christoph

Ever since my family left the small Wisconsin farming community where I grew up, I sought another community that would offer the same stability and neighborliness that I had enjoyed there. I had glimpses of it while attending various universities in Corvallis, Ore.; Ann Arbor, Mich.; even west Philadelphia. But these were just places I passed through on my way to becoming a landscape architect.

After completing my graduate program, I moved to South Laguna, Calif., a 60-year-old beach community of 4,000 tucked between chaparral-covered hills and the ocean. I had found work with a firm that was deeply involved in South Laguna planning and community issues. We worked on the first General Plan for the vil-

lage, and subsequently designed its first park and developed new land-use districts and stricter zoning regulations. Later we wrote a master plan for the community landscape that proposed reinforcing the rustic character of the village and preserving its heritage structures and trees.

Over a nine-year period, I became so involved in community planning, in working with my neighbors to improve our village, that I felt this was my home. I realized that buying a house, with the opportunity to do detailed design and restoration work on it, was an important part of my committed involvement in South Laguna.

My husband Bill Kipper and I eventually found a Craftsman-style bungalow, built in 1933. It was less than 900 sq. ft. in size, with two tiny bed-

rooms (each 9½ ft. by 9½ ft.), one bath, a living room, kitchen and porch (drawing, above). The house is on South Laguna's Heritage Structure Inventory, which means it's among the community's 70 or so original beach cottages. Unlike most, our house had not been altered. It even had the original plumbing fixtures and Art Deco light fixtures.

For the two of us, and for many who visited, this unsophisticated structure felt like a real home, in contrast to the more elaborate but cold, mass-produced tract houses so common in southern California. The skip-troweled plaster walls, the varnished mahogany and fir moldings, the painted cabinets, and expecially the spiraea (bridal wreath) in the backyard evoked my child-

Drawing: Ann Christoph

hood home. Preserving the house's serenity and simplicity depended on changing as little as possible. But the house was designed as a vacation cottage, so we knew that some changes would have to be made to accommodate full-time living and to provide space for my landscape architectural office.

Landscaping—Since the house was so small, I wanted to improve the landscaping first to create usable living space outdoors. This would also expand (at least visually) the space in several rooms of the house, especially in my office, which looks out on the side and backyard. The landscaping would serve too as a laboratory and living portfolio for my design work, giving me examples to show my clients.

My special interest is historical gardens and their restoration, so I based the garden design largely on the concepts of early 20th-century gardens, which emphasized diversity of plants and division of the garden into a series of outdoor rooms. Conceptually, the landscaping is divided into four major areas, each of which takes its theme from an existing tree. The Asian area, outside the front door, is centered around the deodar cedar from the Himalayas (which is one of the trees on South Laguna's Heritage Inventory), and also contains an India hawthorn, a banana shrub, a Himalayan magnolia and camellias, which originated in China and Japan. Besides creating a nice view from the living room, these plantings add privacy by shielding the room from the street and from the house next door.

The fruit area, at the northeast corner of the house, was planned around an old avocado tree. I added other trees that would yield more exotic fruits, not usually found in the supermarket: blood orange, pummelo (similar to a grapefruit), loquat, kumquat and strawberry guavas. Situated just outside our bedroom window, the fruit area screens us from the house next door, yet also makes the lush backyard seem part of the room.

At the back of the lot, there was a marvelous California holly (another tree on the Heritage Inventory) with a nicely shaded area beneath it. This became the native-plant area, which now includes Catalina currant, Douglas iris, bush anemone and lemonade berry. Under the California holly, I put four bent willow chairs and a rustic table, which seats more people than any table inside the house. This is where I serve meals whenever possible.

The fourth major landscaping area is the Mediterranean area, just outside my office. Given that space inside was so limited, I wanted this area to feel like a part of the room. To the olive trees already there, I added a lemon tree, strawberry tree, periwinkle ground cover and rosemary. Inside, I trained a Hoya vine along the window to blur the distinction between indoors and out.

Also included in the landscaping are a shade garden, planted with camellias, impatiens and Kafir lilies; a sun garden that is changed twice a year and that has included flowers alternated with vegetables; and the "memory plants" area that includes bridal wreath, calla lilies, fuchsias, ferns and night-blooming jasmine.

I designed and installed an automatic irrigation system that has both drip and spray mecha-

Nestled in the shade of a California holly tree, the rustic table and chairs get a lot of use—they seat more people than any table inside the house.

nisms. In the garage, there is a digital control box where I can program the times and duration of the waterings.

The drip system has very low flow requirements (between 4 gal. and 10 gal. per minute) and operates at pressures as low as 15 psi. Drip systems typically include a pressure regulator, but a regulator wasn't necessary here because of the already low pressure at our meter (40 psi). This drip system was an economical solution, given our low water pressure and constricted galvanized plumbing, because it makes it possible to irrigate large areas of the yard without designing a whole series of separately controlled systems (with the costly addition of valves and a larger controller).

The flexible plastic tubing (½-in. dia. and ⅜-in. dia. backbone lines, ¼-in. dia. feeder lines) is easy to install because compression fittings are used throughout, so no gluing is required. You can add on to the system simply by punching into the backbone line, inserting a fitting and adding ¼-in. tubing and additional emitters (plastic fittings with a small hole in them). Our system includes a filter assembly into which fertilizer tablets can be inserted.

Irrigation systems like mine are necessary to the maintenance of successful landscaping in our area, and having one to show my clients has helped me demonstrate different methods and options available for their irrigation system. From time to time, I've also been able to test new devices before specifying them for a client's system.

Interior design—While working on the garden, we thought about work to be done inside the house. The house was divided into a series of small rooms. Opening up the floor plan by removing walls, as many remodelers do, would

have been impractical in a house this small—privacy and separation of activities would have been almost impossible. Moreover, the house had no central heating, and having small individual rooms made it more economical to heat. But retaining the basic arrangment of the house and the existing fixtures meant that we had to take full advantage of what little space we had.

We decided to limit our changes to adding built-ins like cabinets, shelving and furniture. But these elements had to be compatible with existing details or, if there were no prototypes in the house, compatible with the era in which the house was built. As research, I studied several decorating magazines from the 1920s and early 1930s, including *Art and Decoration, Good Housekeeping, American Home,* and *Better Homes and Gardens.*

I started the design process by measuring and drawing an overall plot plan at ¼-in. scale. Then I developed drawings at 1-in. scale that showed floor plans and all of the elevations in each room. As I worked on the design, I depended heavily on advice from David Hanson, our carpenter. When I would ask him to look over a detail I was working out, he would make suggestions or disappear to the workshop, returning later with a mockup of the portion in question. In the evenings I built full-size cardboard models of the different elements—shelving, for example—and taped them up for Hanson to see the next day. The design evolved this way.

The home office—As our first major project inside we converted the existing 6½-ft. by 13-ft. laundry/porch into an office. In order to do this, we relocated the water heater, washer and dryer in the storeroom below. Unlike the rest of the house, the woodwork on the porch had been painted. Bill stripped and refinished the porch

Overlooking the olive and lemon trees in the side yard, this converted porch now serves as a landscape architect's office (above left). The influences of that field can be seen in the organic shape of the desktop and in the Hoya vine running under the bookshelf. Directly below the office, in the laundry/drafting room, the layout table folds up for access to the washer and dryer (above).

In the kitchen (below left), the new cabinets on the right match the original cabinets on the left. An island cabinet with a dropleaf mahogany top houses the freezer. The old refrigerator was replaced with two 24-in. units, masked with cabinet fronts, that fit under the countertop (below). The broom closet rolls out on drawer glides, and holds the waste basket, which is accessible through the hatch just above the counter. Above the porcelain drainboards, wall cabinets with slotted shelves and caned doors allow dishes to be stored wet.

woodwork, and later finished the new woodwork to match.

It was important that my office have abundant, well-organized storage. We built in bookshelves, cabinets, a two-drawer legal-size file cabinet and two cubbyhole files for rolled plans.

We made space for floor-to-ceiling bookshelves by replacing a standard door with a pocket door. A bookshelf circles the room above the windows and doors. It hangs from 2x8s bolted into the ceiling joists and mortise-and-tenoned through the shelf, which is then held by square pegs. The through tenons have an opening for the Hoya (wax flower) vine to run through (photo facing page, top left). I knew that periodically I would have to remove the vines for cleaning and retraining, so the bottoms of the tenons swivel open. Behind the shelf and over the windows are louvered light boxes that illuminate the drafting and desk surfaces.

Much of a landscape architect's work involves the design of walkways. Here, predictable walking patterns dictate flowing lines and rounded edges, in contrast to the usual rectangular architectural forms. I developed the shape of the desktop in my office from a study of the walking and writing areas of the room. I tried to maximize desktop space without impeding flow or creating corners to bump into.

Laundry/drafting room—By the time we finished the office, I had hired a landscape draftsman who worked in the living room while I worked in the new office. In order to reclaim the living room for family use, we revised our plans for the laundry room below to include a drafting space. Windows and a glazed door were added. This long narrow room had to accommodate drafting space, a blueprint machine and a photocopier, file cabinets and closet storage, as well as the washer and dryer.

I made 1-in. scale drawings of the room and used paper cutouts of the needed components to try various arrangements. It was clear that only the narrowest washer and dryer would fit.

The top surfaces of the washer and dryer are too narrow to use for spreading out a large drawing, so we designed a 32-in. by 54-in. table that fits over them. The table can be folded up when it's time to do laundry (photo facing page, top right). Hanson built the table with three lengths of 2x12 pine, hinged with two pairs of Soss hinges, and then routed the edges to match the desktop upstairs.

A set of built-in mahogany cabinets running the length of the room provides storage for drafting supplies as well as for household goods. An enameled dropleaf table on the face of the water-heater enclosure cabinet swings up when needed to provide a table for folding laundry.

While I wanted to move the draftsman out of the living room, I didn't want to lose easy communication between us. An intercom wouldn't suffice because we also needed to pass papers and drawings back and forth. So I asked Hanson to cut a hole in the floor (under the desktop, where no one steps) for a pass-through. He built a small trap door to match the flooring and concealed the latch behind a tiny sliding wood panel. The door can be opened from above or below, with no knob protruding above the floor surface. We depend on this "space-age" communications system.

A 1930s kitchen—The existing kitchen had only one cabinet. With three doors leading to other rooms, two large windows, a vintage gas stove and porcelain sink, and a bulky refrigerator occupying much of the room, work and storage space was sorely limited.

To get some ideas, we researched the kitchens of the period. In the early 1930s, the kitchen cabinet was a new household concept. This was a transitional time between the prosperous 1920s—when a number of servants would work in the kitchen and use the pantry for storage—and the Depression—when servants could no longer be afforded. In the early 1930s, kitchens were redesigned for the convenience of the housewife working alone. Pantries were converted to other uses, and storage was consolidated into kitchen cabinets. At first most of these were prefabricated, freestanding pieces that looked like hutches, with retractable porcelain-enamel countertops. Built-in cabinets, based on the prefabricated prototype, came later. Cabinets were supported on legs for easy cleaning underneath. Hinges, latches and supports were clearly visible and accepted as part of the overall design. With their shiny white surfaces, kitchens looked like laboratories.

With all this in mind, we concentrated on the one free corner of the kitchen—the area to the right of the sink, where the old refrigerator had been. A cabinet design based on the prefabricated hutch-like cabinets I'd seen in the magazines seemed like a good solution for this corner (photo facing page, bottom left).

We replaced the upright refrigerator with two 24-in. wide under-the-counter models from Sub-Zero (Sub-Zero Freezer Co., Inc., P.O. Box 4130, Madison, Wis. 53711). These were the only self-defrosting compact refrigerators I was able to find. Hanson made door panels for them that matched the other cabinet doors in the kitchen. The 24-in. width of the refrigerator doors disturbed me, however. I didn't want them to appear too clumsy or different from the other cabinet doors, which are 18 in. wide. So we added a 1x2 strip down the middle, dividing each refrigerator door visually into two panels.

Next to the refrigerators, there was less than 12 in. of space left. We still needed a broom closet, so we designed a roll-out unit that holds canned goods, cleaning supplies, the vacuum cleaner and a waste basket (photo facing page, bottom right). The waste basket is also accessible through a hatch at the end of the counter.

For the countertop surface, I wanted to use porcelain enamel—not only for its authenticity but because it's easy to clean. I found a company not too far away that does this work—Cameo California Metal Enameling Co. (6904 E. Slauson Ave., Los Angeles, Calif. 90022). Ordinarily Cameo does freeway and street signs, but they agreed to fabricate and enamel these custom countertops. I did detailed dimensional drawings of the two tops we needed, one for the original cabinet and one for above the refrigerators. The company matched the beige color of our antique stove for the top surface, and used traditional black for the edge. The total cost for the countertops was $800.

Since the refrigerator units don't have freezer compartments, we built an island counter with a freezer as its base. To interfere as little as possible with traffic flow in the kitchen, we chose a 19-in. by 19-in. U-Line UF-40 freezer unit (U-Line Corp., 8900 N. 55 St., Box 23220, Milwaukee, Wis. 53223). Hanson added wooden sides and a door. On the back of the unit, a framed door with a caned panel allows ventilation of the coils. The freezer plugs into an outlet in the floor beneath it and has enough cord that we can move the unit around a bit.

The mahogany cutting board on top of the freezer was built with a dropleaf so its working surface can be doubled by raising the leaf and sliding it forward on integral runners until the seam is centered on the freezer cabinet.

After all of these improvements, our kitchen lacked one of the items one would expect to find in a remodeled kitchen—a dishwasher. There just wasn't room, and it would have been out of character with the rest of the improvements. But it seemed to me that the biggest advantage of a dishwasher was having a place to store drying dishes. In one of the old magazines, I had seen a dish-drying rack that mounted on the side of the cabinet. So I thought, why not include drying racks inside the two cabinets above the sink drainboards? We made removable mahogany racks and added caned door fronts for ventilation. Dishes can be stored wet, out of sight, and drain into the sink.

In an old hardware store in Los Angeles, whose stock actually dates back to the 1930s, we found hexagonal black glass knobs to match those on the existing cupboards. The original butterfly hinges were steel plated and heavily painted, so we replaced them with new brass ones that we had nickel plated.

While scraping old paint off the kitchen walls, we saw two green stripes around the room about 1 ft. below the ceiling. We imitated these stripes in black paint and again in black tile above the stove. We found 3x6 beige quarry tiles, which matched the stove, to use on the wall behind it for protection from grease. The tile installer cut off the spacing lugs so he could match the narrow grout joints typical of the 1930s.

No trouble at all—As we neared the end of our work on the house, a friend stopped by to check on our progress. He looked closely at the tile work, where we had gone to such extremes to find the right colors and make the grout lines look authentic, and said, "I can see that that was just no trouble at all."

The work wasn't easy, of course. But this house was worth the extra care and effort because it now gives back to us every day the joy of something well thought out and fitting. It is especially satisfying that the house is part of a community that I care about and where I work to achieve the considered decision making that is the essence of good design. □

Ann Christoph is a landscape architect in South Laguna, Calif.

At the entry. The front door of the Honda house leads to the living room at the west end of the house, where the ceiling is open to the rafters. The dining room doubles as a passageway to the kitchen. The railing on the second level is 2-in. copper water pipe, brushed to a satin finish. Note the doors behind the couch—they are sandblasted Victorian doors made of first-growth redwood. The downstairs floors are #2 oak, ¾-in. T&G strips.

The Honda House

Simple construction techniques and a basic plan yield a house with a rich variety of spaces

by James Servais

My wife Gillian and I run a design and construction company, and over the years we have built a number of houses that emphasize energy conservation and livability. We also use a lot of hand-tooled plaster and stucco, which along with the exposed and carved beamwork, gives our houses a sculpted, southwestern feeling.

In July of 1986, a young woman named Deborah Mounts walked into one such house that I was finishing in Oakland, California. She liked the materials and detailing and told me that she had purchased a steep upslope lot on a nearby ridge. It had a great view, and she wanted to build a place on it for herself. She cautioned, however, that expense was an issue and wondered if we could do something within her budget.

Most of the houses that we build are pretty expensive, owing to the steep lots that constitute the remaining building sites in this area, and the amenity-conscious clientele. But it sounded like she might be interested in a project that I had long wanted to build—the "Honda house"—a name that had evolved to describe a house that, like the car, was simple, compact, ergonomic, well built and relatively inexpensive. It seemed like we might have a perfect fit.

Gillian and I had great misgivings, however, about doing contract work again. In the early '80s we had several bad experiences with architects and owners, and for the last few years we have done only spec houses that we design. So we laid it on the line in our contract with Mounts and stipulated that we would design and build the house if, after the approval of the floor plan, we would have full aesthetic control of the project. To our surprise, she signed. We began construction in September of 1987.

Basically a box—The concept of a small simple house constructed of quality materials is hardly new, but it seldom seems to get done—at least here in the Bay Area. The basic shape of the Honda house is similar to lofts and stores I'd worked on or lived in. It's a straight-forward two-story 20-ft. by 46-ft. rectangle covered with a shed roof. There are two bedrooms upstairs that can virtually be combined by opening a pair of wide pocket doors (drawing right). Each floor has its own bathroom.

The living room is 20 ft. wide with a 20-ft. high ceiling at the uphill wall. Its airy feeling is a counterpart to the dining room, which lies in the center of the house, tucked under the bedrooms. The kitchen is along the east wall, where its breakfast table can be seen in a straight shot from the front door (photo facing page). Uninterrupted sight lines like this, along with a high ceiling in one of the rooms, help to sidestep the claustrophobic feeling that can curse a small house.

The house has lots of glass on the long south side. Two pairs of double doors open onto a deck that is on the same level as the first floor, which effectively increases the square footage of the public spaces at a fraction of the cost of enclosed space.

Designing a house such as this is an exercise in restraint. We typically consult other professional designers during the development of a floor plan to see if we've left out something obvious, and to gain general impressions about suitability. This project was no exception to that rule, and we asked several excellent designers for input at various stages of the planning. None of them could resist pushing out walls or adding bays. It seems most designers think that the more complex a house is, the better it is.

We resisted. What we were trying to prove was that simple does not mean cheap. But this

Second floor

First floor

NORTH

0 2 4 8 ft.

meant that setting priorities was crucial. The trade-off in our limited budget was spelled out clearly: For any additional wall or bay, money would have to come out of the finish budget.

Keeping the end in sight—Over the years I have been involved with houses built atop astonishing foundations with elaborate and meticulous framing, only to see an exhausted and over-budget crew struggle at the conclusion of the project. The reality is that with few exceptions, no one cares if the rows of rebar are exactly parallel or if a stepped foundation on a hillside is dead on level. I am not trying to promote shabby workmanship, just an understanding of the tolerances and concessions required at each stage of construction in order to achieve the best possible finished product.

In *Building Your Own House* (Ten Speed Press, P. O. Box 7123, Berkeley, Calif. 94707, $17.95; 440 pp.), Robert Roskind emphasizes the "margin of error" allowed in residential construction and the parameters within which you can work without negative consequences. For instance, Roskind points out that layouts have to be exact, but if a joist is ¼ in. off its mark it's not going to affect the integrity of the structure. This was an important lesson for me when I was learning the ropes. Rookie builders run the risk of missing the big picture when it comes to assembling the skeleton of a structure and often get bogged down because they're too picky about tolerances. Builders never have enough time or money, and being a good builder means knowing how to spend both wisely.

Pier and glulam foundation—Ironically, the first problem to be solved in building this house was how to build a parking space and a foundation for it on a 25° slope. In keeping with its budget-conscious themes, I'd always imagined the house on a flat site, but Deborah's upslope lot upped the ante right away. In addition, she wanted a garage and a storage room. To accommodate both, we sited the house near the top of the lot, where its deck overlaps the storage room and garage (middle photo, p. 89).

Most of the new houses built on the steep lots in this neighborhood are built atop pier and grade-beam foundations *(FHB* 16, pp. 31-37). A few stand on tall-wall concrete pours that act as retaining walls, and fewer still are

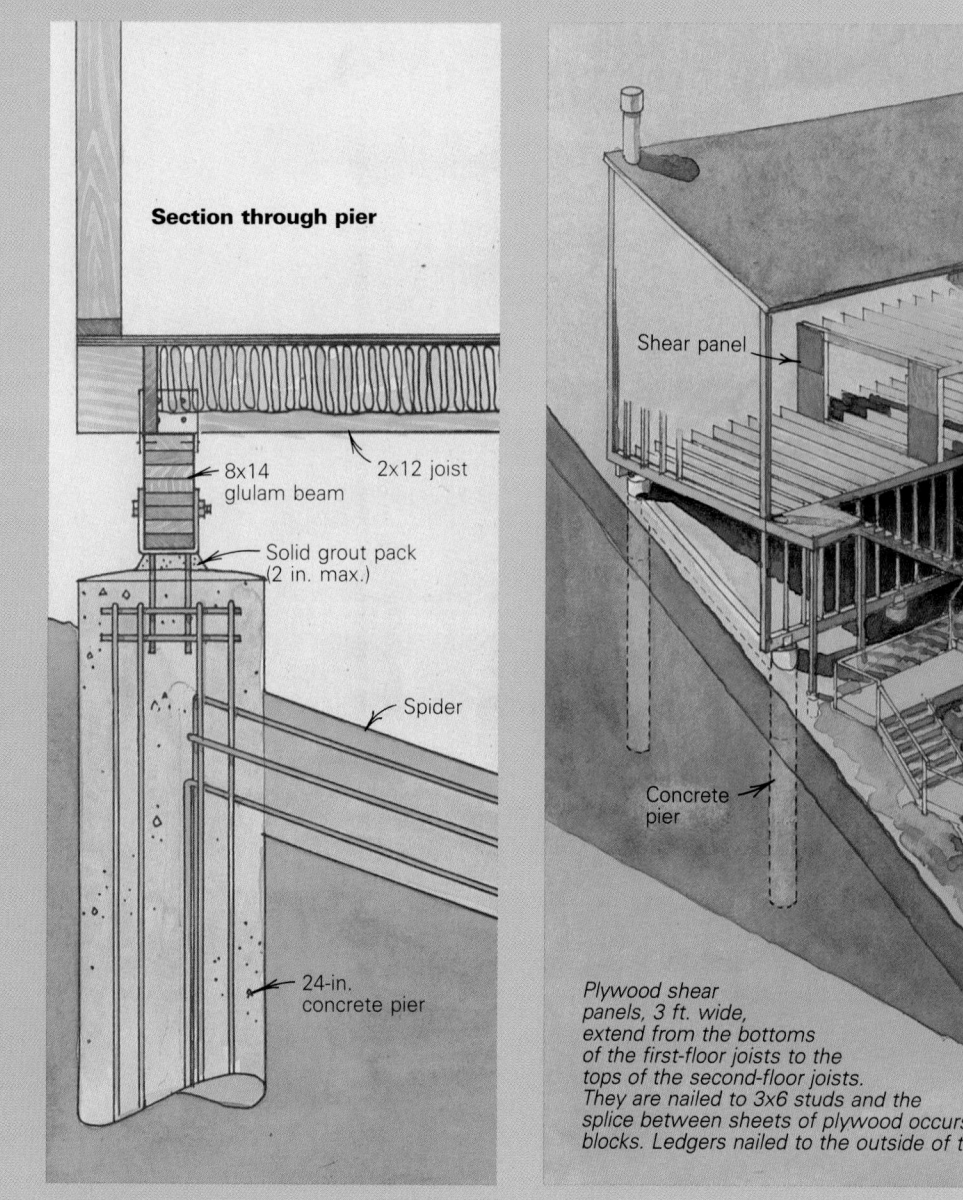

Section through pier

- 8x14 glulam beam
- 2x12 joist
- Solid grout pack (2 in. max.)
- Spider
- 24-in. concrete pier

Honda house revealed

Gunite retaining wall supports corner of house under deck.

- Shear panel
- Deck
- Concrete pier

Plywood shear panels, 3 ft. wide, extend from the bottoms of the first-floor joists to the tops of the second-floor joists. They are nailed to 3x6 studs and the splice between sheets of plywood occurs at 3x6 blocks. Ledgers nailed to the outside of the panels pick up the flooring.

---

built on poles. The foundation that we built for this house uses the best aspects of all three, and for less money.

Much of the house bears on 2-ft. dia. concrete piers arranged in two rows (top photo facing page). We have a phenomenon known as soil creep in these hills, which means the 5-ft. thick layer of topsoil is slowly moving downhill. To hold fast against the creep, piers must extend 10 ft. past the soil into the bedrock. They have to be laced with plenty of steel, and that means large-diameter piers. Our structural engineer, Ken Hughes of Lafayette, California, reasoned that we could cut down on the typical number of load-bearing piers for a house this size because the piers were so big.

Instead of pouring concrete grade beams that extend across the slope to transfer the weight of the walls to the piers, we used 8x14 glulam beams for several reasons. For one, across-the-slope grade beams can impede soils that want to creep downhill. To avoid this, you've got to cast the beams so that they end up a little above grade, which adds to forming time. Even more important is the problem of drilling on a hillside. From past

experience I've found that it is very tough to bore holes exactly where you want them on a slope. When you hit large rocks, the auger deflects one way or another. Stakes get lost under the tractor's treads and piles of dirt further obscure the layout.

Once the holes had been bored for the piers, we hired a crane to lower rebar cages into them. We pumped concrete into the pier holes to within 2 ft. of grade, allowing the rebar to protrude enough for splices. Then we capped each partially completed pier with a Sonotube form, and wired our beam brackets to the rebar of each pier. Sure enough, they weren't in a straight line, but we figured that having the center of a bracket within 3 in. of the axis of a 2 ft. dia. pier was close enough. That gave us 6 in., plus or minus, to work with.

To align and level the brackets, we made a glulam surrogate by scabbing together some straight lengths of 2x6. We screwed it temporarily to the beam brackets and fastened our bracing to the phony beam to hold everything in place as we topped off the Sonotube forms.

The piers are connected by concrete beams called spiders that run with the slope. They are

poured directly on grade, and serve to brace the piers. Because they are oriented downhill, the soil can creep right on by them.

As expected, our two rows of piers weren't quite parallel, but the glulam scheme gave us some room to maneuver. I worried only about making the piers dead level because the floor joists were designed to cantilever a short distance over the beams (drawing above left). This allowed us to build a square platform on top of our beams, where it was easy to control accuracy. You need correction systems like these in hillside foundations.

Parking place—Local codes require an off-street parking place that is at least 18 ft. square, in addition to a driveway. To get a level space this big meant taking a 240-cu. yd. chunk out of the hillside and then building a retaining wall to keep the hill in check. The back wall of the cut was 17 ft. high, and I had no intention of building a formed-concrete retaining wall. The formwork alone would have taken too long, and the form lumber would likely have been unsalvageable.

Instead, we had Hughes design a gunite

Drawings: Malcolm Wells

Photo: Gillian Servais

wall similar to the one that he wrote about in *FHB* #40, pp. 60-63 . Unlike that project, this wall has much more steel in it, and it has a different drainage system. We laid out the steel on the ground, wired it into sections and tilted it into position against the cut (photo top right). We used Miradrain 6000 (Mirafi Inc., P. O. Box 240967, Charlotte, N. C., 28224) to channel away the groundwater that collected against the wall. Miradrain is a heavy plastic material that has dimples in it to create thousands of tiny waterways, and filter fabric on one side to keep the channels from gettting clogged by earth particles.

We tucked the Miradrain behind the rebar and called in the gunite crew. In a couple of hours the job was complete. The garage wall — from excavation to smooth-troweling the gunite — took three weeks. Since it had to be there anyway, we used the back wall of the garage to carry the southeast corner of the house.

Framing — Once we had our square-and-level first-floor platform decked with plywood, we made up our lumber packages into 500 lb. to 600 lb. units and had them lifted by crane onto the platform. I'm a firm believer that carpenters shouldn't have to carry materials to an uphill site. A couple of hours of crane time can save a lot of time and money, and improves morale.

For years now we have framed our walls with 2x6s, 24 in. o. c. The trick is to keep everything in line: studs over joists on both floors, rafters on 48 in. centers. By doing this, not only is there room for more insulation in the walls, but there's about 25% less wood to cut, fewer holes for the plumber and the electrician to drill and a lot more wood left after they do drill. The drawback is, however, that the walls have more wave to them and are heavier to tilt up. To combat the waviness, we use ½-in. instead of ⅜-in. plywood sheathing. Now that we've switched over, 2x4s on 16 in. centers seem to be an historical mistake.

In this house, we had to use ½-in. plywood anyway to meet California seismic requirements. Although not required, we used panel adhesive to help affix the plywood to the wall frame. We even put it where the edges abut one another. It helps seal the house, gives a much stronger shear panel and seems to keep the house straight as the wood dries out.

Because we're in a seismic zone, the building department requires holdowns — or the equivalent — to tie the building to the foundation. I hate holdowns. They have a way of getting installed a little out of alignment, they have to be threaded around conditions that can't always be anticipated, they cost a lot in time and money and, ideally, they have to be retightened after the lumber shrinks as it dries.

So I asked Hughes to devise a way that we could use plywood shear panels to anchor the house to the foundation in lieu of holdowns. To satisfy the building department, Hughes had to show some fancy membrane calculations that probably cost just as much

A web of rebar hoisted against the garage-cut awaits the gunite crew, while a scabbed-together 2x6 drapes across the Sonotube pier forms, aligning the glulam brackets (photo above). Arranged in a composition of simple forms, the "Honda house" relies on color, texture and the repetitious shapes of windows and doors for its exterior style (photo right). Kitchen cabinets were made of vertical-grain Douglas fir by Dave Rasmussen of Dovetail Woodworks (photo below). Sandblasted beams and a T&G ceiling are typical details in a Servais house, as are the plaster walls and the granite counters. In the background, a dropped ceiling conceals the plumbing from the upstairs bath.

ered the entire plywood subfloor with 6-mil poly. This helped in curing the concrete, and kept it from oozing through the plywood to discolor the finish ceiling below. The slab has 6x6 welded wire mesh reinforcing, and control joints divide it into thirds (for more on concrete slabs over wood subfloors, see *FHB #11*, pp. 46-50).

To keep the weight of the structure down a bit, we used a lightweight aggregate for the concrete deck on the second level. It is called Buildex in our area, and it weighs about 110 lb. per cu. ft., as compared to 140 lb. for regular concrete. The aggregate is made of shale that has been heated and expanded.

To promote solar-heat absorption, we used a dark red pigment on the both floors (photo, p. 94). We broadcast 250 lb. of pigment per floor across the slabs, and bull-floated, troweled and sealed the concrete with a wax (Sonosheen) provided by the manufacturer (Sonneborn Building Products, 415 E. 16th St., Chicago, Ill. 60411). Fortunately, this wax also acts as a curing compound for the slab so no additional treatment was needed, other than covering it with construction paper within an hour of waxing. We kept the paper on the slabs throughout the job to prevent damage from subsequent construction activities. The color additive cost an additional $250, but it really makes the concrete look special. The finish floor cost about $2 a sq. ft.—half of what a quarry-tile floor costs around here.

Roof—The hipped roof with gable vents has been common here for a long time. We covered this one with Onduline sheets, a roofing material that is frequently used on farm buildings (Onduline, USA, Route 9, Box 195, Fredericksburg, Va. 22401). It is the only roofing material I know of with a lifetime warranty. The manufacturer promises to replace any sheets that are defective in workmanship or materials for as long as the customer owns the building. The warranty doesn't, however, apply to hail damage.

Onduline isn't expensive, and it's very easy to install. Its corrugated sheets measure 79 in. by 46 in., or 4½ sheets to a roofing square. The sheets are made of organic fibers, corrugated for strength and impregnated with asphalt. It was developed in Europe and has been used for 35 years in more than 60 countries. It is quiet, does not transmit heat and can be installed with simple tools. It also comes with its own sophisticated ABS flashing for roof penetrations. My only complaint is that the flashing is limited to cold-pipe penetrations. We had to make our own flashing to surround the woodstove flue. Onduline costs slightly more than shingles and goes on in half the time.

Windows—Because the design called for such extensive south glazing, we spent a lot of time reviewing the performance of various window types. This was a long, tedious job. With windows and exterior doors eating up over 10.5% of the total project cost, we wanted to be sure of our decisions.

We knew from the outset that the Johnsons didn't want to roll, fold or pull movable insulation in place at night and then remove it in the morning. That led us to investigate the new metallic-oxide coated films used by window manufacturers to reduce nighttime heat loss (see *FHB #20*, p. 22). Based on availability, performance and cost, we narrowed our search down to two products: Heat Mirror 88 by Southwall Technology (1029 Corporation Way, Palo Alto, Calif. 94303) and SunGain by 3M (Energy Control Products, Bldg. 225-4S-08 3M Center, St. Paul, Minn. 55144-1000). Both are nearly invisible films that are enclosed inside double-wall windows. The films allow the sun's radiant energy to pass through the window, and then trap most of it inside by reflecting it away from the window. The films are sold to manufacturers who install it in their own windows, which are available in fixed or operable sash.

Windows that use Heat Mirror contain one layer of the film, while those that use SunGain have two layers. Both products could match or beat the performance of typical night-insulation systems. Quadpane windows with the double layer of SunGain let in more solar energy than those with the single layer of Heat Mirror. Heat Mirror and SunGain windows have comparable R-values—about 3.8.

Because Heat Mirror windows allow less solar energy into a building, they must be "oversized." Conventional double-glazing units admit about 73% of available solar radiation, those with SunGain let in about 63%, while Heat Mirror admits only about 53% of the available radiation. Since a larger window costs more, Lee and Theis had to run extensive studies to find out what these trade-offs meant. Their studies showed that even with larger apertures, the Heat Mirror windows were 15% cheaper than the SunGain windows. We went with Heat Mirror.

Unfortunately, our selection of window manufacturer wasn't a lucky one. The company went on strike, causing a 3½-month delay in getting the windows delivered. Of course, I was told it would take only three weeks when they wanted all the money up front. I've never taped, sanded and painted drywall before installing windows on a job, but I did here. Fortunately, Kansas and drought are synonymous in the summertime, so it didn't hurt too much—except when the windows were shipped and we discovered that most of our rough openings were too small. It seems that the company had two rough-opening sizes for windows with the same nominal dimensions—one for conventional windows and one for Heat Mirror windows. Sending the windows back was out of the question, so we had to tear out trimmers, drywall and plywood just to gain 2 in. of space.

Heating and cooling—For the most part, the Johnson house uses passive strategies to maintain comfortable temperatures—plenty of insulation (R-26 walls, R-57 ceilings), direct gain for heat in the winter, and the 65 cu. yd. of shaded, cool concrete in the summer. But there are two simple active systems to help things along. For one, a pair of sniffer ducts in the living room help to destratify the warm air generated by the fireplace. The ducts, which were pioneered by architect Malcolm Wells, (*FHB #7*, pp. 38-39) look a bit like columns designed to frame a view (photo p. 94). They are made of 1x12 knotty pine, and they lead to heater registers in the tops of the downstairs closets. Each duct has a propeller-type fan mounted near its top, which pulls the warm air away from the ceiling and pushes it downstairs. The fans are barely audible, and cost about $60 apiece. Along with the paddle fan over the stairwell, they do a good job of distributing the heat.

Except for the use of wood and solar heat, this is an "all-electric house." During the coldest part of the first winter of operation, the electric bill was between $60 and $70 per month. This included the use of a dishwasher, stove, hot-water tank and three electric baseboard heaters that we installed as backup on the lower level.

As John Lee points out, "Solar designers

Siting the house on a slope required a 10-ft. retaining wall braced by four buttresses. At left, the formwork for the buttresses divides the lower level of the house into thirds. The architects used these divisions to position the bedrooms and stairwell (drawing, facing page).

Illustration: Victor Lazzaro; Photo: Dan Rockhill

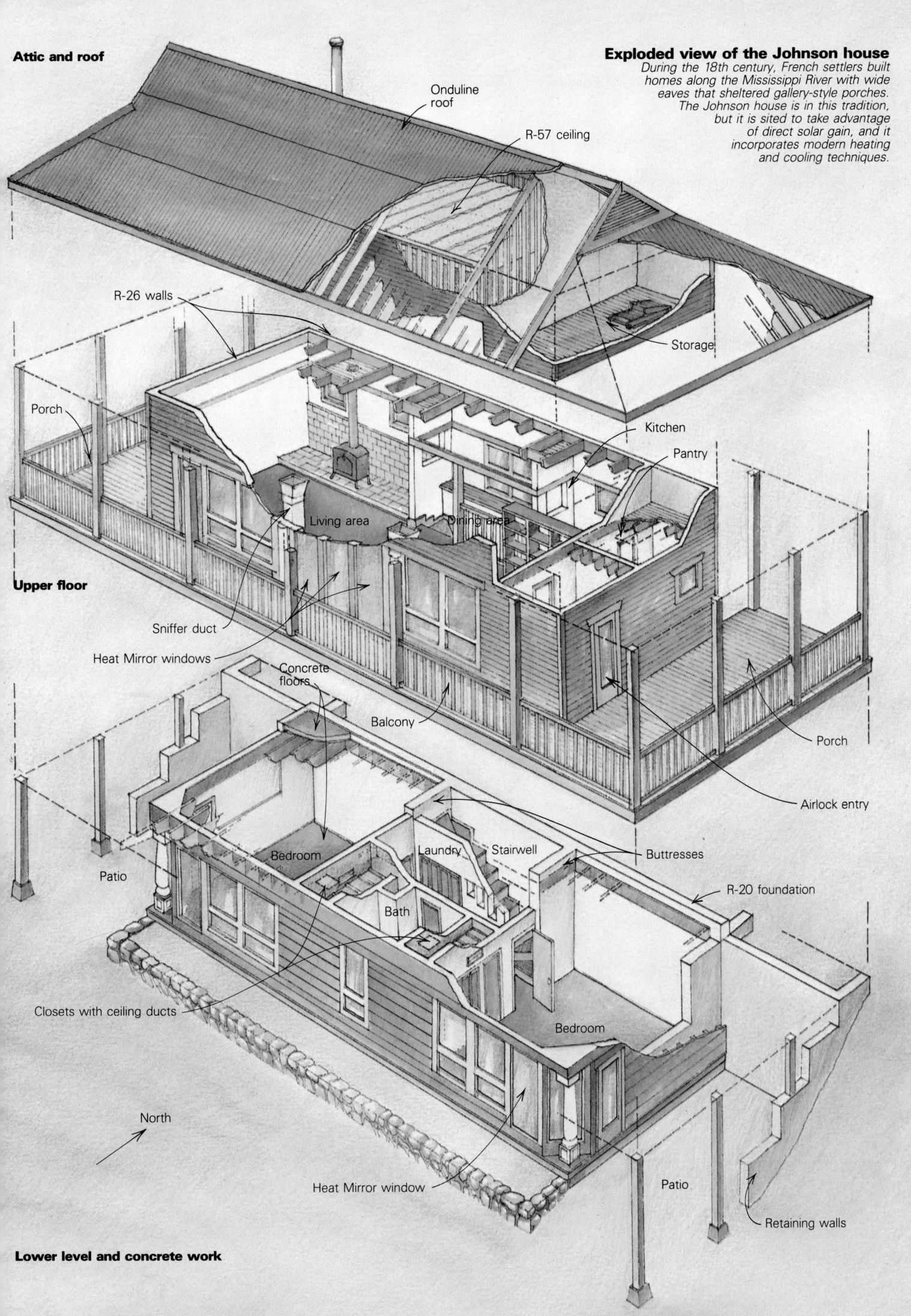

Attic and roof

Onduline roof

R-57 ceiling

Exploded view of the Johnson house
During the 18th century, French settlers built homes along the Mississippi River with wide eaves that sheltered gallery-style porches. The Johnson house is in this tradition, but it is sited to take advantage of direct solar gain, and it incorporates modern heating and cooling techniques.

R-26 walls

Storage

Porch

Kitchen

Pantry

Living area

Dining area

Upper floor

Sniffer duct

Heat Mirror windows

Concrete floors

Balcony

Porch

Airlock entry

Patio

Bedroom

Laundry

Stairwell

Buttresses

R-20 foundation

Bath

Closets with ceiling ducts

Bedroom

North

Heat Mirror window

Patio

Retaining walls

Lower level and concrete work

The floors of the house are finished in dark red concrete. In this view of the upstairs looking east (facing page), the sniffer ducts that help to destratify warm air can be seen on the right, flanking the doors to the balcony. Supplemental heating is provided by the woodstove, which is set into an inglenook that is lined with soil-cement blocks (above).

Four-by-four posts extend up from grade to support the wide eaves that shelter the balcony and porches. The second-level railing is made up of a beveled and grooved 2x4 over a pair of 1x4 skirt boards that sandwich 2x2 balusters.

The soil-cement blocks not only retain the stove's heat and protect the nearby framing, but are a showcase for local decoration. Ann Johnson imprinted the course of blocks above with leaves taken from nearby trees.

Utilitarian detailing in the kitchen is inexpensive and sturdy. A whole-house fan mounted in the ceiling can move stagnant air out of the house in a hurry. On hot summer days, it draws air from downstairs that has been cooled by the surrounding concrete. Beyond the louvered doors, a generous pantry houses canned goods, the freezer and a ladder to the attic.

aren't too worried about keeping a house warm in Kansas. It's keeping one cool that's tough." To that end, the overhangs are carefully calculated to screen out summer sun, and operable windows are placed to take advantage of prevailing breezes. The problem is, when it gets hot here, the wind stops. To generate a breeze at such times, the Johnson house has a powerful whole-house fan (a 5,100-cfm, 30-in. model from Sears) mounted in the ceiling of the kitchen (photo above right). When it's on, the fan draws the downstairs air, which was cooled by the concrete walls, into the upstairs living area, while sending the warm air out the gable vents.

Detailing—Although it wasn't in the budget to buy expensive finishing materials, the Johnson house trimwork draws a good return on investment. Outside, the railing is an example of inexpensive custom detailing that can make a project look special. For both drainage and appearance, we beveled the top of the 2x4 railing cap on the table saw, smoothed it with a power plane, and cut shallow kerfs along its edge to enhance its lines (photo center top). The 1x4 skirt boards below the rail have similar kerfs. The 2x2 balusters are sandwiched by the skirt boards, and the effect is a pleasing blend of perpendicular elements that looks more complicated than it really is.

Inside, we used #3 knotty pine for baseboards, moldings and door and window cas-

ings. We ran a header molding around the entire upstairs, and incorporated it into the sniffer ducts. Once the trim was sanded and in place, the Johnsons painted it with a wash coat of equal parts of white latex paint and water. The finish lets a subtle hint of the grain show through, and it's durable enough to allow stains and scuff marks to be wiped away.

Ann Johnson was responsible for one of the most personal touches in the house. She pressed over 350 soil-cement blocks for the inglenook wall and floor (photo above left) with a Cinva-Ram. This manually operated block press is used mainly in the Third World. It produces 4-in. by 6-in. by 12-in. blocks, and is available in the U. S. from Shrader Bellows (200 W. Exchange St., Akron, Ohio 44309). It costs about $370.

One course of blocks near the top of the wall is made of blocks that look as though they contain fossilized impressions of leaves. Ann made them by placing small mounds of sand on the bottom of the block mold, followed by leaves from local trees. She then added the soil mix, compressed it into a brick, and peeled away the leaves. Once the bricks had dried, she darkened the designs with charcoal (photo above center).

With a building this small, it is possible to pay strict attention to every detail, and in the final analysis it cost as much as most spec homes today. Excluding land costs and architects' fees, it finished out at about $46 per sq. ft.

We were able to build the house so inexpen-

sively for two reasons. First, we were dealing with good clients. The Johnsons interfered very little with the project once it was under way, and encouraged the crew's direct involvement in the detailing. This meant that we could do cabinets, railings, stairs and trim, which kept our interest at a high level. They also helped out with some of the finish work, such as texturing and painting.

The second factor is the concept of building that I call the "one-stop shop." We did most of the work ourselves, subcontracting only, and somewhat reluctantly, the excavation, plumbing and electrical work. I also had some concrete pros help us with the color application on the flat work. We kept costs down some 25% on each trade by not subbing. The sub's costs beyond materials and labor that we refer to as overhead and profit revert back as savings to the owner. In addition, I was called in very early during the design phase. I continually ran down costs and took quotes on windows, floor finishes and construction techniques, and encouraged or discouraged certain aspects of the design based on my knowledge of the costs. Thus we were able to keep the costs of subcontracts down to only 11%, and our own labor at only 34½% of the total project. □

Dan Rockhill is a contractor and associate professor of architecture at the University of Kansas at Lawrence.

Above the Flood
This small house was shaped by local style, energy efficiency and high-water marks

by Brent Smith

I restrict my practice to designing small, energy-efficient homes because I think most of our housing is wastefully out of scale. Occasionally, I teach an extension class on small-house design at the University of California at Davis. Hilary Abramson attended this class because she was looking for a designer who didn't necessarily equate quality with square footage. She asked me to help her design a 1,000-sq. ft. house on a flat, one-acre lot along the Sacramento River. It was important to her that the design share a kinship with the rich history of this area.

The Sacramento River was once a major highway for commerce and travel. Even the great Delta Queen (now on the Mississippi) paddled her way daily from Sacramento to San Francisco. The river used to flood its banks every year, and the early settlements in the valley were designed to accommodate the occasional high waters. The buildings in the original town of Sacramento were built without ground floors, and the old homes all had grand stairs leading from street level up to the front porch.

Today the river is controlled by dikes and

The Sacramento River flowing placidly past this trellis-topped pole house (photo top) was a large factor in its design. In an average year, floodwaters rise to within about 5 ft. of the first floor. A bridge leads to the road atop the ice-plant covered levee in the foreground. Seen from the levee during spring runoff (above), the house presents its private side to the world. In the center of the photo, steps descend to the summertime parking places below the house. The storage room next to the stairs contains the house's mechanical systems, and its triangular shape braces the house against racking. An acrylic panel mounted on a smaller trellis protects the entry from weather.

dams, and only the most pessimistic folks worry about the 100-year flood that might breach the levees and inundate the valley. Nevertheless, not many houses are built on the river side of the levees. Hilary's house was to be one of them.

We took a long and hard look at the old piers, docks, bridges and warehouses along the waterfront. Many of these landmarks were built on poles driven into the mud. The poles run up the exterior of the structure, supporting the floors and roof, and their large scale makes them a dominant visual element wherever they're used.

Hilary and I liked the look of the poles, and everything we had read suggested that they were a relatively inexpensive way to get the first floor 10 ft. above the ground—the height required by code to bring the house above the 100-year flood stage. Whether the big flood comes or not, the poles would still be periodically submerged about 5 ft. all winter long, and their relatively narrow profiles would allow them to stand up easily to the slow-moving current along the bank at flood stage. The alternative foundations used most frequently

Photo facing page and small photo above: Brent Smith; Illustrations: Frances Ashforth

around here are 10-ft. concrete block walls, but they look a little out of place in this riverside context.

Contradictions and compromise—Hilary wanted her house to be well insulated and to take whatever solar advantage it could of its southern exposure. But she also wanted a large bank of windows to the north overlooking the river. And for privacy's sake, she was adamant about having a minimum number of windows on the south, facing the road.

These requirements, simple as they sound, presented a program that was at odds with the climate and the site. Although winters are mild in the Sacramento Valley, summers are torrid—temperatures average 93°F, and heat waves with even higher readings are common. A generous bank of windows overlooking the river to the northwest—exactly where the summer sun goes down—would act as solar collectors at just the wrong time of the year. All summer long, direct sunlight and sunlight reflected off the river would bombard this northwest wall. On the other hand, the solar orientation to the southeast faced the elevated levee road—just where windows would violate the owner's privacy.

These conditions, along with the raised first floor, put to rest any thought of a standard passive-solar configuration. And the more the design progressed, the more I realized that energy efficiency, economy and pole construction were in conflict with each other.

For the poles to be used most economically, they would have to support both the roof and the floors. The walls would then be merely infill—non-structural skins. But if the walls were to be heavily insulated (2x6 studs with R-19 insulation) the wall structure alone would be strong enough to support a three-story house, making the poles unnecessary from the floor up. However, most houses that are not pole-framed, but merely rest on a pole-supported platform, tend to look like birdhouses. So we chose aesthetics over economy and decided to run the poles all the way to the roof, on the outside of the house. There they would carry a gable-shaped trellis that helps to moderate the interior temperatures. The trellis supports wisteria vines that screen out the summer sun, then drop their leaves in the fall to admit the winter sun. At this point the basic form of the building began to emerge.

For light, heat and ventilation, I designed an operable skylight clerestory that faces southeast, and sits along the northwest side of the house. It acts as a solar chimney, so that in summer, vents in these wells can be opened to allow hot air an easy way out. This air is replaced by air from a roof-mounted cooler. In winter, the low-angled sunlight can bounce off the white north walls to be absorbed by the 3-in. thick concrete-slab floor (for more on

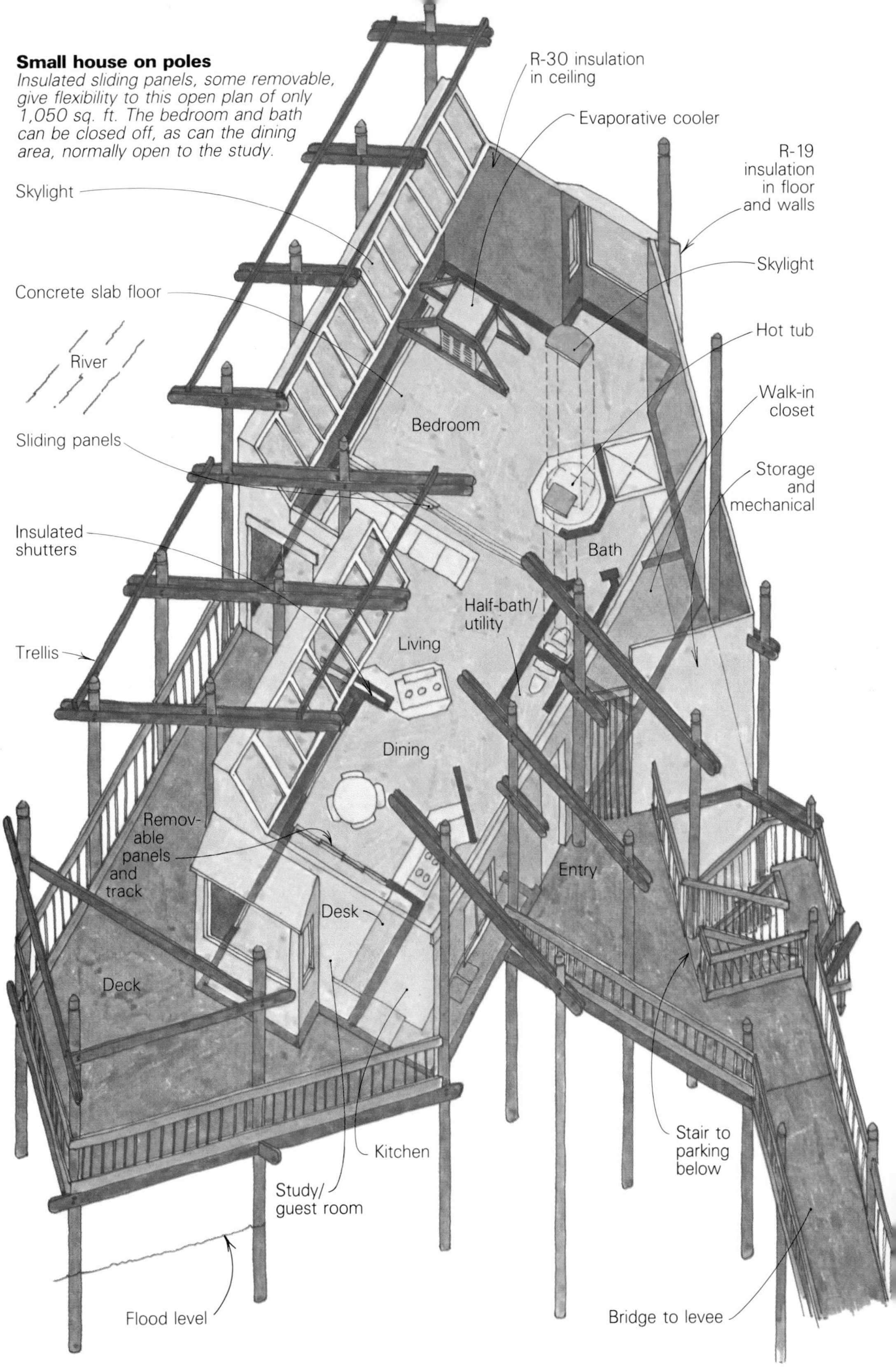

Once the 2x12 beams were bolted into notches cut in the poles, standard stud-wall construction techniques were used to finish the framing. Seen here from the river, a worker stands in what will be the dining-room doorway.

From *Fine Homebuilding* magazine (October 1983) 17:40-45

Small house on poles
Insulated sliding panels, some removable, give flexibility to this open plan of only 1,050 sq. ft. The bedroom and bath can be closed off, as can the dining area, normally open to the study.

- Skylight
- Concrete slab floor
- River
- Sliding panels
- Insulated shutters
- Trellis
- Removable panels and track
- Deck
- Desk
- Study/guest room
- Kitchen
- Flood level
- Living
- Dining
- Bedroom
- Half-bath/utility
- Bath
- Entry
- R-30 insulation in ceiling
- Evaporative cooler
- R-19 insulation in floor and walls
- Skylight
- Hot tub
- Walk-in closet
- Storage and mechanical
- Stair to parking below
- Bridge to levee

An open plan. The living room and bedroom occupy one large space that can be closed off with sliding doors, shown in the center of the photo at left. Against the wall behind them is a gypboard pocket that houses a 12-ft. door used to seal off the adjacent windows. Horizontal shutters ride in tracks screwed to the ceiling, and regulate the light and airflow through the skylight wells. The sliding shutter at top right opens to a roof-mounted evaporative cooler. Pebbled concrete is the finished floor throughout, as seen in this view south from the bedroom, right.

mass in wood-frame structures, see *FHB* #11, p. 46). During winter nights and summer days, insulated shutters mounted on the ceiling are used to close off these light wells.

Since most of the windows in the house face the northwest view of the river, I designed an assortment of sliding interior shutters to cut heat loss during the winter, and to block out the sunlight during late summer afternoons. Windows that face the levee also have insulated shutters, in this case, for privacy.

Floor plan—I think flexibility is the key to making a small house feel larger than it really is. Except for the closets, utility room and bathrooms, the house is one continuous space that can take on a number of forms, depending upon need. The heated portion of the house totals about 1,050 sq. ft. The living room and sleeping area are usually open to one another (photos above), but by closing six 3-ft. by 9-ft. panels, the bed and bath become private. The utility room near the front door doubles as a half-bath for guests.

The dining area is quite small, but it's next to the study/guest room. By moving the portable sliding partitions to tracks in front of the built-in desk, the dining area is expanded into a larger and more formal room.

The space under the house is used for parking when the ground isn't wet. An exterior stair leads up to the house. At the entry, an unheated storage area is set diagonally to the rest of the house. Its prow-like wall continues to ground level, where it's tied to its own small concrete foundation. The wall forms a structural diaphragm and a visual anchor. Along with the stair and entry bridge, it gives the building greater racking resistance, eliminating the need to cross-brace the poles.

Insulated sliding doors—The success of the open plan of the house would rely in large measure on the effectiveness of the sliding doors and the shutters. They had to be lightweight and easy to operate and move to other areas of the house. They also needed to be attractive, easy to build and still offer substantial insulation.

I chose 1½-in. thick expanded polystyrene (beadboard) for the core of the sliders because it doesn't give off the dangerous gases associated with some other foam insulations. The panels were cut to fit into a 2x2 fir grid, then sandwiched between two sheets of ⅛-in. tempered hardboard (drawing, facing page) using panel adhesive and drywall nails. Joint compound was used to fill the nail dimples, and the doors were finished with wallpaper. A ¼-in. Teflon runner screwed to the bottom of each door rides in an oak track installed flush with the surface of the concrete-slab floor. A corresponding track on the ceiling guides a 1x1 oak runner fixed to the top of the door. The door is removed by lifting it up as far as possible and tilting it out at the bottom.

The largest sliding door in the house is 12 ft. wide by 7 ft. tall. It covers the living-room windows in the northwest wall. It's built like the smaller doors, but it's too heavy to push around on Teflon runners. Instead, the door is hung by rollers (mounted on the top of the door) that run in a metal track. When it isn't in use, the door slides into a gypboard pocket along the bedroom wall.

This door was a problem, and it had to be built twice to get it right. For the first try, we used vertical 2x2s, 2 ft. o.c., as an interior framework. The hardboard overlapped the horizontal supports at top and bottom, so it was strong enough, but the panels between

the vertical supports would expand so much when the sun hit them that the door sometimes appeared to be pleated, and it wouldn't always fit into its pocket. We solved the problem by adding horizontal 2x2 nailers, 2 ft. o.c.

The ceiling shutters (photo above left) that close off the skylight and evaporative cooler are also made with beadboard. They're sheathed with resawn plywood on the bottom where they face the room. These shutters are closed to retain heat in the winter. In the summer, the shutter for the evaporative cooler is left open, but the skylight panels are closed to keep the heat out. The top of these shutters are finished with a layer of heavy aluminum foil, glued to the insulation. The foil bounces a lot of the direct solar gain right back where it came from. When the house begins to get hot, the skylight shutters are opened about an inch to allow hot air to escape through windows in the skylight well.

The window shutters on the northwest wall of the study/guest room are painted white on their exterior to reflect heat. On the inside they are paneled with resawn fir plywood to match the walls. These shutters are counterbalanced panels. Flush with the plane of the wall, they slide up and down on airplane wire, and meet in the center of the window when closed. Further details on their construction are given on p. 100.

Raising the frame—The house was built by Ananda Construction of Nevada City, Calif. They are good craftsmen and very patient, which was a real advantage because this was the first pole house that I had ever designed, and the first one they had built. One pole house doesn't make us experts, but we did pick up a few tips on setting the poles just by

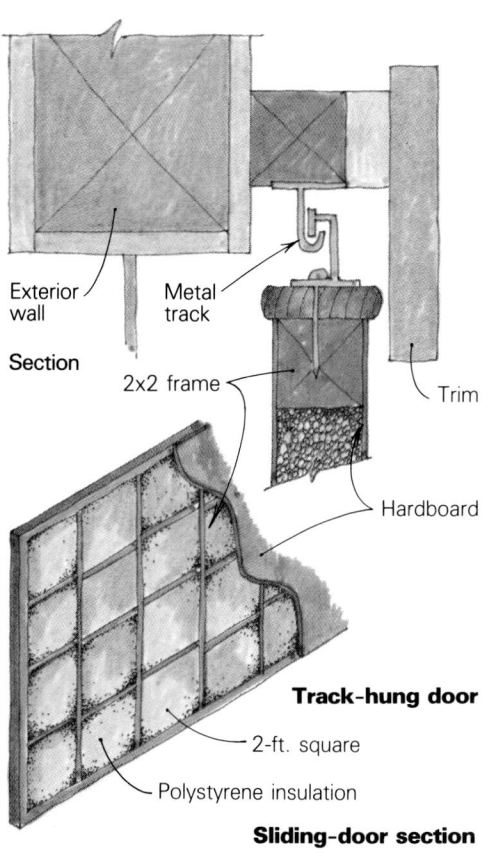

Section

Exterior wall

Metal track

2x2 frame

Trim

Hardboard

Track-hung door

2-ft. square

Polystyrene insulation

Sliding-door section

2x fir track

1x1 runners

1x3 redwood trim

2x2 fir frame

⅛-in. tempered hardboard

1½-in. polystyrene

Drywall nails

¼-in. Teflon runners attached with countersunk flathead screws

¼-in. fir shim as needed

Ski wax to reduce friction

1x oak track with ⅜-in. deep grooves

Plywood spacer

Subfloor

2x redwood

Concrete floor

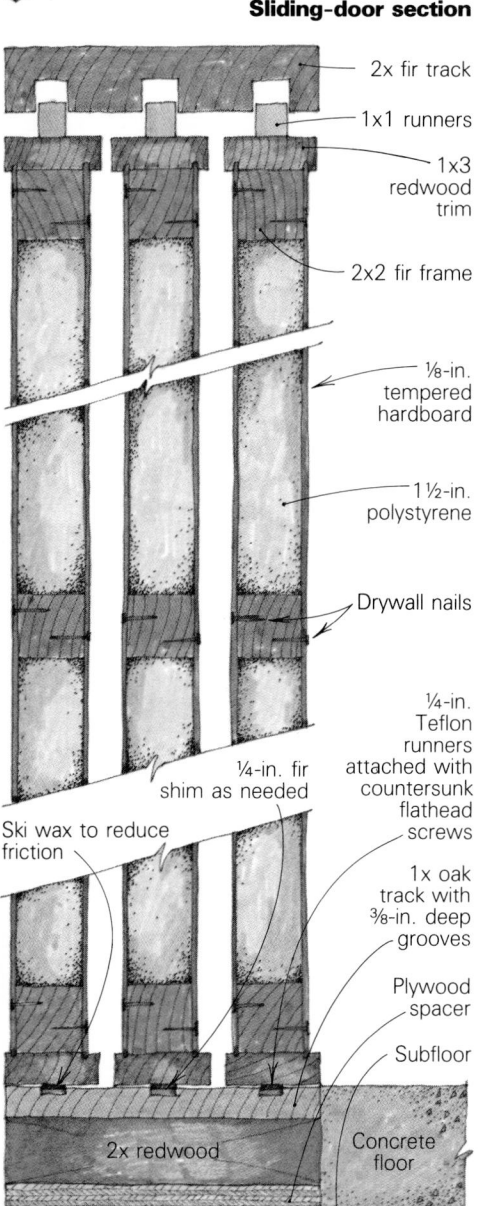

Insulated sliding panels. In the dining area, movable insulated panels on the ceiling, between rooms and over exterior doors control heat loss and gain, and add flexibility to the plan. The overhead shutters are operated with a rod that hooks into eyelets screwed into the edges of the shutters. Windows in the light wells are opened in the summer for ventilation. Both track-hung and sliding doors have beadboard cores sandwiched between hardboard, as shown in the drawings.

Making counterbalanced, vertically-drawn window shutters

The windows on the northwestern wall of the study/guest room were needed for light, but privacy and nighttime heat loss called for some type of covering. Insulated wood-covered shutters would serve those purposes and give the room a nice break from gypboard, but I wanted something more than typical shutters. I began to experiment with running the shutters floor to ceiling, so that they were almost a part of the wall. By using hardware in ways it was never intended, I came up with counterbalanced shutters suspended on airplane wire cable. They meet in the center of the window, leaving matching panels of plywood showing above and below. Open, the shutters cover these panels and expose the window (photo below).

As on the other shutters in the house, we used a 1x2 pine frame and a 1½-in. beadboard core. We measured and cut the frame and insulation carefully because to get counterbalanced shutters to work properly, they have to be identical in size and weight. We covered the exterior side of the frames with hardboard and painted it white to reflect heat. The interior covering was ⅜-in. resawn fir plywood. At 2 in. thick, these shutters fit flush in a 2x6 wall. The wall is framed with 2x4 sills and trimmers, and a 4x6 header (drawing, below). The bottom and top plates required some notching so that the shutters could be fully opened to the floor and ceiling.

With the 3-ft. by 4-ft. windows in the study/guest room, which were centered in the standard 8-ft. framing, we needed only a single sheet of plywood for both the shutters and the panels. We cut a 1-ft. by 8-ft. strip off the plywood, and set it aside for trimming out the inside of the opening around the panels and the sides of the shutters. The remaining 3-ft. by 8-ft. piece was cut into four 2-ft. by 3-ft. sections. I labeled them to keep track of the matching grain patterns, and built the two shutters with sections 2 and 3. Sections 1 and 4 were used for the panels top and bottom. The shutters were completed with the addition of 1x2 trim that served both as a closure strip and handles.

A length of ⅛-in. stainless-steel airplane wire with an electrical terminal crimped on the end was screwed to each side of the top shutter. The free end was then threaded around a pulley mounted near the top of each jamb. The pulley is actually a wheel from a sliding door. The shutters were then held in their closed position in the opening, centered vertically in the window, and the two wires pulled down to the bottom of the lower shutter. The wires were secured by threading them through the electrical connectors that had been mortised into the bottom rail of the bottom shutter on each side in 1-in. diameter holes. Tightening the setscrew on these connectors suspended the shutters in the opening while we checked them for fit. They should be level, and fit together well in the middle of the window. Tightening or loosening the wires changes the angle at which the shutters hang.

Once the shutters were properly adjusted, the wires were stapled to the bottom rails and the setscrew given an extra turn. The sides of the opening were cased with 1x4s to keep the shutters in their tracks and hide the hardware. The bottom and top were trimmed with 1x6s. —B.S.

Counterbalanced shutters insulate two 3x4 windows in the study/guest room. Each shutter is 2 in. thick, so the 2x6 sill plate is notched accordingly to let them fit flush with the wall. One 4x8 plywood sheet is just enough material to make shutters, panels and trim for each window.

working through the snags and surprises on this job.

First of all, be sure to hand-pick the poles at the yard if at all possible. Poles will range from crooked to straight, and it's much easier to work with the straight ones. While at the yard, mark the straightest poles for use at the corners of the building—they become guideposts for aligning the others. Try to get your supplier to bring along a forklift when the poles are delivered, and have him deposit each pole near its designated hole. Moving poles that weigh 1,000 lb. apiece even a short distance is no picnic.

Lay out the pole location with great care, and be there when the holes are drilled. Try to find a drilling rig with a plumbing device that ensures a vertical hole, and help the auger operator as much as possible. A hole that is out of plumb will give you fits. If a hole is drilled slightly out of place, don't try to refill it and drill it over again. Instead, widen it with a shovel, and once the pole is set, fill the mistake with gravel or concrete.

I had detailed a decorative shape to be carved on the top of each pole. This tapered cone with a notch below it would have been easy to carve if the poles were on the ground, but the depth of the holes varied so much that the poles had to be topped and carved once they were in place. That problem could have been solved by using a transit, and string lines above the holes to establish a level reference point. Then accurate measurements could have been taken to the bottom of each hole, and the poles cut to finish length and marked for later installation.

Our engineer specified gravel as backfill material. Once the poles were positioned in their holes, the gravel made it pretty easy to adjust the poles to plumb. The crew rented a small crane to lift the poles, and as each one was placed, about 2 ft. of gravel was shoveled around the base of the pole while it was held roughly plumb. This was enough gravel to hold the pole firmly while several workers hauled on lassos tied to its top to get it as plumb as possible considering its rough tapered exterior. Then the hole was filled with gravel and four sacks of dry-mix concrete poured on top of the gravel and moistened. Once the mixture had set up, a tapered concrete collar was formed and poured to shed water and increase the rigidity of the pole.

When the poles were all in position, pairs of 2x12 beams were notched into them and then bolted in place. The notches were cut by first making repeated passes with a circular saw set at a depth of 1 in., and then dressing out the joint with a chisel. The crew worked on ladders while cutting the notches, and it was a time-consuming job. It would have been worth going to the trouble of building a scaffold for this chore.

We let the beams run long, and radiused the ends for a finishing touch to echo the roundness of the poles. These little cantilevers, which can be seen in the photo on p. 97 were handy brackets for holding scaffolding for sheathing and trimming the exterior walls.

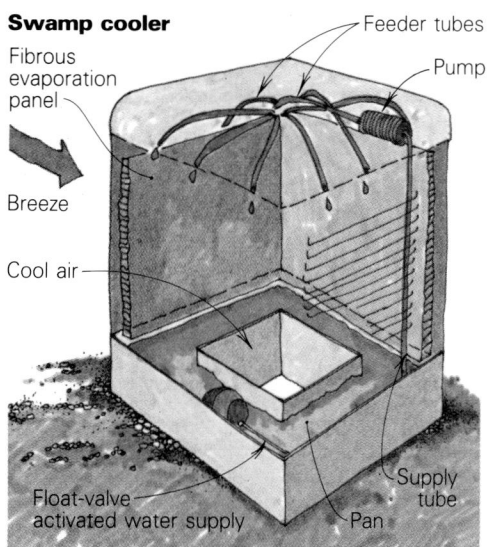

Swamp cooler. Inside the basic box (drawing), a network of feeder tubes and absorbent panels cool incoming air by evaporation. On the roof (photo), acrylic panels shelter the cooler from weather and leaves, yet allow exposure to the prevailing breezes.

Swamp cooler—When I was a kid growing up in Sacramento, most houses had an evaporative cooler, or "swamp cooler," mounted on roofs or in windows. This device (photo above) is about the size of a dishwasher and has absorbent panels that hang behind louvered screening. A small pump transfers water from a pan at the base of the cooler to feeder tubes at the top of the panels. The water trickles down the panels to be recycled, and what evaporates is replaced by a float-valve activated supply line. A fan mounted inside the cooler pulls hot air through the wet panels and pushes air cooled by evaporation into the interior of the house (drawing, above). It's about as simple as an appliance can be, costs about $400, and works well in hot regions with low humidity. Swamp coolers are made by The Williams Furnace Co. (225 Acacia St., Colton, Calif. 92324) and by Arvin-Air, 500 S. 15th St., Phoenix, Ariz. 85034); write the companies for local distributors.

Although most homes in the area have air-conditioning, this house seemed like a perfect place to install a swamp cooler—the climate is right, and the cooler's low energy consumption fits the spirit of the house. We made the installation even more basic by removing the fan and its motor. This way the cool air flowing out the bottom of the cooler simply falls into the room through an opening controlled by an insulated shutter in the ceiling. This flow is boosted by the negative pressure caused by hot air escaping through the windows in the skylight well.

The cooler works fine until the temperature rises to about 100°F. At that point the breezes usually die down, the humidity from the evaporation chamber causes too much discomfort, and a backup heat pump takes over. Since the average temperature is not quite that hot, the cooler is useful for most of the summer.

In retrospect—If I were to do this building again, I would try to get more mass into it. The concrete floor is attractive and has a durable finish, but it could be even more useful as a thermal storehouse if it had a layer of concrete blocks under the slab. I would arrange the blocks into air channels, much the way Stephen Lasar uses Flexicore panels to form plenums under concrete floors (see *FHB* #1, p. 43) and then I'd pump heated air from the skylights through the floor in the winter. In the summer, the system would be reversed and cool night air sent through the floor. And instead of gypboard, I'd use stucco on the interior walls to add a more even layer of mass throughout the house.

The crew waited until the building was nearly completed to pour the floor, reasoning that wear and tear during construction would damage the finished surface. They wouldn't do it that way again. Concrete got slopped on the walls, and it had to be laboriously removed later. The pebble finish meant that the surface had to be hosed down as it set up, making more of a mess. Because the building was enclosed, it took a long time for the concrete to cure enough to seal. Finally, working with the highly volatile sealer indoors was a smelly and awful task, and it took four coats to do the job. The floor should have been poured as soon as the platform was finished, and then protected during the framing stages with the plywood roof sheathing.

My feeling now about pole structures is that they should be used only where they solve a special problem—a steep hillside, a flood plain such as this site or a tidal-basin site. We found the cost of a pole house quite high, especially when we added the expenses for the heavy hardware required by California's earthquake-conscious design criteria. This house cost $80 per square foot in 1979. If it had been built on a continuous concrete foundation with block walls, I think it would have been closer to $70 per foot. But even though it cost more to use poles than concrete, I'd use them again for this project. They fit the site and they solved the problems well. □

Brent Smith is a designer/contractor. He lives in Loomis, Calif.

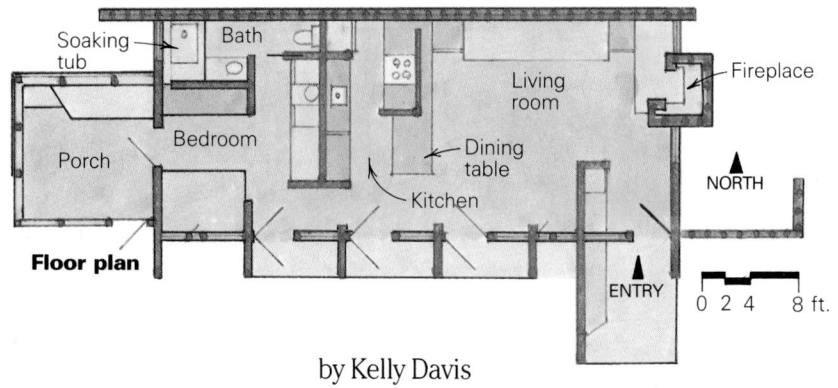

Wisconsin Wizardry

Crafty design creates an energy-efficient house with a lean footprint

Floor plan

Soaking tub · Bath · Fireplace · Living room · Bedroom · Dining table · Porch · Kitchen · NORTH · ENTRY · 0 2 4 8 ft.

by Kelly Davis

I've always been drawn to the intimacy and sense of human scale that small spaces can evoke. As a direct result of their size and scale, such spaces are often more conducive than big spaces to everyday activities and interactions—for reading, for conversation, for quiet winter evenings in front of the fire. But as an architect, I've also long been fascinated with the manipulation of space to make it appear larger than it is.

In designing my own small house, I was determined to merge these two seemingly disparate qualities and create a warm, intimate space that would also be as unconfined and fluid as possible. At the same time, I wanted my house to be easy to maintain and relatively inexpensive to heat and cool. Because all these goals had to mesh with a modest budget, they had to be accomplished through the creative use of common, readily available materials.

In a house where mistakes are not camouflaged by molding or covered by wallpaper, careful design must always be accompanied by sensitive craftsmanship. I was fortunate to be able to enlist the help of Charlie Vanasse, an anthropologist-turned-builder, and carpenters Steve Heselton and Jim Wenum. They rose to the challenge and did a masterful job of turning two-dimensional plans into three-dimensional reality.

Drawings: Frances B. Ashforth

Seclusion with a view—I envisioned the house to be a cabin-like, year-round retreat from the workaday world, so the site was critical. I was lucky to find a beautiful 35-acre mix of woods and fields on the Wisconsin side of the St. Croix River, just a few miles from my office. The heart of the site is a southwest-facing slope overlooking the river valley, with a grove of 20-year-old red pines on top and a bird's-eye view of a limestone bluff in the distance. Naturally, I hoped to capture this view, but I also wanted the house to nestle into the natural landscape, thus offering protection on blustery winter nights when the wind whistles out of the north.

The solution was to design a slab-on-grade earth-bermed house (photo facing page). Notched into the hillside, the house turns a windowless north wall and a low shed roof to the elements, while a glazed south wall and angled clerestory admits sunlight and carefully orchestrated, though somewhat restrained, views. The best view is focused at the end of a 50-ft. long, 8-ft. wide deck set perpendicular to the house and cantilevered over the hillside. I've traveled to Japan a number of times and have admired the traditional architecture there. The narrow deck embodies the traditional Japanese concept of revealing vistas gradually, culminating with an element of surprise.

Taking this concept a few steps further, the house itself is approached on foot. Cars are parked at a garage/studio/ guest room about 300 ft. away from the house. This enhances the feeling of retreat, creating a distinct transition between the outside world and home, between public and private places. It also masks the size of the house—attaching the garage to the house or locating it nearby would have revealed immediately how small the house really is. Equally important, visitors are treated to a walk through the woods and then to glimpses of the house and the view beyond before descending steps to the front door. This approach creates a sense of drama and unfolding space that is powerful and somehow unexpected with such a small building, and it's vital to its success (though it does tend to limit the number of visitors during the winter).

Room enough for two—The house totals 944 sq. ft.—big enough for one or two persons— including a screened porch off the west end (floor plan, facing page). Anything smaller would face diminishing returns. Heating, electrical and plumbing systems are all givens, and beyond a point, they don't get substantially less expensive with a reduction of square footage.

The main entry is a 7-ft. wide alcove in the southeast corner of the house. It's defined by the longest in a series of wing walls that intersect the south wall at 8-ft. intervals, and by a 12-ft. long bench (photo facing page). The bench is bisected by a 1-in. thick panel of insulating glass in the south wall, yet appears to be continuous from the exterior to the interior of the house. The effect is to amplify the apparent scale of this diminutive space.

Here, as well as in several other locations throughout the house, there is no jamb where the glass meets the wing wall. Instead, the edge of the glass fits into a slot in the bevel siding and sheathing, concealing the metal glazing channel. This again minimizes the visual transition from exterior to interior.

The entry opens into an ample living room that's anchored at one end by a massive concrete fireplace. Built-in seating and shelving run the entire length of the north wall (photo left, next page). At the opposite end of the living room, the dining area is defined by a built-in table. The kitchen, as tight as a ship's galley, is adjacent to the dining area and is partially open to the living space.

The bedroom, visually screened from the living area by a wing wall, is reached by way of a low, flat-ceilinged passageway. The ceiling is an exension of a wide exterior continuous soffit that runs along the south side of the

house. A built-in double bed is tucked beneath this ceiling, which provides a nice sense of shelter, an important contrast to the long-distance views seen from the large bedside windows (top photo, p. 105). Opposite the bed are a built-in desk, bureau and bookshelves. Wardrobe and utility closets separate the sleeping space from the kitchen. The bedroom fronts a small bath with a deep soaking tub and connects to the screened porch for summer use.

In a northern climate, a screened porch can be visually cold and unsightly during the winter months. Placing the porch at the far west end of the house made it as inconspicuous as possible. Its existence, in fact, often surprises summer visitors. Sheltered from the elements by wide overhangs, the porch fits almost entirely beneath the same wide ceiling that canopies the bed (photo below). The porch is an area where people are often seated, so its low ceiling is appropriate and actually seems to stimulate conversation. Just beyond the porch walls, the hillside drops off in two directions, creating the sensation of a protected treetop aerie.

Should the need arise, the house is designed to accommodate a second bedroom and bath to the north of the existing bathroom; heat ducts and plumbing lines are stubbed out, and two vertical courses of concrete block can be removed to make way for a door opening. This addition would extend and emphasize the perpendicular axis established by the deck out front.

Stretching the limits—Besides the design techniques already mentioned, there are a few other methods I used to expand the house visually. For instance, ceiling heights vary throughout the house. The low overhang along the south wall measures just 6 ft. 6 in. high, emphasizing the horizontal while serving as a display shelf (bottom photo, p. 105). The roof, on the other hand, measures 12 ft. high at the clerestory peak but only 5 ft. 8 in. high along the north wall. The high ceiling in the center of the living room relieves the sense of confinement created by the overhang below, while the low ceiling along the north wall gives intimacy to the seating area.

Because sound transmission was not a primary concern, many of the interior partitions don't reach the ceilings and, in a similar vein, are held 6 in. or more shy of the outside walls. One result of this is an uninterrupted diagonal sight line almost 50 ft. long from the northeast corner of the living room to the southwest corner of the bedroom, unusual in a house of this size (bottom photo, p. 105). In addition, I at-

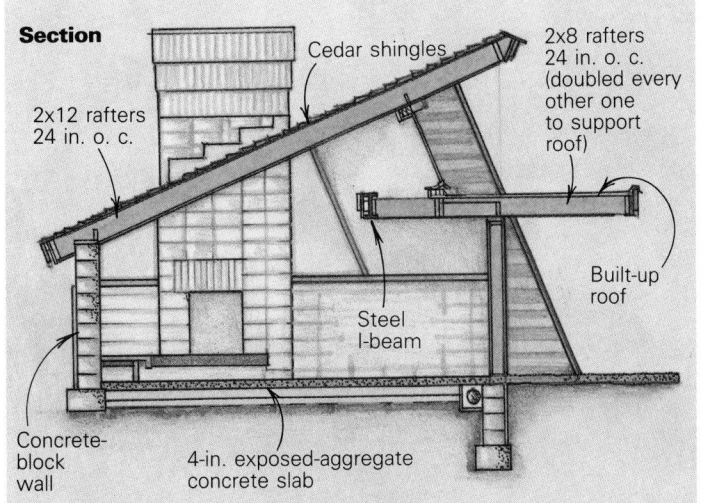

Section

2x12 rafters 24 in. o. c.

Cedar shingles

2x8 rafters 24 in. o. c. (doubled every other one to support roof)

Built-up roof

Steel I-beam

Concrete-block wall

4-in. exposed-aggregate concrete slab

Notched into a hillside, the long, narrow house (photo facing page) embraces the outdoors through a continuously glazed south wall and clerestory. The screened porch (photo below), located at the west end of the house, lies dormant during the winter, yet becomes a haven for sleeping and sitting during the summer.

The interior is characterized by varied ceiling heights, lengthy sight lines and the careful combination of readily available materials. At left in the photo, the kitchen counter and shelves key into the masonry coursing, exemplifying the author's careful detailing.

In the bathroom, there's a soaking tub. It's made of pressure-treated plywood covered by a vinyl liner concealed beneath clear T&G cedar.

tempted to blur the boundaries between spaces. For instance, the bathroom door is the only interior passage door in the house. As a result, it is hard to tell where one space ends and another begins.

Sight lines from the interior to the exterior are equally long. The configuration of the deck, for instance, creates a view almost 70 ft. long from the back wall of the living room to the end of the deck. An equally long diagonal view exists between the back wall of the screened porch and the far corner of the deck.

Making ceilings float—The house is forthright in its use of materials (drawing previous page), due at least in part to cost considerations. The flooring throughout consists of a 4-in. thick exposed-aggregate concrete slab over (from top to bottom) a 4-mil polyethylene vapor barrier, 6 in. of sand and 1-in. thick extruded polystyrene foam insulation (XEPS). This makes for an inexpensive, attractive floor that doubles as a source of thermal mass.

The north wall is made of 12-in. concrete blocks, laid in a stacked bond with carefully raked joints. The exterior of the wall is coated with Hydrocide Mastic (Chem Rex, Inc., 57-46 Flushing Ave., Maspeth, N. Y. 11378; 800-433-9517) to repel water, and insulated with 1½-in. thick XEPS. A foundation drain at the base of the wall transports water away from the house. For added insulation, block cavities are filled with vermiculite. The joints are reinforced horizontally every other course with Dur-O-Wal (Dur-O-Wal, Inc., 3115 N. Wilke Rd., Suite A, Arlington Heights, Il. 60004; 708-

577-6400) and vertically with #4 rebar spaced 32 in. o. c.

Once all the block was laid up, the interior surfaces were lightly sandblasted, a process that took just a few hours yet completely transformed the material aesthetically. Sandblasting removes the chalky layer of surface lime from the blocks, exposing the aggregate and enriching the color. The fireplace, also of concrete block, was built using several standard shapes and sizes, then sandblasted.

The only complicated framing in the house was for the low flat roof over the south wall. While supporting the shed roof above, the overhang appears to float above the glass wall with no window or door headers visible. To achieve this, a steel I-beam was installed 6 feet in from the face of the south wall, running the full length of the house. The I-beam supports the inboard ends of the rafters, allowing the outboard ends to cantilever 6 ft. beyond the south wall. The weight of the roof above counteracts any tendency toward sagging. The rafters are 2x8s spaced 24 in. o. c., with every other rafter doubled and bearing on structural mullions. As a result, conventional door and window headers were unnecessary and glazing was carried right up to ceiling height. The single intermediate rafters primarily serve as nailers for the finish materials. Outside, the overhang is topped with built-up roofing. The overhang is finished underneath with drywall: standard ⅝-in. drywall inside the house and ⅝-in. exterior ceiling board outside. The latter, made by the U. S. Gypsum Co. (101 S. Wacker Dr., Chicago, Il. 60606-4385; 312-606-

4000) is a weather-resistant board designed for exterior soffits and other applications with indirect exposure to the elements.

Keying in the details—The house is laid out on a 4-ft. module. Wing walls, doors, windows, concrete blocks, redwood battens over the drywall ceiling joints and redwood dividers in the flooring are all placed on a 4-ft. grid. This creates a rhythm that marches through the building and contributes to its orderliness and spaciousness.

Before a spade was turned on the job site, every detail in the house, from the layout of concrete blocks to the towel racks, was committed to paper. All walls but the exposed masonry surfaces are covered with three different widths of clear redwood bevel siding oiled inside the house, and are finished outside with Cabot's Bleaching Oil (Cabot Stains, Inc., 100 Hale St., Newburyport, Mass. 01950; 800-877-8246). The widths are coursed randomly, or at least seemingly so, making it possible to key other architectural elements into the siding. In the kitchen, for example, mahogany countertops, backsplashes and open redwood storage shelves key into the siding courses (photo above, left). These elements are in turn aligned with the living-room bookshelves, which key into the concrete block courses. This correlation of horizontal lines occurs throughout the house. Each connection is subtle in itself, but the sum total has an impact.

Much of the furniture and lighting in the house is built in. This reinforces the overall design and makes the house feel uncluttered

From *Fine Homebuilding* magazine (Spring 1991) 66:36-39

and more spacious. The furniture and cabinetry, built of mahogany plywood and redwood, is detailed in the same way throughout the house. The scale is low and horizontal, another attempt at masking the diminutive nature of the house. Equally important, it was more cost-effective to have the major pieces of furniture built in as opposed to buying them.

Soaking in the bathroom—Tucked into the northwest corner of the house, the bathroom holds the same character and detailing as the rest of the house (right photo, facing page). Its site-built soaking tub is another idea borrowed from Japan. Measuring about 2 ft. by 3 ft. by 30 in. deep, the tub consists of a pressure-treated plywood box lined on the inside with a vinyl sheet (typically used for shower pans) concealed beneath clear T&G cedar. The cedar is held in place by ½-in. square cedar stops fastened to it at the corners with brass screws. A cedar duckboard floor is removable for cleaning. Trim around the tub is oiled redwood, fastened to the tub with brass screws so that it can be dismantled if the liner ever needs replacing.

The trapezoidal window in the bathroom displays a small outdoor planting area adjacent to the soaking tub, created by extending the concrete-block wall beyond the confines of the room. Instead of specifying an operable window for ventilation, I had a narrow hinged insulated panel installed next to it, a trick devised by one of my partners. The panel is a 1-in. thick core of XEPS faced on each side with ⅜-in. saw-textured redwood plywood. Properly weatherstripped and fitted with standard butt hinges, bronze casement locks and a fixed exterior screen, this system makes an energy-efficient, cost-effective alternative to operable windows. The vent allows the bather the pleasant sensation of a cool face while immersed to the neck in steaming hot water. Similar vents were placed in the bedroom and living room.

Regulating the indoors—The house is heated by an electric forced-air furnace and heat pump supplemented by simple passive-solar detailing and an energy-saving custom fireplace. The back of the fireplace's firebox is a ⅜-in thick steel plate with an air chamber behind it. Warm air heated by the fire is drawn under the floor slab by a duct fan and into the return-air plenum of the furnace for recirculation. Energy bills average only about $50/month.

In winter, the concrete-block north wall absorbs heat during the day and radiates it well into the evening. Conversely, in the summer the overhangs on the south side of the house shade the interior, and the concrete-block wall helps moderate warm temperatures and keep the house comfortable. Four standard awning windows in the clerestory and four custom-built redwood doors in the south wall can be opened to improve natural ventilation. □

Kelly Davis is a principal with McGuire/Engler/ Davis Architects P. A. in Stillwater, Minnesota.

A built-in bed is tucked beneath the low overhang that parallels the south wall of the house. Ventilation is provided by a small door installed between the inoperable glazing panels. The bedroom also serves as passage to the adjacent screened porch.

Through the use of low interior partitions, the author created a 50-ft. long sight line from the living room to the far corner of the bedroom. Also, the partition separating the kitchen from the living room (straight ahead in the photo) is held about 12 in. shy of the back wall, again to create an expanded sight line.

A House in Friday Harbor

Balancing daylight and view with a string of gabled rooms

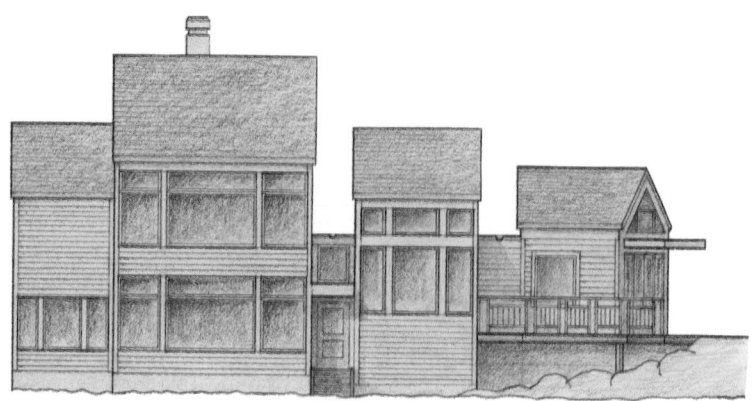

by Gordon Lagerquist

Sometimes studying a mistake is good way to find inspiration. I was reminded of this when I began working on a design for Claire and William Eagers' new house and found a compelling example of what not to do—their old house. Blessed with a view of a picturesque harbor in Washington's San Juan Islands, it had windows on only one side of each room. As a consequence, the house was a collection of dark, cavelike spaces with glaringly bright views on one wall. The house that was to replace it needed to strike a balance between the seaside panorama outside and the natural light inside.

Simple program, daunting site—The Eagers wanted the new house to be informal in character and full of light (photo below). They wanted the public spaces to flow easily from one to another. This meant the living room, dining room, kitchen and entry could be designed as one space or as a series of interconnected spaces. The master bedroom and bath were to be separate from the rest of the house, and a guest room was to be located off the living room. They needed a garage space for one car. While they didn't have a particular style of house in mind, they wanted its scale, shape and finishes to fit into the existing neighborhood of beach cottages converted to year-round living.

Between a road and a steep hill, the Eager house stretches out in a string of gabled rooms that conforms to a narrow strip of buildable land. In this elevation from the west, you can see the gable windows that balance the daylight in the house.

The site measures 100 feet square and lies between the lane and the water 50 ft. below. It has a level buildable portion at the top, 30 ft. wide by 100 ft., along the lane. Because of the steepness of the hill and the location of the other houses on the lane, there are no required front-yard setbacks.

Their old beach house sat at the west end of the level area, hard against the streetside property line. Because the site is on a slope, which falls off to the north toward the water and is heavily wooded with fir and madrone, the only exposure to the sun is in the afternoon from the west. On the water side of the site a steep trail runs down to the shore and an existing dock. The trail is cut into the rock and switches back and forth on its way to the water.

The view to the rocky shore below and the islands beyond is spectacular and the Eagers naturally wanted to take advantage of it. This meant that a large portion of the glazing had to face north, toward the view, but away from the available sunlight—just like the old house.

Another constraint shaping the house was the relationship of the site to the street. The lane is narrow and heavily used by both automobiles and pedestrians. The new house would sit almost on the edge of the pavement, so we needed to buffer the living spaces from the lane.

Plan follows roadbed—I first visited the site on a bright sunny day in February of 1985. As I look back over my early sketches I see that they contain the seeds of the eventual solution: a series of similar, boxlike rooms topped with gable roofs that would stand slightly apart from one another, linked by low, flat roofs, allowing light to enter the house through windows in the gable ends (elevation drawing, facing page).

The plan that eventually emerged begins at the west side with a one-story room for the kitchen. To conform to the road, the kitchen meets the dining room at a 15° angle (drawing right). This allowed us to keep the house closer to the street and build right up to the edge of the existing house during construction. While we wanted to put the new house as close to the old one as possible, we didn't want to tear it down before the new house was ready. Both the Eagers and the crew used it through the entire construction period.

For visual and acoustic privacy, the south wall of the kitchen has no windows. Instead it has a long counter that includes a small sink where helpful guests can participate in food preparation. Cabinets and shelves above and below this counter provide storage for most of the kitchen's utensils, appliances and cookbooks. The kitchen is sort of a double "Pullman" layout, with an island in the middle. The half nearest the water is the domain of the chef—whoever wears the hat that day—and contains the electric range, refrigerator, and double sink. Circulation to the terrace and lounging space for kitchen guests is accommodated on the south side of the island.

The kitchen is open to the dining room (photo next page). While the wall plate height is 10 ft. in the kitchen, it jumps to 12 ft. in the dining room. A continuous 7-ft. high storage wall along the south side of the dining room buffers street noise. Above this storage wall a band of 3 ft. high clerestory windows helps to give this volume a light airy feeling.

The dining room is followed by a still larger two-story gabled box for the living room and the master bedroom. The master bedroom is a half level above the kitchen/dining-room level and is reached by way of a stairway from the dining room. The front door to the house is located here, between the dining room and the stair to the master bedroom.

In keeping with our strategy to use secondary spaces to buffer the street, the bathrooms are adjacent to the stairway on the south side of the house. Downstairs the bathroom is split in two. The upper portion is off the master bedroom, and contains a large walk-in shower, lavatory, and toilet. It is connected by a narrow stair that parallels the main stair to another lavatory and toilet. This lower powder room is behind a door off the main stair, two steps above the entry level. The reason for this split bath is to allow a guest to use the powder room and then be able to reach the shower in complete privacy. A lockable door at the top of the narrow stair assures the owners of their privacy. The entire bath area is isolated from the rest of the house by a glass roof.

The last gable in the chain is on the east end, where it shelters a garage at street level and a guest bedroom on the main floor. Except for the garage, each gable is separated

from its neighbor by a 4-ft. wide section of flat roof (bottom photo, p. 109). The roofs of the individual gables, on the other hand, are at an 8-in-12 slope. They make a strong visual connection to the surrounding evergreen trees and distant Olympic and Cascade mountain ranges.

Beginning with a bang—Because we matched the floor levels to the existing grades, the job didn't require much excavation—at least until we got to the guest room. Here we had to blast away approximately 175 yards of rock. The estimates for this work varied between $5,000 and $20,000. The low bidder had an excellent reputation for working with dynamite in close quarters, so I signed him up. When the dust settled, every tree and shrub all the way down to the water had been stripped of most of its foliage. Claire was so depressed by the apparent devastation that she climbed on the next ferry and headed back to the mainland. But the cavity in the rock was perfect for the guest room. The damage to the plants and trees was superficial, and the site and the client have now recovered completely.

Glazing the gables—After exploring several elaborate schemes to support the roofs we settled on a simple solution that left the interior volume of each gable completely open. The gable ends are trusses consisting of 6x10 top chords and ⅝-in. dia. steel tie rods as the horizontal bottom chords. The tie rods run through grooves in the window muntins and are welded to steel brackets (top drawing, p. 109) at the intersections of the 6x10 top chords and 4x6 columns in the wall. This

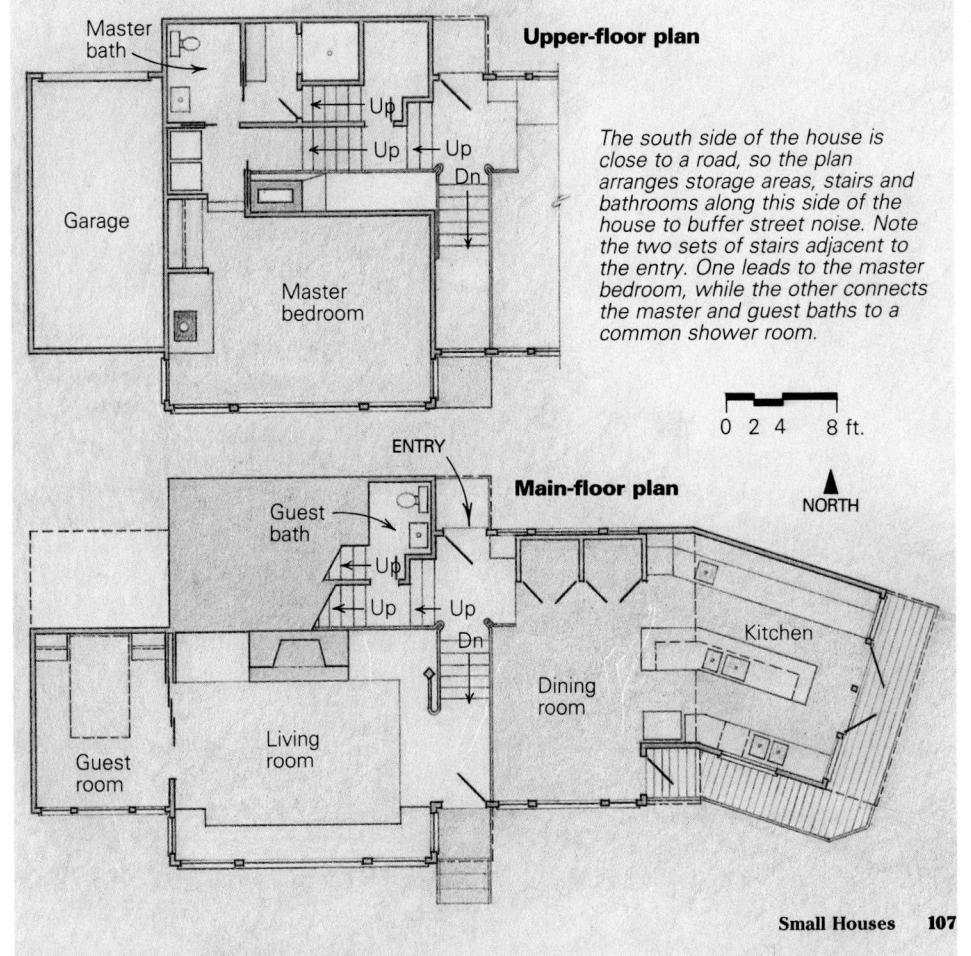

Upper-floor plan

Master bath

Garage

Master bedroom

Up
Up · Up
Dn

The south side of the house is close to a road, so the plan arranges storage areas, stairs and bathrooms along this side of the house to buffer street noise. Note the two sets of stairs adjacent to the entry. One leads to the master bedroom, while the other connects the master and guest baths to a common shower room.

0 2 4   8 ft.

ENTRY

Guest bath

Up
Up · Up
Dn

Main-floor plan

NORTH

Kitchen

Dining room

Guest room

Living room

allowed us to eliminate the double top plate common to stick-framed walls, and as a consequence, install windows with very narrow muntins above and below the plate line (photo facing page). In addition, the trusses eliminate the need for posts under the ridge beams, allowing a large triangle of glass at each ridge that is uninterrupted by vertical framing members.

The rods were welded, full length and without turnbuckles, to their brackets at a metal shop on the island. Contractor Dave Smith and his lead carpenter, Dave Diffner, installed the brackets into shallow mortises cut into the framing members at the building corners (top right drawing). By way of the brackets, the tie rods transfer the lateral loads from the roof trusses to the ground through the shear walls at the gable ends.

Paired 3x8 common rafters span from the ridge beam to the outside walls. A single 4x8 would have worked structurally for the rafters, but to tell the truth, I'm bored with the ponderous look of 4x rafters in a building of this scale, and 2x material looks too skimpy. Doubled 3x's cost a little more, but I think the extra expense is justified when the rafters are such prominent visual elements.

The exposed ceiling atop the rafters is made of 2x6 T&G select hemlock decking. To meet Washington's energy code, we insulated the roof with 3½ in. of Thermax (polyisocyanurate) rigid insulation. Skip sheathing for the cedar shingles went over the top of the insulation.

I come from a long line of carpenters, and even though I spend most of my time at a drawing board these days, I still like to get my hands on some portion of a construction job. On this one, my wife Audrey and I cut out three different fancy-butt shingle shapes for a decorative border several courses above the eaves of the three main roofs (bottom photo). This "petticoat" adds a pleasant ornament to an otherwise plain exterior.

Windows, trims and finishes—We chose furnituremaker Spencer Horn of Seattle to construct all the windows for the house. His studio is across the street from my office and this proximity helped us accomplish the difficult task of building window frames up to 20 ft. wide and 9 ft. high. Spencer went to the site and measured the framed openings and then laid out each of the largest windows at full scale on his studio floor. The largest frames, those for the master bedroom, had to be shipped by flatbed truck in two sections.

We kept embellishments in the house to a minimum, but added a few touches here and

The dining room lies between the kitchen and the two-level portion of the house that houses the living room and the master bedroom (photo facing page). Note the intersection of the wall and the ceiling in the upper left of the photo. The delicate horizontal window muntin conceals a steel tie rod that acts as the bottom chord of a roof truss.

From *Fine Homebuilding* magazine (June 1990) 61:50-54

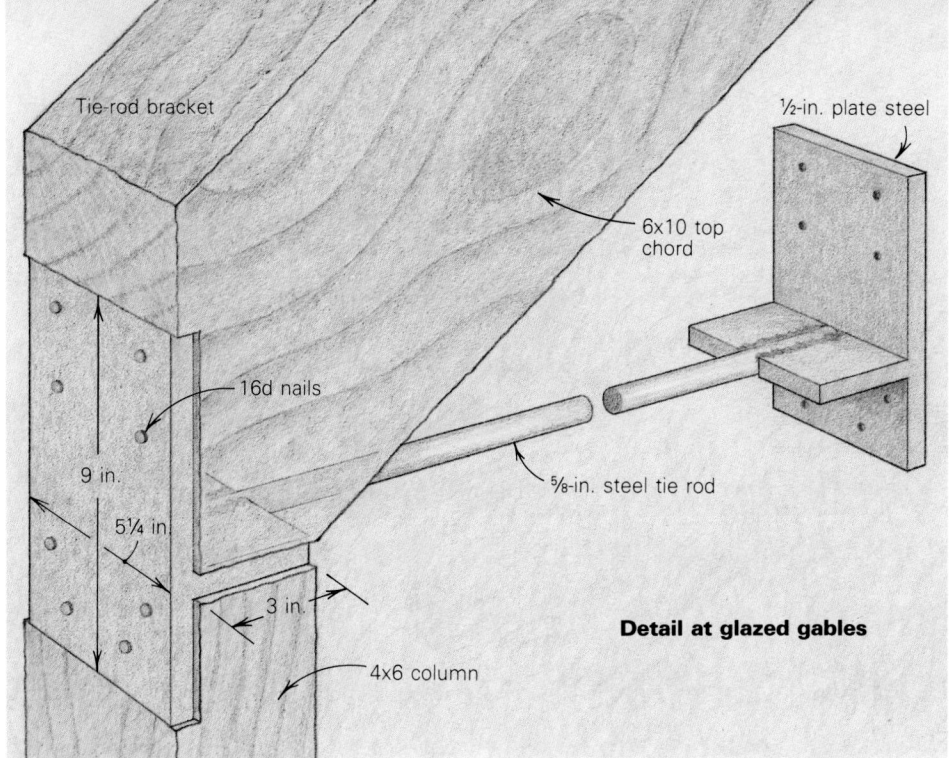

Detail at glazed gables

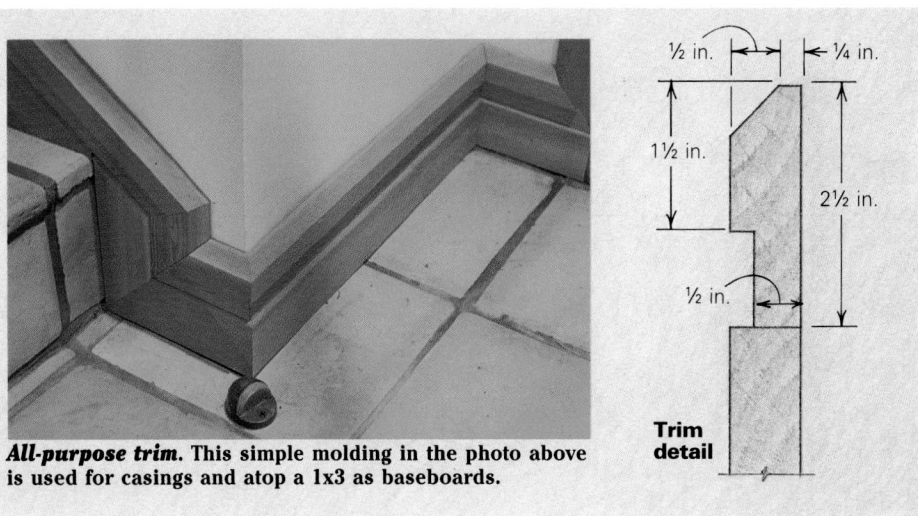

All-purpose trim. This simple molding in the photo above is used for casings and atop a 1x3 as baseboards.

Trim detail

A 4-ft. wide flat roof separates the dining-room gable from the living-room gable and cantilevers beyond the exterior wall to shelter the front door (photo below). The siding is Douglas fir, finished with Olympic Weathering stain. The folded creases in the copper gutters keep them straight and add a decorative shadowline. Custom-cut shingles form a decorative "petticoat" at the base of the roof.

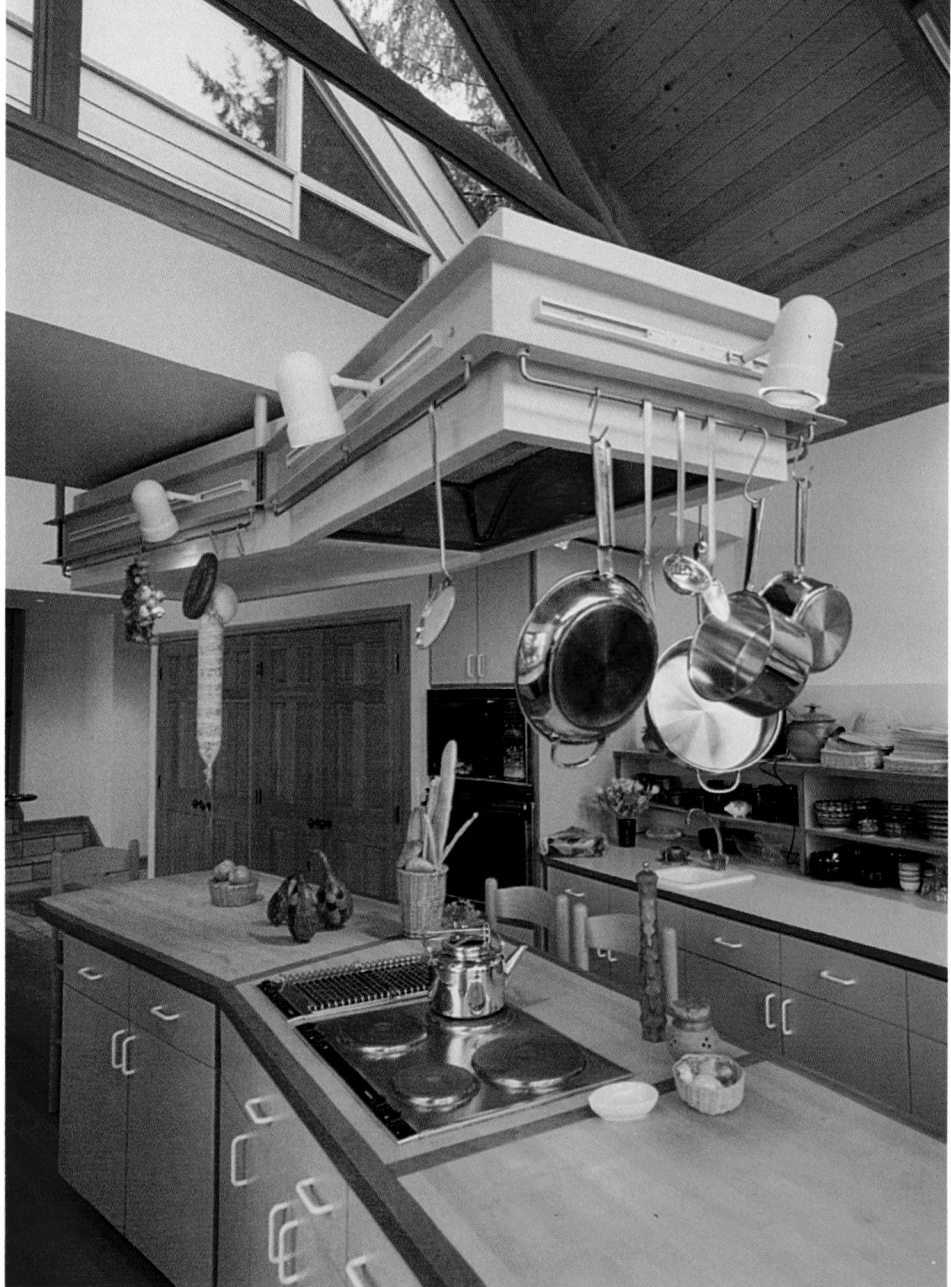

Bent pot rack. Above the kitchen island a cantilevered pot rack built on a steel framework also serves as a light standard and hood range. The hood is held aloft by lag bolts run through the flanges of the C-channel framework and into a pair of 4x12 beams in the flat ceiling.

Mostly earth tones. Mexican paver tiles cover the stairs and the passage through the house from the front door to the back steps. Teal blue steel handrails are the only architectural deviation from a palette of warm colors. Below the stairs to the master bedroom, firewood is stored in a cast-concrete bin formed during the foundation work.

there to make it evident that the building was assembled with care. The trim detail around the windows, doors and baseboards (top photo, previous page) is a simplification of a baseboard molding from a turn-of-the-century Seattle house that I used to live in. Its simple profile casts not only an assertive shadowline but also a highlight along the chamfered edge. It can be used by itself as a casing or in tandem with flat stock depending on the situation. Contractor Smith had the trim made up at a local mill shop, but it's simple enough to make with a router.

Plank 1x6 cherry floors cover the dining room and kitchen. They are screwed and plugged, and finished with Glitsa, a Swedish floor finish that wears well and shows off the grain of the wood (for more on Swedish finishes, see *FHB* #36, pp. 42-45).

Cloudy grey skies are a usual part of the landscape in the San Juans. Warm tones are therefore an important part of an interior color scheme, along with an occasional bright color for some variety. We had a good start on warm colors with the cherry floors, fir windows and trim and the hemlock ceiling. We added to this palette by choosing unglazed 12-in. square Mexican paver tiles for the bathrooms, entry and stairs (bottom photo). They are treated with a water-base sealer and then waxed.

Pot rack—As a final touch to complete the kitchen, I designed a combination pot rack-rangehood-light fixture to serve the kitchen's island. I didn't want to clutter up the high ceiling with support brackets for the rack, and yet the rack had to project well beyond the low, flat-roofed portion of the ceiling between the kitchen and the dining room. The solution turned out to be a cantilevered frame made of 1½-in. by 4-in. steel channel (top photo). Hung at one end from the low ceiling, the rack follows the same 15° dogleg of the kitchen and its island. Pots hang from ¼-in. stainless-steel rods that we had custom-bent at a local metal shop. The rods are anchored to the pot-rack frame by way of metal collars that are welded to the C-channel. Hexagonal-head set screws tapped into the collars hold the rods in place.

A painted MDO plywood box is affixed to the inside of the steel framework. It houses the copper-hood liner and the ductwork that leads to a 1,000 cfm fan unit mounted on the flat roof. This keeps most of the noise from the fan motor away from the kitchen. We added a rheostat as soon as we discovered that the fan, operating at full power, was pulling smoke out of the fireplace in the living room and the airtight wood heater in the master bedroom.

Once the new house was finished, most of the original one was removed. We kept the old foundations in place to take on a new use as retaining walls for a brick terrace off the kitchen, on the sunny side of the new house. □

Gordon Lagerquist is a partner in the architectural firm of Lagerquist and Morris in Seattle, Washington.

Capital Gains

Adding light, space and spirit to a tiny Georgetown rowhouse

by Edward S. Fleming, Jr.

By the summer of 1981 I was ready to pull up my roots, which had been growing in the tropical soil of New Orleans for six years, and return home to Washington, D. C. I'd spent those years earning an architecture degree and working as an intern architect. I had also completely renovated the apartment I'd rented during my stay, making my landlord alternately happy with and confused by my efforts.

The early 1980s were difficult times for intern architects to find jobs, but I finally secured a position with a Washington firm. The only thing missing was a place to live. An old friend, who belonged to a real-estate investment group that owned several houses in Georgetown, told me by phone that a small rowhouse the group had been renting to students would soon be vacant. They had intended to renovate and sell it, but found that they couldn't make a profit. I suggested a variation on the agreement that I'd had with my New Orleans landlord, and my friend liked the idea.

The offer was this: I'd live in the house rent-free and would design and build the renovation myself. The investment group would pay for materials, and once the work was complete, we'd sell the rowhouse together and divide the profits. Having the energy of a young man who didn't exactly know what he was getting into, I thought this seemed like a fantastic deal. The only thing that echoed in my ears as I packed for the move was the tone of my friend's voice when describing the house as "rather small." No problem, I thought; designing is fun, building your design is even more fun, and anyway, someone used to say that less is more.

More or less a house—Washington, D. C., a lovely city anytime, managed to have beautiful fall weather when I arrived. I saw the house for the first time on one of those clear, crisp days. The definition of "house" as I knew it was a structure surrounded by space and light. But here was a "house" that was one of eleven units all sharing the same brick front wall, which was set back about 15 ft. from the sidewalk (top photo). Each house had a party wall between it and its neighbor's and a small

The street facade of the author's rowhouse in a historic district could only be repointed and painted (top photo), but the interior underwent a major transformation. Fleming excavated under the rear dogleg in order to make three floors out of two. The old foundation wall is visible in the new study (bottom photo). A new kitchen and bedroom are located on the top two floors.

indentation at the rear that produced the only relief to this solid mass. There were yards, but they were tiny yards. This, I discovered, was a rowhouse.

What amazed me was that the house measured only about 10-ft. 11-in. wide at its widest and as little as 7-ft. 4-in. at the rear dogleg. It was 36 ft. end to end, making the whole house under 700 sq. ft. The interior was typical of a rowhouse, with high ceilings at the first floor and a sidewall stair that wound once to a dollhouse landing on the second floor (drawing, next page).

Someone had made "improvements" to the house in the early 60s, as I discovered when I ripped out some old plaster and found a clipping from *The Washington Post* that described one of Jackie Kennedy's evening dresses. At that time, the kitchen was moved to the front of the house, where it effectively blocked most light from reaching anywhere else. The little light that managed to creep in was blocked by the stairway. Two small windows at the rear, which faces east, lit the living room. On the sunny day that I first walked into the house, I had to turn on lights to see clearly. The kitchen contained an old gas furnace that spit fire, and an electric stove with a ground wire that had been gnawed by rats and that would send a tingle up my arm if I happened to touch it and the refrigerator at the same time—not hard to do in such a tiny space.

My excitement started to give way to the blues as I faced the prospect of living through the winter in this dreary shoebox. As I wandered through the house, feeling like Alice in her large stage, I thought that it would take a miracle to turn *this* into something special. Shortly after my move, I talked with my friend about what would make the house more marketable. The house cost little to hold on to, so time wasn't critical. As long as I improved the house and kept the cost of materials down, I was free to have my own fun.

Planning and design challenges—While I worked on the house, I would also be working fulltime for an architecture firm and studying

Floor Plans

Level 5 and roof plan

Bedroom #2

Skylight

Levels 3 and 4

HVAC

Kitchen — Dn — Up — Open

Up — Skylight

1 in. gap between wall and floor

Bedroom #1

Skylights

Levels 1 and 2

Dn

Study — Up

Dining

Sitting area

Dn

Living area

NORTH

0 2 4 8 ft.

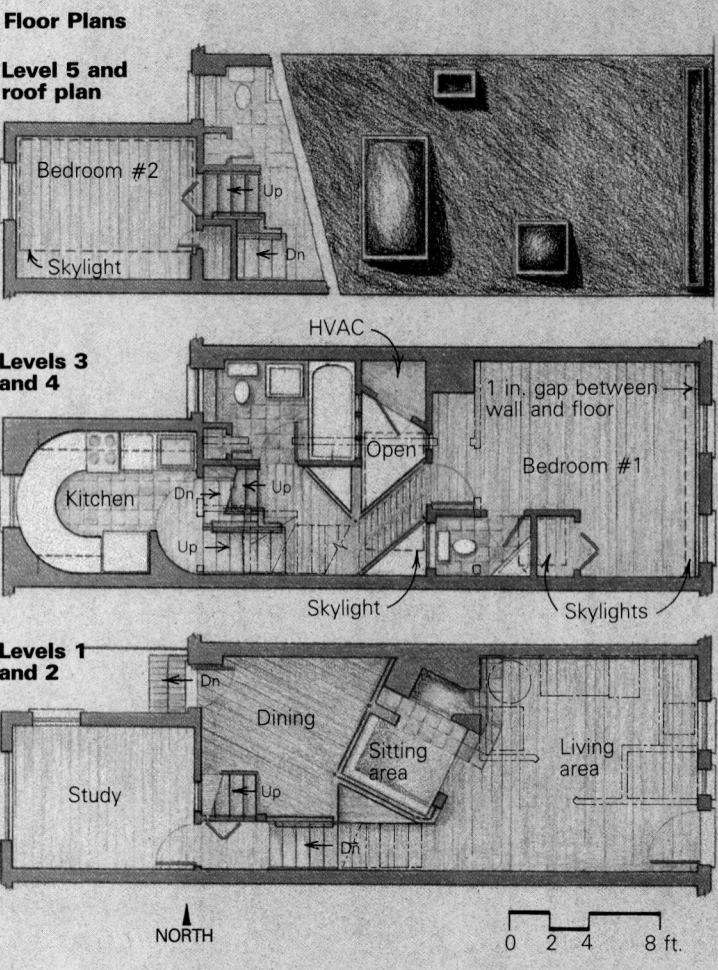

Only the flooring in the living room (foreground of photo, top left), parts of the masonry fireplace and the location of the back door (behind the dining table) remain of the original construction. A grey door to the left closes off the study and the new kitchen is above. The existing upper level was cut out and reframed to make a bridge between rooms (photo left). Bedroom #1 is to the bottom of the photo. A skylight above the bridge makes a central light shaft. Interior windows with floating casings extend views and bring in light, unless blinds are shut for privacy. The tub/shower is behind the three narrow windows to the upper left.

Showered with light. Windows in the shower (photo above) open to the light shaft and the bedroom beyond. The ceramic soap/shampoo holder was custom-made.

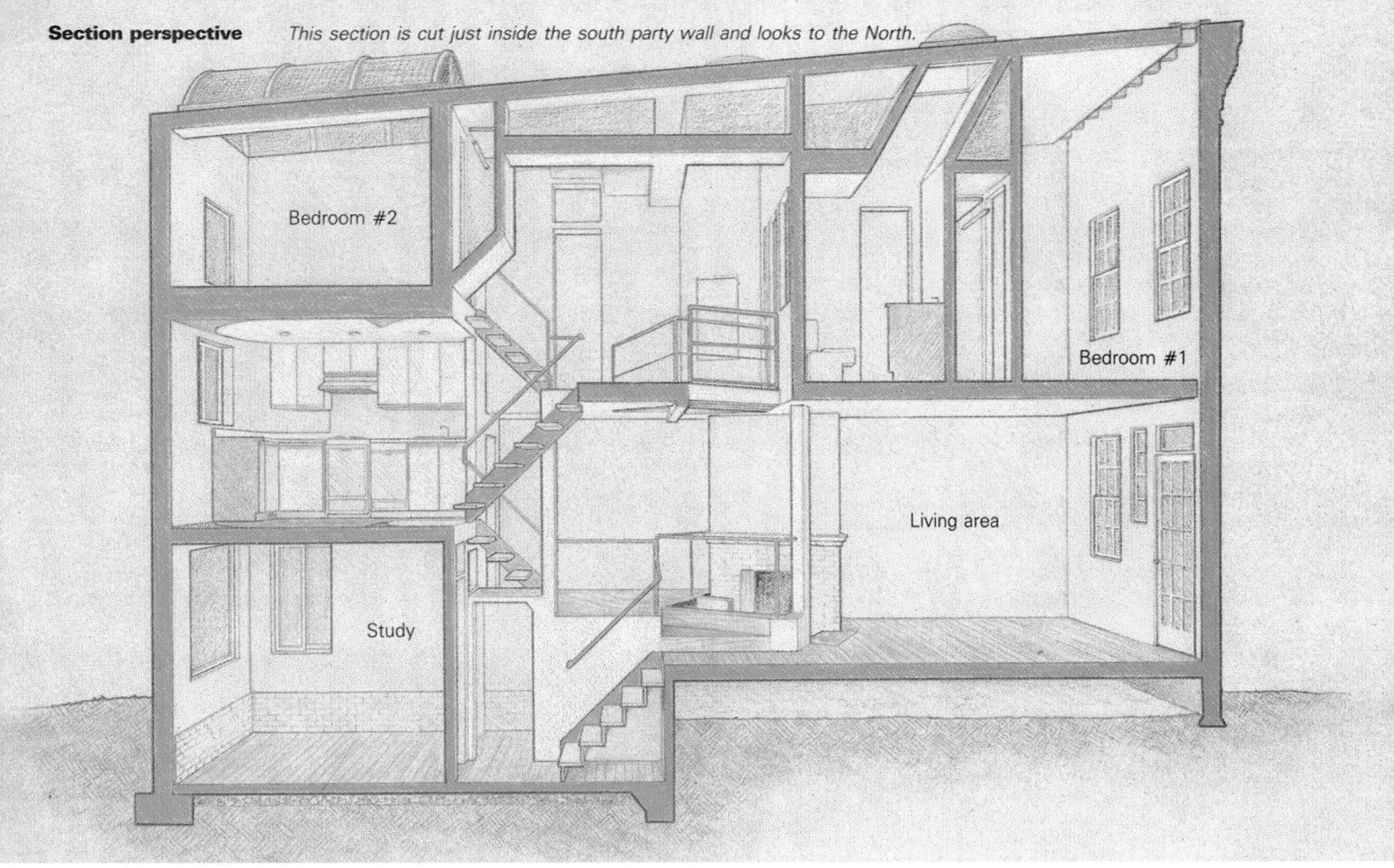

Bedroom #2

Bedroom #1

Living area

Study

for my licensing exams. I had to juggle my time well enough to keep these balls in the air and stay sane. For that reason, I intended to limit construction to small areas, but as work progressed, I had less and less normal living space. No problem, for I'd become less normal myself and was acclimated to my disaster area. For the time being, however, I arranged a living area near the fireplace, then tore the back finish and risers from the stair to allow some daylight in. I slung my hammock in the front upstairs room, set up my drawing board in the 7½-ft. wide upstairs back room and started designing.

The two most obvious design challenges were to deal with limited space and almost nonexistent natural light. The building is in a historic district, which meant that nothing visible from the street except paint color could be changed without approval. But I could add skylights as long as I kept them out of sight. To start out, I planned to excavate under the narrow dogleg to add another level. This would allow space for a second bedroom and more storage. Then I designed a series of intermediate levels that, along with a switchback stair, would tie the new three-story section to the two-story section (drawing above). The new dining-room level would sit a few feet higher than the living room and a sunken space to the side would serve as built-in seating around the fireplace (photo facing page, top).

In order to increase lines of sight, it made sense to open up as much of the house as

possible. To increase the perception of depth, I layered spaces and elements. I designed openings in the walls of the various levels, and planned to cut out the floor space to make a bridge (photo facing page, lower left). The idea was to create a forced perspective of greater distance and an energetic sense of motion. The framed views from a multitude of levels would create foreground, middle ground and background from inside the house to the sky in order to make the spaces seem bigger than they are. The geometry of the floor areas, openings and the stair and its railing would create a sense of twisting or rotating of the whole volume of the house.

Bringing in natural light would not only throw off the gloom, but the movement of sunlight and the passage of clouds would create a sense of motion in the solid forms. Interior windows would lend light from one space to another. For example, three windows on the shower wall capture light for the bathroom from the skylight above the bridge (photo facing page, bottom right).

I went quickly from sketches to large-scale cardboard models to test ideas. I tested the models with lamps and the sun to study the effect of light. These models were a huge help in refining the plan to match the ideas that I had been sketching. I presented a finished model and drawings to the owners and got the green light on the design. After we worked up a cost estimate, I had a ceiling-breaking ceremony in February of 1982.

Digging in and under—My first major task was to excavate under the back part of the house. I pulled up a section of flooring and rigged a board-covered path to move excavated earth to the backyard, using a wheelbarrow balanced on the middle of a 2x12 plank that spanned the excavation pit. For the next two months I'd come home from work, eat dinner and start digging. I'd fill up the wheelbarrow, back it around my living room, zoom out the back door and roll it up more planks to the growing pile of earth in my tiny backyard. My new neighbors watched wide-eyed as a good-sized ski slope slowly took shape. In all, I dug about 6½ ft. down and moved 26 cu. yds. from inside to outside. Then my brother helped me load it, shovelful by shovelful, back into the wheelbarrow, down a 3-ft. alley into my truck, which we'd unload in a nearby lot.

The grade I had to reach to fit in a new level was below the bottom of the existing foundation, which was a flared 14-in. wide portion of the brick bearing walls. So I learned about underpinning (see *FHB* #39, pp. 38-42, for more on underpinning a D. C. rowhouse foundation). I was lucky enough to meet an old Italian mason who told me about drypacking mortar (making a very dry but bonding mortar) for the last joint between the new and old foundation walls to reduce movement. In the three and one-half years since the job's been finished, I haven't seen any cracks in the walls.

Finally, in May I was ready to pour the slab. I rented a portable mixer and wheeled sand, cement and gravel in the front door, through the house and into the backyard. Bright and early one Sunday morning, I started up the motor and began mixing the concrete. This was how I discovered the limit to my neighbors' patience and why I had a slab party as soon as it cured.

During this time, I met my future wife, Catharine, who supported what had become an obsession for me. It wasn't long before she, too, was pulling down walls and watching the dust fly. It was wonderful to be able to share the daily progress and watch, together, as my idea inched its way toward reality.

Unsteady as you go—In order to reframe part of the existing second floor to make a bridge, I removed some of the floor joists from under the bathroom and cut off the upper half of the old stair. I put up stilts to support the old tub, toilet and sink and ran planks across the gap in the framing. This meant that to take a shower, I'd walk up the half-stairs, heave myself up to a plank and swing around a corner and into the 4-ft. by 4-ft. cast-iron tub, with its swaying 10-ft. legs and garden-hose drain. Friends who would visit amidst the rubble would shake their heads in total disbelief.

The new walls and floors went up quickly during the summer as I developed my skills at solo framing. I was lucky to find rowhouses nearby that were being gutted and, after getting an okay from the foreman, I salvaged enough lumber for all my floor framing, plus three flights of battered stairs. I had to hire subcontractors to do electrical, plumbing and HVAC work (licensing restrictions kept me from doing myself). They were at first perplexed by the design, but quickly took an interest in the job and made everything fit beautifully. By fall, most of the mechanical and electrical systems were roughed in. One day in September, three months after my first architecture licensing exam, I got the letter I had been alternately waiting for and dreading that told me I had passed.

As the rough work drew to a close, living seemed to become a little easier and less dangerous. But I reached a point about halfway through where I wondered if I'd ever finish. Sometimes I'd stand in the middle of the space and feel as if I could see through everything with X-ray eyes, knowing what had been done and how much more remained. I'd feel an overwhelming sense of heaviness—almost as if I were being submerged. Occasionally, though, I'd realize that an idea was actually taking form.

In late fall, I took about seven weeks off from everything to cram into my head all the architecture I could, then flew back to Louisiana to take the second part of the exams. I finally got the news in February that I had passed and was now able to go out on my own. Maybe so, but I still had another eight to twelve months left to finish the house.

A time-keeping skylight—One day in early spring, I was walking down the street in front of the house and heard the university clock tower strike noon. I looked down and noticed that the shadows from the street lamps were exactly parallel to the curb. Of course, at solar noon the sun shines from due south and, as L'Enfant planned for Washington, D. C., all the numbered streets (mine was 35th) run north and south. It dawned on me that this rowhouse design should respond to the coincidence of sun angles and the French engineer's city plan. So I designed a narrow skylight along the front wall, which is parallel to the street. I also decided to stop the upstairs floor an inch shy of the front wall. This would create a long, narrow gap between floor and wall, and I had great plans for it.

At solar noon every sunny day, sunlight would descend through the skylight, through that gap and onto the wall in the living room downstairs. I had to build a low skylight so that it wouldn't be visible from the street. So I used insulated glass panels in a wood frame, rubber gaskets and a 2x3 wood sill. The existing roofing was metal, making flashing and waterproofing easy.

I spent hours aligning the furring for the front wall, installing window and door trim (recessed so it wouldn't cast shadows) and figuring the proper width for the skylight and the opening in the floor. I wanted the skylight to appear to be the same width as the narrow slot in the bedroom floor when viewed through that slot from the living room. The skylight turned out to be about 8-in. wide.

The moment of reckoning finally came, with the skylight glazing set, the floor slot finished, the sky clear and the time 11:30 a.m. When I saw the first wide band of sunlight begin to creep down the wall below the skylight, I danced on the roof like a crazed Druid, then rushed inside to watch an angled band of light move down the wall and slip through the slot in the floor. At noon, the entire wall was washed in strong bands of sun (top photo, facing page). Seconds after noon, the light quickly vanished like cellophane being peeled off the surface. The idea worked. The angle of the sunlight on the front wall changes with the seasons, making the equinoxes and solstices visual celebrations.

Danger on the job site—By late spring, when I finished the skylight, Catharine and I had become almost comfortable with a house that still didn't have what most people would call basic necessities. But we still asked friends and family over to share what was becoming a sort of protracted birth. One weekend when we were expecting guests for dinner, I was getting things squared away in the kitchen and Catharine was getting ready upstairs. Suddenly I heard a shout and saw, out of the corner of my eye, something falling from above. In the first split second I thought that Catharine had knocked a piece of furniture off the yet-to-be-railed bridge. Then I

looked down to the hearth below the bridge and my heart stopped. There she was, sprawled on the plywood floor. For the most excruciating twenty seconds of my life I thought she was dead. This project I'd been so obsessed with caused the most crushing loss I could imagine.

Just as I thought my head would explode, Catharine opened her eyes and told me not to move her, but to call an ambulance. When I got her to the hospital and all the injuries were tallied, she'd suffered a broken collar bone and many cuts and bruises, but no other damage. She'd fallen head-first 10 ft. from the bridge, missing the sharp edge of the dining platform by inches. We'd become so comfortable with what was really a dangerous site that I never thought to install temporary railings, thinking that the finished railings would be in soon. The first thing I did when we returned home was to hammer on a railing. Luckily, Catharine was strong and was almost back in shape in seven weeks.

A ceramic stream—Towards the end of the summer, as the rowhouse neared completion, I started thinking in detail about finishes. Catharine is a ceramic sculptor so I suggested during her convalescence that she design and make a custom ceramic countertop for the kitchen and several pieces for the main bath. She came up with a drawing of curvilinear porcelain pieces formed into a swirling mass that would follow the circular geometry of the kitchen. We enlarged the sketch to full scale on large sheets of tracing paper and laid them over one huge slab of clay that we'd rolled out over the plywood base. Once the tracing paper pattern was in place, we gently retraced all the lines of the design, leaving a clear indentation in the moist clay. Then, we carefully peeled off the tracing paper and, with kitchen knives, cut through the impressions to the plywood underneath. We covered the top with plastic sheeting and loaded it with a layer of plywood and dozens of bricks. Once a day for about three weeks, we'd lift off the covering and mist the slowly drying clay. We lost a number of pieces to cracking, but were able to retrace and cut new pieces to replace them. As the clay dried, it shrank, giving us the space we needed for grout joints. Once the tiles were completely dry, we carefully carved a code number on the back of each corresponding to its location on the paper pattern. We transported the tiles on pallets to Catharine's pottery studio where we glazed and fired almost 1,100 pieces.

Setting the tile was a lot more complicated than setting the square manufactured tiles we used in other areas. We worked with an epoxy mastic to ensure that the tiles would stay put, but it had a very quick drying time. We applied the adhesive with a notched trowel, then worked in a panic to fit the pieces in the right places, guessing at proper joint spacing.

Eventually, the countertop and backsplash (including some tiles with pawprints added accidentally by our dog and cat) came out level and strong. The design looks like a shimmering stream, bending around the curve of the kitchen wall (bottom photo, background). It was well worth the two-and-a-half months it took to complete.

The case of the floating window—I built the new stairway from new 8/4 oak stringers and I restored the treads of the salvaged stairs, which I'd stored in my mom's basement for the previous year. I blind-mortised the treads into the stringers and left the risers open in keeping with the notion of framed views and to allow light to pass through (bottom photo). The pipe railing (built before the local code was changed to require intermediate rails) was designed to look fluid, like a line twisting up and around with the stair, accentuating its ascent.

One of the last details I attended to was the casing for the remaining doors and interior windows. I wanted to make the casing appear movable, as if it could glide through the partition or wall (bottom left photo, p. 112). To do this, I held each drywall edge back from the rough opening about ½ in. and finished the edge with steel casing bead. The edges of the rough framing, perfectly squared and set back from the wall surface by the thickness of the drywall, were covered with metal corner bead before the drywall or casing was installed. The casing was simply 1x clear white pine projecting about one inch beyond each face of the drywall. This left a narrow reveal between casing and drywall. I routed a channel in the center of the door jambs for the hinge knuckles so that the doors could be set in the center of the opening and not detract from the edges of the casing. We painted the walls bone white and the casings warm gray. Then, with a small brush, I painted the reveals a very dark, high-gloss gray to exaggerate the shadow of the joint, making the casings appear to float in the walls.

Tallying the cost—In the new year, I completed the house by repointing brickwork and installing storm windows on the inside of the original divided-lite windows. We finally had our "whew, it's finished" party in February for everyone we could think of—almost two years to the day from when I started construction. The total construction cost, including subcontracted work, was $26,000. When the owners sold the house, they walked away with a respectable profit, and I felt as if I'd given up my only child for adoption. But, my hands-on education had given me some understanding of how complex building really is, as well as a deep respect for builders that, unfortunately, is usually not promoted during a strictly academic architecture education. □

Edward S. Fleming is a partner in Architect-nique, Washington, D. C., where he is designing modular housing. Photos by Tom Guidera.

Noon beams. **At noon on June 7, sunlight creeps through the 8-in. skylight and down the bedroom wall (above), then through the 1-in. gap between floor and wall to the living room below. Open risers and railings let views and light flow between rooms (below). A custom-made tile countertop and backsplash follow the curve of the kitchen wall.**

Hawaiian Ohana House

A flexible plan allows a small guest cottage to double as a photography studio

by Sue Ellen White-Hansen

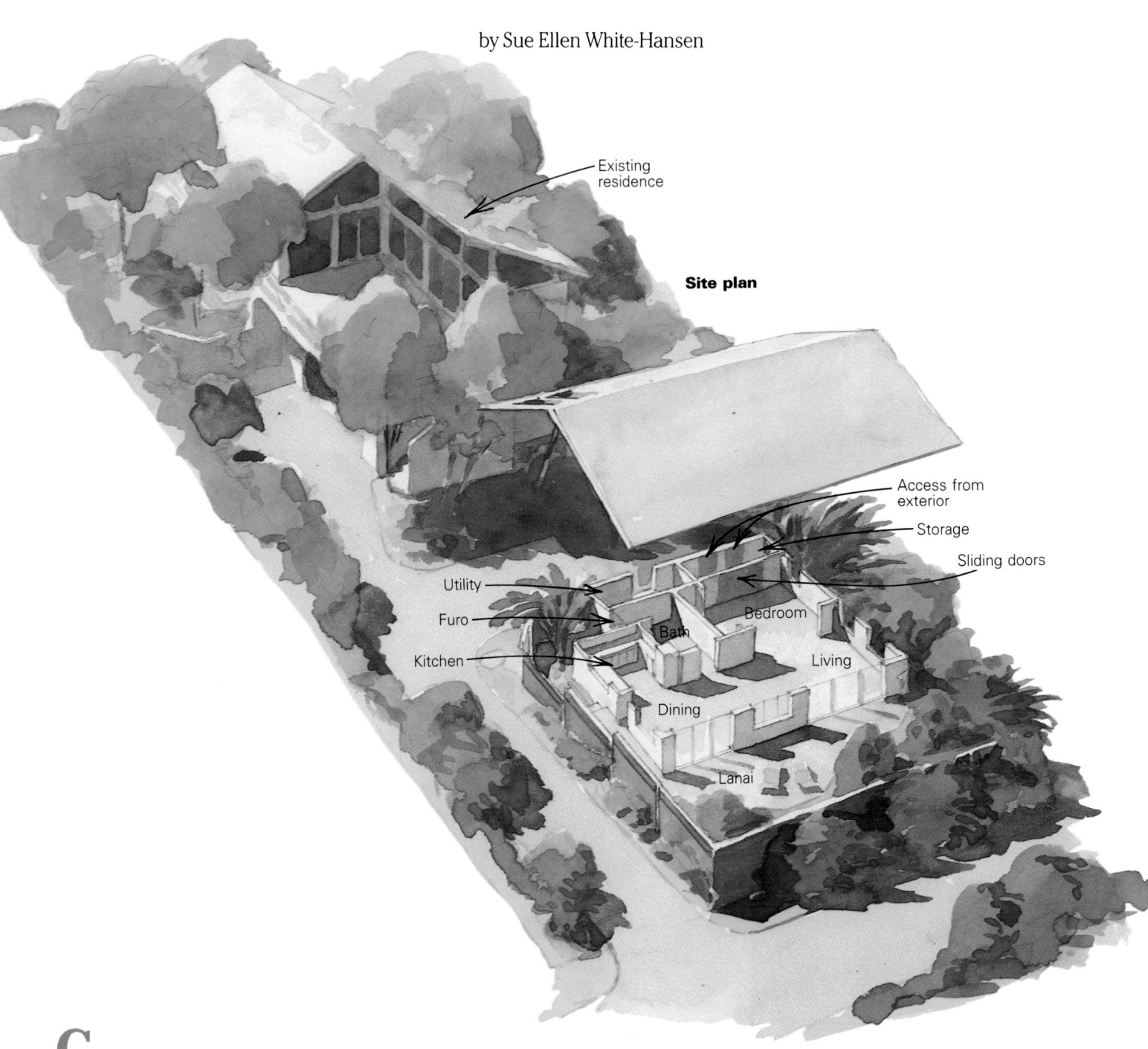

Site plan

Existing residence

Access from exterior

Storage

Sliding doors

Utility

Furo

Kitchen

Bath

Bedroom

Living

Dining

Lanai

Carol Ann Davis and Walter Briant have lived on the Hawaiian island of Kauai for more than 25 years, in the community of Poipu on the sunny southern shore. In that time the couple has seen their neighborhood grow from a few beach-front homes pressed against the water's edge by the sugarcane fields to a world-class resort area with golf courses, retirement homes and hotels nibbling away at the cane fields.

Development in paradise is always a mixed blessing, and for Kauai residents its impact has been to decrease the number of homes available for full-time occupancy and to raise rapidly the price of the limited amount of build-able land. Kauai property prices commonly exceed the cost of building a house—even though the availability and cost of materials on Kauai are enough to give most mainland builders nightmares.

The ohana house is one solution to the is-land housing shortage that has evolved from the tradition of close Hawaiian familial ties. *Ohana* means extended family, and a dwelling that bears this name was customarily a small resi-dence adjacent to the main family house, in-tended for the use of grown children beginning their own families, or by other relatives.

Walter and Carol Ann had just enough room toward the front of their lot for a small house

Drawing: Malcolm Wells

(drawing facing page) that fits within the ohana-house zoning restrictions. While its main function is as a rental cottage for visitors and guest quarters for friends and family, it also leads a double life as a photography studio. Carol Ann is a professional photographer who specializes in school portraits, and she needed both studio and equipment storage space. So the problems of storage and control of light had to be balanced with the need for privacy, ventilation and the desire for an inviting space.

Hidden by the hedges—The lot is 60 ft. by 180 ft., with the main house placed well back from the street. To preserve everybody's privacy, the ohana house is sited close to the road on the east, but far enough back (20 ft.) to provide a place for an outdoor sitting area that faces the morning sun. The north wall is as close to the property line as is allowed by code (5 ft.). Along both of these borders, the house is secluded behind thick, tall hedges. The driveway to the south further limited the 25-ft. wide by 32-ft. long footprint of the house.

Within this rectangle, Walter and Carol Ann, working with architect Stefan Schweitzer, developed a plan with less than 800 sq. ft. that has a large, open space occupying the eastern half of the house. Furniture groupings divide this room into dining and living areas, and two pairs of sliding-glass doors open it to the secluded patio between the house and the road (photo below right).

The bedroom is in the northwest corner of the house, with jalousie windows for ventilation along the north wall. The windowless west wall, which faces the main house, conceals a generous storage closet for photography gear that can be reached through lockable bypass doors in the bedroom or through doors on the outside wall of the house. This makes the transition from studio to rental easy and provides equipment access when others are occupying the ohana house. A separate closet serves the bedroom.

When it's functioning as a bedroom, this space is isolated from the rest of the house by a trio of sliding shoji screens that extend to cover the 10-ft. opening (photo above right). When Carol Ann is using the house as a studio, the shoji screens are retracted to open most of the house into one large, L-shaped workspace. The doors (L. A. Shoji and Decorative Products, Inc., 4848 West Jefferson, Los Angeles, Calif. 90016) are mounted adjacent to the header on tracks that are provided by the manufacturer. To keep them from swaying when the tradewinds blow through the house, the shoji interlock at their bottom rails.

At the sunny end of the house, the dining corner is open to a simple U-shaped kitchen (photo next page) with full-size appliances. The washer, dryer and water heater are in a service closet next to the storage area, where they can be reached through an exterior door.

With a budget of about $50,000, or $60 per sq. ft., money had to be carefully allocated.

From *Fine Homebuilding* magazine (June 1990) 61:58-61

The main room of the house is divided by furniture groupings into a dining corner and two sitting areas. A trio of sliding shoji screens shield the bedroom from the public portions of the house.

A curving concrete lanai, 10 ft. across at its widest point, provides an outdoor space that can be reached from two pairs of sliding glass doors from the the primary room of the house. The ends of the rafters and the lintel above the gate share a graceful S-curve detail. On the house, the exposed rafter ends are protected from the weather by copper caps.

Any amenity would have to make a tangible contribution to the livability of the house or the longevity of the structure. On the simple side, the house has a straightforward single-gable form with a composition roof on a 4-in-12 slope. The plumbing runs are minimal, the cabinets are off-the-shelf factory units and the lighting and plumbing fixtures, drywall, and T-111 plywood siding are all relatively inexpensive.

On the other hand, the house has a few touches that added to the basic expenses. For example, it has an open beam ceiling with exposed wood decking to enhance the feeling of space and to promote better ventilation. The floors are paved with ceramic tile, and the bathroom has a custom tub with a view of a lush garden (more on the tub later).

With climate in mind—Prevailing tradewinds from the northeast keep Kauai's climate from being overly hot in the warmer summer months, so air-conditioning is not a necessity in a structure designed to take advantage of this natural cooling. To that end, jalousie windows are widely used in tropical and subtropical climates because they provide plenty of ventilation. They also leak much less than other types of windows when left partially open in driving rainstorms. And though they leak air, keeping heat in is not a problem here. Along with the other windows in the house, the glass jalousies are made of tinted bronze glass, which reduces solar gain by about 30% in addition to reducing glare. The jalousies in the bedroom, front door and sitting-room windows are redwood, finished with four coats of urethane varnish.

Except for the north wall and the storage area on the west, the house is surrounded by 4-ft. deep eaves. There are pros and cons to such deep overhangs. The advantages are protection from storms, shade in a climate noted for its blazing sun and semi-protected exterior places for sitting or storing things out of the rain. On the negative side, deep eaves can shade an interior too much if there aren't any skylights or windows high on gable-end walls. High windows in the wall above the kitchen sink let sunlight into the south end of the house, leaving the north end (where Carol Ann does her photography) free of the harsh glare and direct sunlight that plague photographers. Paper window shades that diffuse the daylight hang over most of the windows in the studio portion of the house, allowing her to further control the light.

The house is built on a concrete slab atop gravel fill in direct contact with the earth. This helps to maintain a relatively cool and constant temperature, and provides ideal moderation in this climate, where daytime temperatures almost always average in the low 80s. White glazed ceramic tile covers the floor, bath and counter surfaces, adding to the cooling mass. The reddish-brown grout between the tiles closely approximates the color of the pervasive Kauai soil, which seems to color everything on the island. The tiles are easy to clean with a mop, and the grout always looks fresh.

Insulation is not commonly used in residential construction in Hawaii unless the structure is to be air-conditioned. In the ohana house, however, Walter and Carol Ann wanted to promote the natural cooling afforded by the slab and the overhangs by insulating the roof and walls to keep the heat out. A layer of 1-in. foil-faced Thermax insulation (an isocyanurate foam) helps to reduce heat transfer from the shingles to the ceiling decking. It was laid between 2x2s nailed to the exterior surface of the decking. A layer of ½-in. plywood atop the 2x2s provides a nail base for the composition shingles. The reflective surface of the Thermax helps to bounce radiant heat away from the roof, while the foam reduces conductive heat gain. The east and south walls were insulated with 3½-in. fiberglass batts.

House in a box—When a typical North American winter begins to sting the face and numb the fingers, many carpenters dream of pounding nails under a subtropical sun cooled by gentle tradewinds. John Goertzel, a builder from Washington state and a friend of Walter and Carol Ann, got his wish for just such a working vacation when he signed on to build this cottage.

Goertzel's first task was to investigate his sources of building materials on the island. He knew from previous experience that materials typically cost considerably more than mainland prices, and that shortages and delivery delays are the norm. Therefore, to reduce costs, control quality and assure availability, Goertzel decided to ship by sea nearly all the

A small U-shaped kitchen at the south end of the house shares the sunshine with the eating area. The grout between the white glazed tiles is the same color as the red Kauai earth, making it easier to keep the floors looking clean.

materials from the mainland in a cargo container. Several companies on the West Coast specialize in shipping custom packages of building supplies to Hawaii, including Container Home Supply (P. O. Box 522, Woodinville, Washington 98072). In a package, it's possible to save between 10% and 40% on materials, depending on the item.

The task of ordering every possible item, down to the nails, for use 3,000 miles away is not as formidable as it seems. Any builder who bids a job goes through essentially the same process. The biggest challenge comes in trying to make changes as the structure evolves. For example, you can move a window, but it's tough to change its size. Thoroughly conceived plans are a must for container-delivered materials, and unforeseen circumstances call for creative improvisation.

In keeping with contemporary building practices in Hawaii, Goertzel specified treated framing lumber for the ohana house. Because of the pervasive termite problem, the Hawaiian building code specifies that treated lumber be used wherever it touches concrete, but most current construction in the islands is done with pressure-treated lumber for all framing and exterior sheathing. Plate stock for the ohana home was hemlock, rated at .25 CCA, which means that .25 lb. of chromated copper arsenic was pressure-forced into each cubic foot of wood. This concentration is the minimum Hawaii retention standard for aboveground use. The frame was built of treated Douglas fir. Even the roof sheathing is pressure-treated plywood.

When the entire construction package arrives all at once, storage can be a problem—especially in Kauai's climate of sudden downpours. Goertzel kept a supply of heavy tarps on hand for covering supplies. Also, he divided the materials into two shipments, timed seven weeks apart, to ease the storage problem.

The first load included framing lumber, roofing, drywall, siding, windows, exterior doors, sliders, roof decking, paint, plywood, roof and wall insulation, nails and tools—everything necessary to enclose the house. The second shipment contained appliances, prefinished interior doors and wood trim, cabinets, plumbing fixtures and lighting fixtures.

A custom soaking tub—Because most of the materials and fittings were ordered well in advance, the house was built almost exactly as conceived. One change, however, was the built-in shower and soaking tub in the bathroom (photo above right). The original plans called for a 3-ft. by 4-ft. shower, finished with ceramic tile. But Walter decided to replace it with his design for a more versatile and appealing ceramic shower with a sunken tub. Its inspiration comes from the Japanese furo—a traditional soaking tub. Central to the use and effect of the tub are its depth (about 22 in.), the sloping back (essential for comfortable soaking) and the combination step/seat for ease of entry and exit. The level of the step/seat is the same as the bathroom floor.

To build the furo, an area about 4 ft. square was blocked out during the pour for the slab floor of the house. The drain was positioned 12 in. below the finished floor of the bathroom. Next, a male form was constructed, representing the shape of the tub. The top of the form extended 12 in. above the finished floor. To make sure that the angle was right for reclining comfort, Walter got in and out of the tub cavity to rest his back against the sloping plywood form board before casting the final form in concrete.

The first concrete pours created the vertical surfaces. After the form was stripped, the floors of the shower and the step/seat were filled to provide a base for the tile and the proper drainage slopes (bottom photo).

The tub has no waterproof membrane. Any water that seeps through the concrete or around the drain eventually ends up in the rock fill under the slab, where it can't do any damage to the house. As is traditional, water comes from a hole in the side of the tub rather than a spout.

The furo and shower walls were tiled with 2¼-in. sq. ceramic tile, set in a latex thinset mortar and grouted with latex-fortified grout. Goertzel cautions that tiling the many angles and planes of the furo was a labor-intensive project, requiring over 60 hours of work. But considering the cost of high-quality prefabricated soaking tubs, the clients know the outcome was worth the expense. □

Sue Ellen White-Hansen is a free-lance writer living on Whidbey Island in Washington State.

The furo

A concrete and tile soaking tub called a *furo* tucks into the corner of the bathroom, hard against an outside corner of the block foundation. The vertical walls were poured in stages, using plywood form boards that were adjusted in small increments to get the angle of the backrest right. Then the seat and step were built up with concrete slightly sloped toward the drain. The tub has no waterproof membrane—any moisture that finds its way through the cold joints in the concrete seeps into the gravel fill under the slab.

The substrate for the tile walls is Wonderboard over 15-lb. felt embedded in wet patch-roofing compound over waterproof drywall. A strip of white tile next to the blue ground of the top step/seat warns bathers of the change in levels. —S. E. W.

Planning the darkroom.

Planning the darkroom. I designed my workspace so I could handle everything from film development through drymounting in one room. Only exhibition editing was to be left for another room and accomplished in natural daylight.

There is no pattern to my darkroom schedule. I'm as likely to develop two rolls of film a week as I am to spend 15 hours a day making 16x20 exhibition prints. This room had to be responsive to my habits by being an independent element in the house.

With the combination of earth berming and insulated foundation walls, the Trombe wall keeps the room comfortable. In the summer, it's always between 68° and 70°, and in the winter the temperature fluctuates between 55° and 65°. When I want to get to work, I need only bring the room up a maximum of 10° with the radiant electric heaters. With this system, I can also take advantage of the sun's warmth without admitting direct sunlight, an ideal passive solar system for a darkroom.

A thermal-storage wall requires a southern exposure, but only limited space. It will effectively radiate heat 15 ft. to 20 ft. into the room behind it. I now know that for my purposes, my 1-ft. thick wall is thicker than I need. It stores a lot of heat, and moderates temperature fluctuations in the room, but the way I work, I'd rather have the warm air in the room as soon as possible. Trombe walls can probably be as thin as 8 in., and if I were to build mine again, I would pour it about that thick.

One of the best tools you can have for designing the darkroom of your dreams is a list of the drawbacks of other darkrooms you have worked in. Like many photographers, I'd worked in kitchens, bathrooms and flooded basements. I knew what I *didn't* want my darkroom to be like. One typical oversight concerns the placement of light switches. Most rooms have a single switch near the door. I made sure there were three-way switches near the enlarger and print washer so I could flick on the room lights to look at prints without trotting over to the door.

A darkroom needs lots of grounded outlets for the timers, safelights and other appliances. I have ten outlets on the exposed joists overhead, above strategic counter and shelf areas. On the one wall faced with gypboard, there are four outlets in the 30-in. space by the enlarger.

I also used overhead space to suspend racks of 1-in. by 1½-in. pine for storing large flat items like trays, picture frames, matboard and shipping crates. In other darkrooms I've had, this stuff always wound up piled on precious counter space. Under the center island, which faces the print washer, opposite the 16-in. deep sink, is room for print-drying racks. The drymount press is on the counter itself, along with a second enlarger for multiple printing.

Three wall cabinets, for paper and equipment storage, are hung on the gypboard wall. I covered the concrete walls with white-glazed American Olean tile for a bright reflective surface. Quarry tile on the floor resists damage from chemical spills, and rubber mats ease leg strain. The sodium vapor safelight makes the room feel as bright as day, and eliminates the possibility of eyestrain.

The wet sinks are large enough to hold the trays for developing my 16x20 prints, and they are continuous, which puts an end to the inconvenience of fixing and toning prints separately.

I included a greywater line in the drainage system of the house. I wanted darkroom wastes to bypass the septic system and go directly to the leach field. I use only small quantities of chemicals, and I flush my trays with fresh water to dilute the solutions when I dump them, so they won't harm the environment. But I didn't want them killing beneficial bacteria in the septic tank. —R.G.

The solarium (facing page) is bright and airy. Temperatures near the glass reach 80° on sunny winter days. The spiral staircase saves space and keeps the open feeling of the room.

The concrete walls in the living area were board-formed to look like weathered barnboard (below right). One channel in the concrete carries the wiring; another holds a wood strip for hanging pictures. The vertical boxes are site-built cold-air returns. Upstairs (right), a wall of translucent glass block admits morning light into the bathroom. The guest nook is a recess in the hall's south wall.

workspace, while at the same time preventing the sunlight from entering the room. Rather than painting the concrete, I coated it with Maxorb, a foil material oxidized black on the side that faces the sun and left shiny on the other to help keep heat from seeping back outside through the concrete wall when the sun isn't shining. Maxorb is made by Ergenics (681 Lawlins Rd., Wyckoff, N.J. 07481). It is usually used in solar collectors. Properly applied, it should never need replacement or retouching, a necessity in my design, because there is no room for me to get between the glass block and the concrete to repaint.

The solarium behind the glass block is the airiest room in the house. It's a 10-ft. by 24-ft. space that's open to the sloped ceiling. I'd originally planned to build a standard staircase at the solarium's west end, leading up to the office, but I decided during construction that it would take up too much space. I went shopping for a circular staircase but found that most commercial models are either rickety or incredibly expensive. I finally had a sturdy one made for me by the Leslie Iron Works of East Pawlett, Vt. The $750 I paid was about $300 less than the cost of some manufactured units I had seen.

I wanted my windows and glass doors to be unprimed on both the exterior and the interior so I could treat them exactly as I wished. Luckily, the only manufacturer willing to supply them this way was nearby (Rivco, in Penacook, N.H.). I use the central French doors during the summer, but enter through the airlock at the solarium's east end when it's cold. This entry warms up quickly in the morning, and if I open the inner door at about 9 o'clock, I can let a quick shot of warm air inside.

In a small house, you really must clarify your priorities. My darkroom and office are big—about 14 ft. by 15 ft. each. My kitchen, on the other hand, is moderate—an 8-ft. by 14-ft. galley, separated from the solarium by a concrete wall that drops to counter height to let light through and allow conversation. It works, even for large parties, because it is open-ended. I installed a soapstone chemistry-lab sink that I bought from a bankrupt college, and energy-efficient appliances. A half-bath and laundry are in the small utility room off the kitchen's east end. It also connects to my darkroom (sidebar, facing page).

I set up the dining table either in the solarium or in the area just to the west of the kitchen. Both spaces also make nice sitting rooms, the solarium because of its brightness, and the

Modest housing: working with the Farmers Home Administration

In Vermont, where the average annual income is $14,000, the Farmers Home Administration (FmHA) is a much appreciated lending agency. Listed in the telephone book under the U.S. Department of Agriculture, the FmHA has a loan program to help people whose income is below a certain level build, buy or improve their homes.

Current FmHA requirements for a loan include being ineligible for conventional financing—"non-bankable," in other words. Your debts must not be excessive, and your credit history must be good. A work history in my nonprofit organization has kept my income low, and my IRS statement was evidence enough that no bank would accept me for a mortgage. Mortgages are written for a fixed interest rate over 33 years. Interest charges may be subsidized if your income level is low enough, so the rate you pay may be anywhere from 1% up to the full rate specified in the contract, currently 13¼%. The eligibility range in southern Vermont has just risen from an adjustable maximum income of $17,500 for a subsidized mortgage to an absolute maximum income of $23,000. This is good for medium-income people, but means more competition for loans. At the outset, the FmHA wants a credit application, an IRS statement of income and verification of employment (also called "reliable income").

Three important qualities. Getting an FmHA loan as an owner-builder or owner-contractor is tough. In fact, in many offices, it is impossible. In the Windham County office, the supervisor is selective. Two of the 20 housing starts last year were owner-builder projects. This sort of decision is entirely at the supervisor's discretion, and I'm glad I was dealing with a thoughtful and flexible person. Nonetheless, I realized early on that the first quality an owner-builder needs to secure an FmHA mortage is perseverence.

At preliminary meetings with the FmHA staff, it may seem that they are just trying to make your life difficult. But keep their position in mind. One of the things the FmHA worries about most is that the stress of building or contracting is so extreme that it can affect other aspects of an inexperienced person's life, which in turn can make the loan a bad risk. If you have any friends who have built their own houses, you know this isn't far-fetched. It's hard to carry on a normal life when you're not only hammering nails, but also managing money, material deliveries and subcontractors, not to mention handling the almost daily crises that come up in any building project. Relationships can suffer, and so can your performance on your paying job.

It's a fact that a lot of owner-builder projects never quite get finished. The FmHA staff will probably feel when you begin talking to them that taking an additional loan to cover the cost of a contractor's fee is well worth it when spread over payments of 33 years. They prefer that their clients continue with their jobs and normal lives, and not take on the time-consuming and pressured task of building. This isn't unreasonable. After all, if you fail, the FmHA is left holding the bag. They feel much more comfortable working with a reliable professional contractor they know will recognize a tight budget and come

in on deadline. You'll have to persuade them they don't have to take this tack with you.

The second necessary characteristic you have to have, then, is confidence. And you must communicate this to the FmHA staff. Preparation is vital. Certainly, my two woodshop courses in college didn't make me a carpenter. But I knew my house. I read everything I could, from passive solar theory and economical construction practices to how to use a framing square. I went to the Shelter Institute, and after 50 hours in a two-week program for contractors, I knew my terms and how buildings go together. I also became committed to building the most energy-efficient and thoughtful house I could. I knew no one else would attend to details the way I would.

The FmHA responded to my apparent building expertise. I exhibited great confidence and determination in every conversation, and could understand what the staff was talking about at all the meetings. The supervisor came to feel that I had developed enough knowledge about the building trades to be a contractor, and to bring this particular project in on time and budget.

Third, the FmHA supervisor recognized that I had management experience. In my own design and publishing business, I had worked with budgets, cash-flow charts and production schedules and had supervised a staff. I would be able to organize the job and run the books on the site, keeping track daily of the expenses and the progress of construction. Many professional tradespeople have trouble with this, and it was an enormous advantage for me in the supervisor's eyes. If you have similar experience, be sure to talk about it in your early discussion.

Design. When I built my house, there was only one other FmHA home in my region that had "solar features." Washington is now encouraging the regional offices to consider modest solar proposals. The design they recommend is just a box with a bit more insulation and a few extra windows on the south side, but the plans are a useful reference. The FmHA's job is helping low-income people get housing, not setting architectural trends. You'll have to justify your design by these criteria.

The FmHA provides guidance from the earliest meetings by handing out a 20-page booklet entitled "Information for Contractors." It includes everything from septic-tank specifications to a simple kitchen plan, and covers HUD Minimum Property Standards for such things as counter dimensions and insulating values. Use the booklet before you come up with a design of your own. FmHA is flexible on house plans, and the requirements are not meant to intimidate. I, for example, went for an open floor plan for efficiency and a sense of light and space. Just don't get too idiosyncratic. FmHA does have to make sure that the house is salable if you decide to move.

My house turned out to be one of the rare projects that actually came in completed within the FmHA's nine-month contract and for the allocated amount. As the supervisor said recently, "We'd let you run a job for us any time." —*R.G.*

darker space because of the coziness in front of the stove. As a photographer, I also have an affection for middle grey, the color of this area's board-formed concrete walls.

Upstairs, the office overlooks the solarium, and an 8-ft. wide hallway leads to the bedroom, passing the bathroom and guest nook. I installed a double-glazed patio door in the office's west wall. If I ever add on, access to the new space will be through here.

The guest nook is a recess in the hall's south wall, with a Velux skylight overhead. I use its walls to store books and papers. The bathroom is across the hall. My sink is scavenged, but I gave a lot of thought to its fixtures because I find most bathroom faucets and handles fussy and inefficient. I wanted handles I could work with my wrists or elbows, and a faucet I could get my head under. I wound up with American Standard lever handles and a gooseneck spout—industrial fittings that most stores would have to special-order. I insulated the bathtub by laying Styrofoam around it as we put it in. We also kept all the plumbing on the inside surface of the walls, boxed with a pine pipe chase that resembles the cold-air returns. I can leave the house for days at a time during the winter without worrying about frozen plumbing.

Behind the tub is the bedroom wall. For this partition, I reverted to high-tech and installed translucent glass block. Besides being a look I like, the block wall lets daylight into the bathroom and lets me get away with only a small, triple-glazed window on the exterior (north) wall. The glass block forms the bed's headboard on the other side of the wall, and we installed another Velux window overhead, so I can look at the stars at night. The angle of the bedroom wall creates a sunny sitting area, and the space is bright and cheerful in the morning—a good way to start the day.

Before hanging drywall throughout the house, we installed Therma-Ray radiant electric heating panels in the ceilings of most rooms. Radiant electric heat is reasonably economical, but I've used it primarily to raise the temperature in the darkroom from 55° or 60° to 65° or 70° during the winter. I've rarely needed it in the rest of the house. I do feel that photovoltaics or even wind power may become practical for my location in the not-too-distant future, and if that happened, I would be delighted to hook up to grid-free electric power, flip on the Therma-Rays and cart wood only when I felt like it. My current utility bill ranges between $20 and $30 per month, to cover the use of 300 to 550 kilowatt-hours of electricity.

Right now, no windows in the house have insulating shutters. The glass block has an air-space over 2 in. thick, and the other windows are double-glazed, with additional storm windows on the north, east and west in winter. But a lot of heat leaves the house through the glass on cold nights. I was originally willing to put up with this because I like the broad expanses of glazing, and I didn't want to clutter things up with shutters or shades. I've recently calculated, though, that I could cut my heat loss by as much as 50% with insulated curtains, so I've decided to install them. □

Building a Multi-Purpose Room

Thoughtful details stretch the limits of a small house

by Louaine Collier Elke

Three years ago, the non-profit Ecumenical Association for Housing of San Rafael, California, with the support of the City of Fairfax, sponsored a housing project designed for low- and moderate-income families in Marin County. Nine adjacent lots on a steep site were purchased, and nine low- and moderate-income families worked together to build a house on each lot under the direction of a licensed contractor. Upon completion of the project, each family had the option to buy one of the houses or to be financially compensated for its work.

My husband and I decided, with the enthusiastic support of our three teenagers, to participate in the program. I had a longstanding interest in architectural design, and my husband was experienced in construction. Besides, we both enjoyed working with our hands.

The three-story houses were all basically the same: 1,300 sq. ft., three bedrooms, two baths, with an open floor plan for a prototypical family consisting of a young couple with two small children. The design called for the main living areas and one bedroom to be clustered on the second floor, with the other two bedrooms to be located on the third floor. Though we intended from the beginning to buy one of the houses (and ultimately did), we had doubts about how well our lifestyle would mesh with the floor plan. It was an attractive plan but provided few walls and therefore few private spaces for activi-

ties, such as drawing and sewing, and it provided limited space for storage. A garage would have circumvented some of the problems, but because of the steep slope of the lots, it would have required very expensive retaining walls.

Once we moved into our new house, our short-term solution to the storage problem was to continue to rent public storage space for the things we used seasonally. I also maintained a studio away from home where I did textile-design work and prepared the curriculum for the art class I taught at a local college. But the cost of these amenities strained our budget. The solution we finally devised centered around designing the maximum utility into the minimum amount of space. In the end, we accomplished the work on a small budget, doing the work ourselves in stages and using existing furniture and appliances wherever possible.

Making room—Deed restrictions would not allow us to increase the footprint of the house, and the second and third floors were well used already. That left us with the first-floor entry and utility area as the only places in the house suitable for remodeling. The area measured about 8½ ft. by 11 ft. and encompassed the entry hall, a coat closet and a small room, which housed a washer and dryer behind bi-fold doors (floor plans below). That didn't give us much room to work with, but the laundry

room was flanked by a dead space on the west side and by a sloped crawl space behind the north wall (between the second-story floor and the steep hillside). By shifting the laundry appliances into the dead space, tearing out the coat closet and the interior wall in the hallway and building a storage area into the 9-ft. by 11-ft. crawl space, we would have enough room left for a carefully designed workroom incorporating a sewing and hobby center and an all-important art studio (drawing next page).

Structural concerns—To accomplish the job, we had to contend with three imposing structural elements. First and foremost was a 6x12 Douglas fir beam between the original laundry room and the crawl space (floor plans below). A 2x4 stud wall bearing on the beam supported the second-story floor joists. Instead of tinkering with the existing framing, we left the beam and the wall in place and designed around them. We decided to install a pair of full-extension drawers below the beam which would open into the new work space, and to frame the lower floor of the storage area behind the beam, flush with the top of the beam.

The other complicating structural elements were a pair of sloping grade beams on either end of the 6x12 which would encroach upon the new work and laundry areas. Our solution to that problem was to box in the ex-

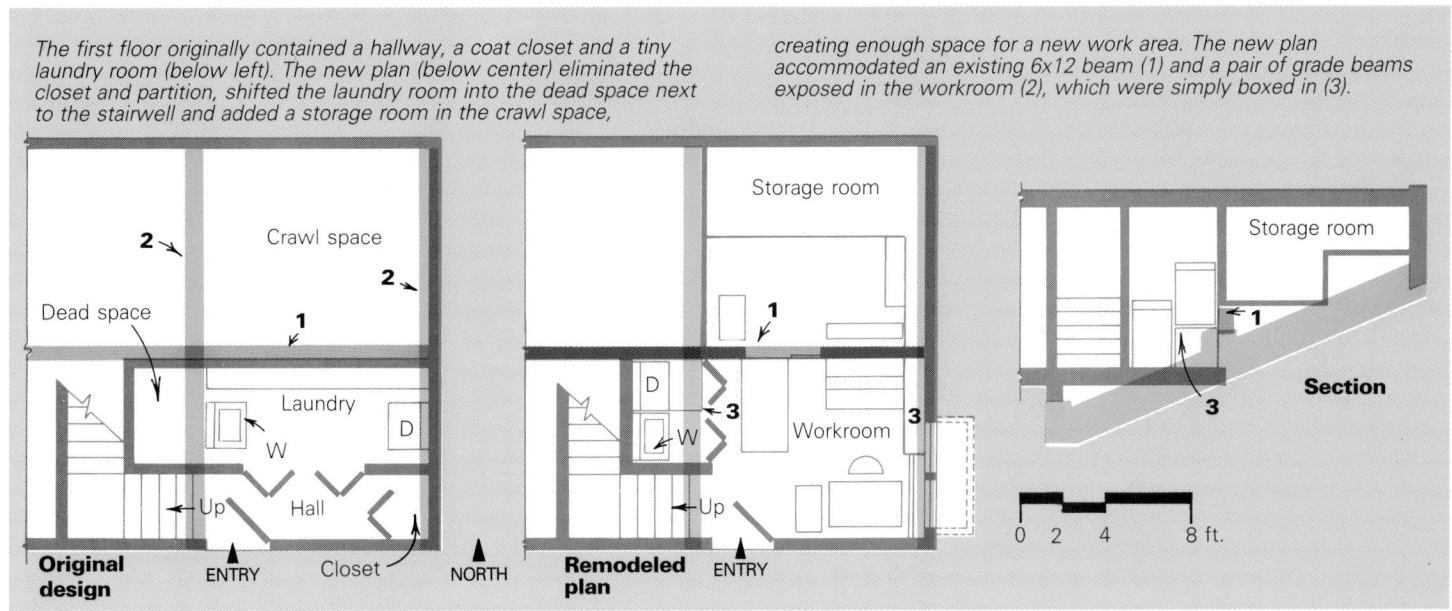

The first floor originally contained a hallway, a coat closet and a tiny laundry room (below left). The new plan (below center) eliminated the closet and partition, shifted the laundry room into the dead space next to the stairwell and added a storage room in the crawl space, creating enough space for a new work area. The new plan accommodated an existing 6x12 beam (1) and a pair of grade beams exposed in the workroom (2), which were simply boxed in (3).

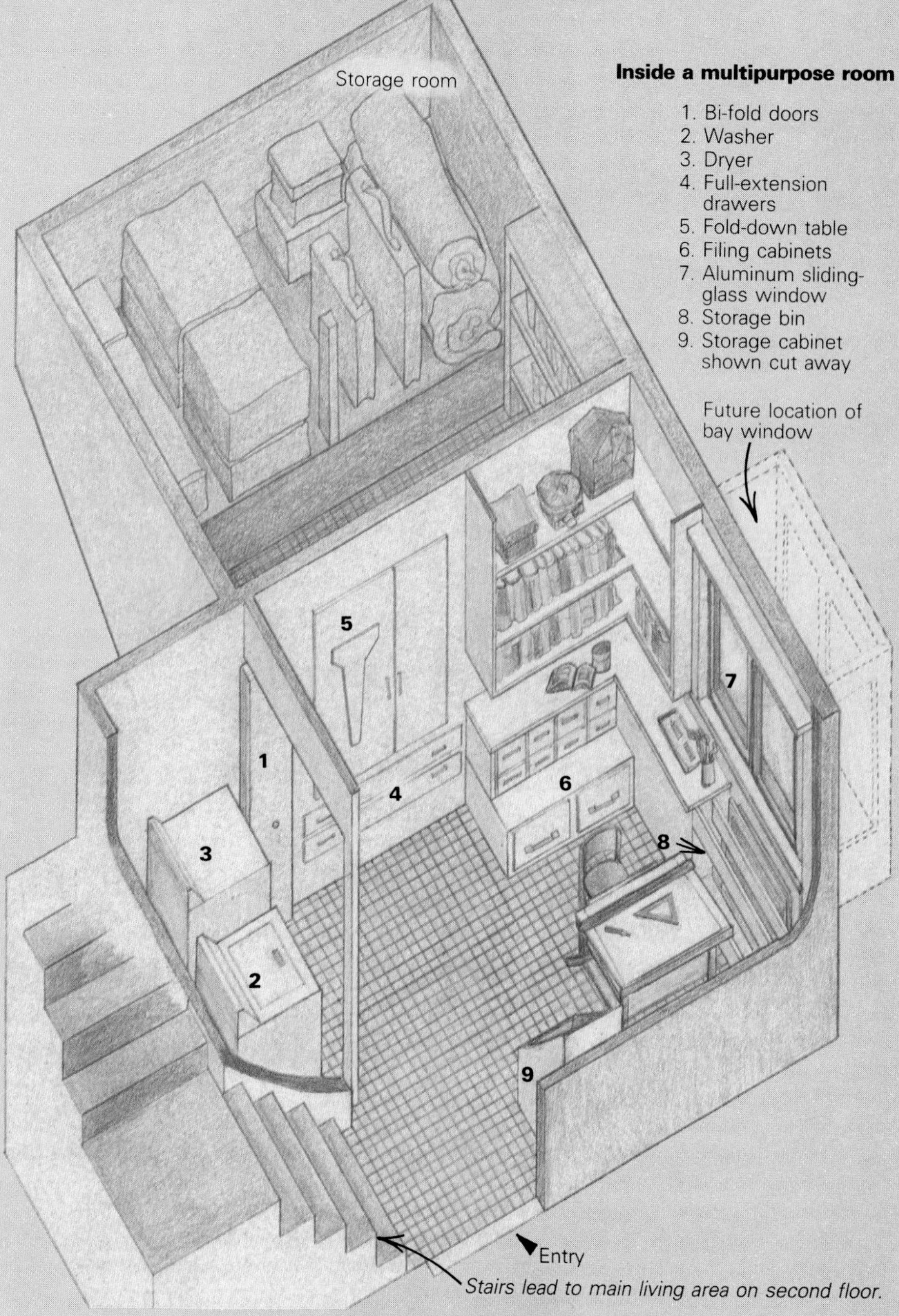

Inside a multipurpose room

Storage room

1. Bi-fold doors
2. Washer
3. Dryer
4. Full-extension drawers
5. Fold-down table
6. Filing cabinets
7. Aluminum sliding-glass window
8. Storage bin
9. Storage cabinet shown cut away

Future location of bay window

Entry

Stairs lead to main living area on second floor.

Drawing by author

posed portions of the grade beams. The boxed-in beam in the laundry room would support the clothes dryer while the one in the work space would serve as a shelf for a radio and other items.

The laundry alcove—The new laundry area, which is along the west wall, measures a scant 54 in. wide by 44 in. deep. The boxed-in grade beam and dryer occupy the right half and a compact Whirlpool Design 2000 washer sits on the floor to the left of the dryer (photo facing page, left). Standard size appliances wouldn't have fit into this space. Fortunately, our existing dryer was 27 in. wide instead of the standard 29 in. wide, and the new full-capacity Whirlpool washer we bought is 24 in. wide to fit into narrow spaces like this one. A stacked washer and dryer would have been a good solution for this small alcove, but our old dryer was still in good shape. The controls are on top, but the shortest member of our family is 5-ft. 6 in. tall, so this elevated dryer has worked out for us.

Above the washer, we installed a rod for hanging clothing and put in a shelf for laundry products. A Closet Maid vinyl-covered steel shelf (Clairson, Int'l., 720 S. W. 17th St., Ocala, Fla. 32674) hangs above the dryer for our two laundry baskets. We used this grate-like shelving so it wouldn't interfere with ventilation, which is handled by a fan in the ceiling. When the laundry appliances aren't being used, they hide behind a pair of bi-fold doors.

Split-level storage—The split-level design of the storage area allowed us to extend it clear to the back wall of the house. Both levels of the storage room are supported with vertical 2x4s hanging from the second-story floor joists. The finished flooring is 1x6 Douglas fir, which was easier to install than plywood in this confined area. A simple pull-chain fixture lights the area.

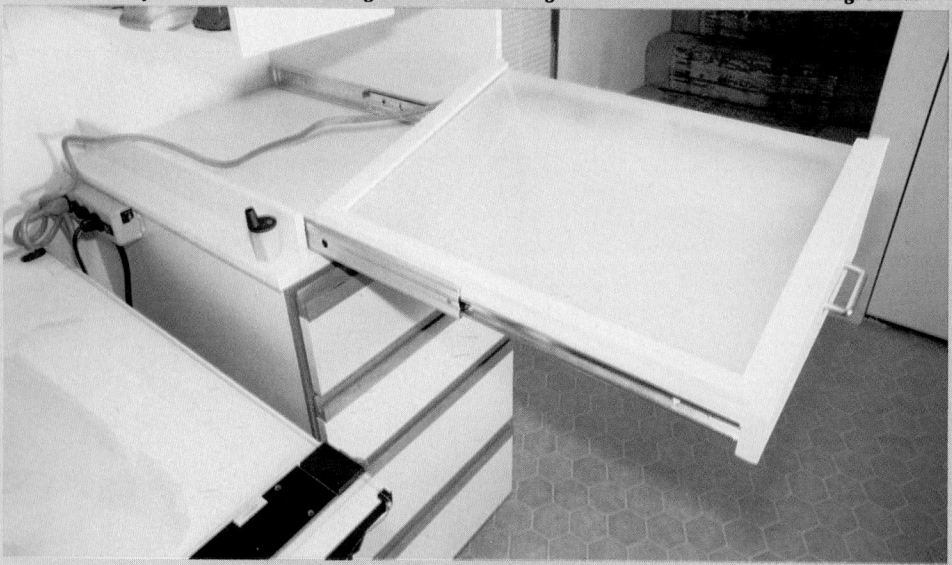

The light box (photo below) sits atop a commercially manufactured base cabinet located just inside the main entry. In use, the light box slides out beyond the face of the cabinet on a pair of full-extension drawer slides; the slides are fixed to a pair of cleats screwed to the cabinet top. The main entry and the stairs leading to the main living areas are visible in the background.

The top drawer of a base cabinet houses a handy fold-out ironing board (photo below). Directly above the cabinet, a built-in storage unit combines bookshelves with storage for art supplies. To the left is the drafting table.

The oversize access doors for the storage area are more than their appearance suggests. The door on the right is hinged at one side and swings out of the way conventionally. The door on the left, however, is hinged at the bottom and drops forward to serve as a sewing and design/layout table (photo below center). Support is provided by a single fold-out leg hinged to the front of the door. Because it's necessary to scale the 6x12 beam to gain entry to the storage area, a small stepladder is tucked just inside the right-hand door.

The size and placement of the fold-out table was critical. The design allows me to sit at the right-hand side of the table while someone else uses either the drafting and study area behind me or the laundry area to the left of the table.

Behind the fold-down door, we hinged an old three-drawer dresser to use as a sewing cabinet (photo below center). The top drawers are used to store patterns, yardage and mending projects. We discarded the bottom drawer, leaving a cavity big enough to house the sewing machine and related attachments. When we need to pack large items into or out of the storage area, we unlock the slide bolt on the side of the cabinet which engages a hole drilled in the floor, and swing the cabinet back into the storage area and out of the way (photo below right). Behind the right-hand door, we mounted a small rack on the trimmer stud to hold spools of thread.

Under the 6x12 beam are two wide, shallow, drawers. The drawers slide out on metal tracks that allow them to be fully opened. The drawers are usable even when the table is down. The plywood drawer cabinet hangs from the storage-area floor joists. We used side-mounted, full-extension, 90-lb. capacity Grant drawer slides (Grant Hardware Co., High Street, West Nyack, N. Y. 10994). I use the drawers to store my large-sized art papers, which is a big improvement over storing them in suit boxes under the bed as I did in the past.

The northeast corner of the workroom is occupied by an old wooden filing cabinet, a card-filing cabinet and the other boxed-in grade beam, with an L-shaped bookcase above (drawing facing page). The small drawers of the card-filing cabinet are fitted with solid wood bottoms in place of the slotted wood bottoms typical of old card files. The drawers are great for housing art materials, such as tubes of paint, pencils and small jars of adhesives. As with almost everything in the room, the filing cabinet is painted an off-white to unify it visually with other built-ins and furniture as well as to furnish the maximum reflected light to the room. The hanging bookcase is built of ¾-in. fir plywood, and all exposed plywood edges are faced with ¼-in. by ¾-in. screen molding. Adjacent to the boxed-in beam on the east wall is a bin for vertical storage of portfolios and picture-framing materials.

Originally, we had hoped to install a bay window in the east wall, which would extend out 2 ft. to make the room look bigger and to allow me to have a window garden (drawing facing page). But due to the expense of bay windows, we decided instead to install a 4-ft. high by 5-ft. wide double-glazed aluminum sliding window and to replace it with a bay window later. Louvered shades are installed over the window and over the main-entry door.

My drafting table sits in the southeast corner of the room, complete with a shelf underneath to hold tracing paper and project references (photo facing page). On the wall above and behind the drafting table is a cork board for pin-up references, reminders and visual favorites to personalize my work area.

Ironing board in a drawer—Between the drafting table and the front entry, we installed a commercially manufactured four-drawer kitchen cabinet and built a wall-mounted storage unit directly above it. The side of each that's nearest the entry is covered by a continuous sheet of ¾-in. plywood.

The top drawer of the base cabinet (photo facing page) contains a Swedish fold-out ironing board (distributed by Water, Inc., 129 Arena Street, El Segundo, Calif. 90245-1227). There are several small ironing boards of this type on the market, but of those we evaluated, we liked this one best. The light-duty board works well for ironing our laundry and is handy for my sewing projects as well. The remaining three drawers are filled with drafting equipment and art supplies.

The wall-hung cabinet above consists of two book shelves on the left side facing the drafting table, and a vertical opening in front for storing drawing tubes and mounted presentations. Beneath the upper cabinet, a light box sits on top of the base cabinet (photo facing page, left). When needed, the light box slides out beyond the front surface of the cabinet on a pair of full-extension drawer slides screwed to a pair of wooden runners.

The relationship of the storage unit to the rest of the work area is as important as the unit's function. In order for me to work efficiently, I need to avoid a sense of crowding or cramped space. The cabinet was placed 11 in. to the left of the door to provide comfortable entry into the house. This placement also allowed the ironing board to be used either by itself or in concert with the sewing table. The 80-in. high cabinet also provides some degree of privacy from people entering and leaving the house via the stairway to the second floor. Alternately, it keeps my work on the drafting table from serving as the first impression for our visitors. □

Louaine Collier Elke is a textile designer and a teacher at the College of Marin. She lives in Fairfax, California.

The washer and dryer (which sits on a boxed-in grade beam) are designed to fit into tight spaces like this one. A ceiling fan, assisted by grated shelving, provides the ventilation. Bifold doors conceal the laundry alcove.

The left-hand door to the storage area is hinged at the bottom and swings down to become a work table (photo below left). A single leg hinged to the front of the door provides support. Once both storage-room doors are open, entry is gained by pivoting the hinged dresser behind them back into the storage room (photo below right). A stepladder is stored to the right of the dresser.

Mandating Energy Efficiency

This test home gets high marks from both owner and builder

by Gerry Copeland

In early 1984 I was selected by the Washington State Energy Office to design and build one of 228 houses conforming to the new Model Conservation Standards (MCS). These standards were developed by the Northwest Power Planning Council, operating under a 1980 act of Congress, to promote energy-efficient construction. The house I built was part of a test to see if these standards were cost effective and if the expectations of energy savings could be met. At that time, the Northwest Power Planning Council was pushing to have the Model Conservation Standards written into the building codes. This movement was opposed by the home-building associations in the state, who were afraid that the increased cost of building to these standards would hurt the home-buying market.

Since I've been a local proponent of passive-solar, energy-efficient design and construction, I was very receptive to the MCS guidelines. These standards seemed to coincide with what I'd been learning through my own experience. So I built a 1,250-sq. ft. house for Bill Hewes near Colville, Wash., following the MCS guidelines. The house (photo above) has been occupied, and its energy performance monitored, since December 1984.

Solar construction in the Northwest—Before my involvement with the MCS program, I was designing and building solar houses. I carefully calculated each house's heat loss and balanced the equations with the proper-sized glass

This electrically heated 1,250-sq. ft. house was built as part of a program to test standards for energy-efficient construction in the Northwest. Total heating costs for the first full year of occupancy were $131.

area, heat mass and insulating shades. My figures and formulas came from books by Edward Mazria, David Wright, the U. S. Dept. of Energy and others. But the energy performance of the houses didn't meet the design expectations.

For instance, one all-out solar design with much south-facing glass was uncomfortably bright on sunny days and noticeably colder when the sun wasn't around. Insulating window shades weren't installed because of their untraditional appearance and their expense—hard to swallow at a project's finish. Another house, an earth-sheltered solar design—dubbed "passive lunar" by the owner because the moon's light extended as far into the house as the sun's—had uncomfortably cold floors, and the owner was never home to operate the shades.

I questioned whether these solar-gain strategies were cost effective. Of course, compared to the standard 2x6-framed energy-efficient homes built in the area, both of the above homes perform quite well, because of the extra insulation, high-quality windows and doors, and other features of their construction.

The energy performance of these homes fell short of my calculations for several reasons. Here in northeast Washington, there isn't much

sunshine in November, December and January. This is a cold, 7,400 degree-day area, and in December, there are only 279 Btu/day/sq. ft. of sunshine, compared to 1,041 Btu/day/sq. ft. in Phoenix, Ariz. In itself, this figure is low enough to be significant, but because of the mountainous terrain, microclimates can occur here that reduce the incoming sunshine even more.

Other factors that undermined my calculations were inconsistencies in the owner operation of the insulating window shades and the mechanical systems controls, maintenance of weatherstripping and so on. Even if the home owners have high energy-conservation ethics, they might be away from home for twelve hours at a time, or even for a number of days.

So after my experiences with solar energy, I welcomed the MCS design principles—less glass, more insulation, a near-perfect air/vapor barrier (.1 air changes per hour), an air-to-air heat exchanger, higher-quality windows and doors, and more meticulous workmanship. One element of the MCS approach that impressed me was the interrelationship of all the design elements. This allows trade-offs between south orientation, thickness of insulation and amount of glass. It's a very sophisticated approach that allows considerable design freedom.

A plywood vapor barrier—The Hewes house is built over a crawl space with typical foundation and floor-framing details. But for the subfloor, we glued and nailed ¾-in. T&G plywood

From *Fine Homebuilding* magazine (October 1987) 43:60-63

over the floor joists, with adjoining ends glued to a common joist. All the T&G edges were caulked with Tremco Acoustical Sealant (Tremco Inc., 10701 Shaker Blvd., Cleveland, Ohio 44104) before we shoved them together. It's a very sticky black caulk that remains flexible over time, ensuring an airtight joint. But it must be applied in just the right amount in the right place, or it eventually gets all over you. Plywood sheathing with joints sealed this way is a very effective vapor barrier.

After covering the ground in the crawl space with a layer of black 6-mil poly, we installed 10-in. fiberglass batts (R-30) between the floor joists, held in place with insulation rods. These are simply short lengths of stiff wire, sized for either 16-in. o. c. or 24-in. o. c. layouts. When flexed slightly, they will fit between joists or rafters, bite into the wood and hold insulation in place. Then we stapled Tyvek housewrap across the undersides of the joists, with all joints overlapped 18 in. and double stapled.

Double walls—A dominant strategy of the Hewes house design is the 10-in. thick exterior wall construction. In order to have enough insulation for a high R-value and to install an unpenetrated vapor barrier, I chose to build double walls: 2x6s at 24 in. o. c. outside and horizontal 2x4s at 24 in. o. c. inside, with a 6-mil polyethylene vapor barrier between them (photo above). This fairly simple system allows the outer wall and sheathing to "breathe" and the inner wall to

The dominant feature of the Hewes house is the 10-in. thick exterior wall construction. It is a double wall with a continuous vapor barrier run in between. Interior wall framing runs horizontally for extra strength and easier plumbing and wiring.

act as the raceway for electrical and plumbing. It eliminates the need, as in other techniques, for gaskets and caulking at all penetrations of the vapor barrier. However, subsequent programs promoting MCS encourage the use of the Airtight Drywall Approach (ADA)—an easier and more cost-effective way to do the vapor barrier (for more on ADA, see *FHB* #37, pp. 62-65).

We framed the exterior walls using "advanced framing techniques," which eliminate superfluous framing members—backing for partitions, double headers, cripples, etc. (Note: Although structurally sound, these framing techniques are not universally accepted, so check with your local building inspector before using them.) We laid out the 2x6 wall at 24 in. o. c. with roof trusses lined up directly over each stud. This alignment was critical because we used a single top plate. At all corners and butt joints of the top plate, we pounded in 5-in. by 9-in. truss connector plates.

Exterior corners were framed with just two studs, one at the end of each wall, so that the insulation could run to the outermost stud. We also eliminated backerboards for partition walls, again permitting full insulation along the exteri-

or. Corner clips were used later to hang drywall in these areas.

For exterior-wall headers, we used one 2x10 let into the side studs with no cripple or trimmer studs. For openings up to 5 ft. wide, one 2x10 was sufficient. We used two 2x10s nailed together for bigger openings (5 ft. to 10 ft.) and filled the remaining space with high-R foam insulation. We used unfaced fiberglass batts (R-19) for the exterior wall insulation, and were careful to fit them snugly between studs.

We used 24-in. deep parallel-chord trusses for the roof, which gave us a cathedral ceiling over the main living area (photo, p. 131) and left space for the R-50 blown-in cellulose. It also left space above the insulation for ventilation between the soffit and ridge vents, as well as room for the insulation installer to crawl through the truss spaces. We extended the plywood sheathing up to cover the ends of the trusses and keep the insulation from pouring into the soffit.

The 6-mil polyethylene vapor barrier was run with an extra 6 in. left on the floor at the base of the wall. Later, just before the interior-wall base plate was nailed down over it, this flap was sealed to the floor with acoustical caulk. At the top, we left an extra 12 in. to be sealed to the ceiling vapor barrier. All sheeting joints were overlapped, caulked and stapled to solid backing if possible.

For the interior wall, we installed horizontal 2x4s on edge 24 in. o. c., and we took care to ensure that the spacing would be right for the drywall. Running these 2x4s horizontally made it easier to run plumbing and wiring and also strengthened the wall. Except for the bottom plate, which was nailed directly to the floor, the 2x4s were nailed to the 2x6 studs with 5½-in. barn nails. We used short boards as spacers to hold the 2x4s in place while we drilled through them edgewise to accept the big nails. Whenever a hammer blow missed and punctured the vapor barrier, the hole had to be patched with an oversized piece of polyethylene caulked to the surrounding sheet.

The interior wall was also insulated, but unfaced batts wouldn't stay in place. So we used R-11 fiberglass batts faced with kraft paper and stapled them in place. These were carefully fitted around all electrical and plumbing obstacles.

The MCS approach required a separate piece of polyethylene lining around the inside face of window and door openings. When the window or door was installed, the lining was sealed with acoustical caulk and stapled to the frame, then turned back on the inside of the opening and tacked down over a bead of caulk to the vapor barrier around the rough opening.

Because of the 24-in. o. c. framing, we used ⅝-in. drywall for a stiffer wall surface. At the inside corners of the exterior walls, and where partition walls met the exterior walls, we used corner clips to hold the drywall. Using these clips slowed down the installation process a bit, but the extra insulation and the savings on lumber were worth it.

When we installed the drywall on the ceiling, we had to be especially careful of puncturing the vapor barrier. We did, of course, make several holes and had to patch them with a piece of poly and the ubiquitous acoustical caulk.

The ceiling insulation was blown carefully into the truss spaces to get a uniform thickness and fill all voids around the truss members, ducts and pipes. We made sure it was full depth over the exterior wall plates. With loose insulation installed on an angle, there was some concern that it would slump toward the bottom. But a recent inspection showed no such problems.

The heat exchanger—We installed the air-to-air heat exchanger inside the vapor barrier, so that only the exhaust and intake ducts penetrate the vapor barrier. We used a Star model 100-B, 150 cfm capacity (Star Heat Exchanger Corp., B-109 1772 Broadway St., Port Coquitlam, B. C., Canada V3C 2M8) and put it in the quasi-attic space over the hall. This location gave it easy access to all rooms. The laundry, bathroom, kitchen and hall have stale-air return ducts. The bedrooms, bathroom and living room have fresh-air supply ducts. The fresh-air intake is located in the south-side soffit. The exhaust-air vent is in

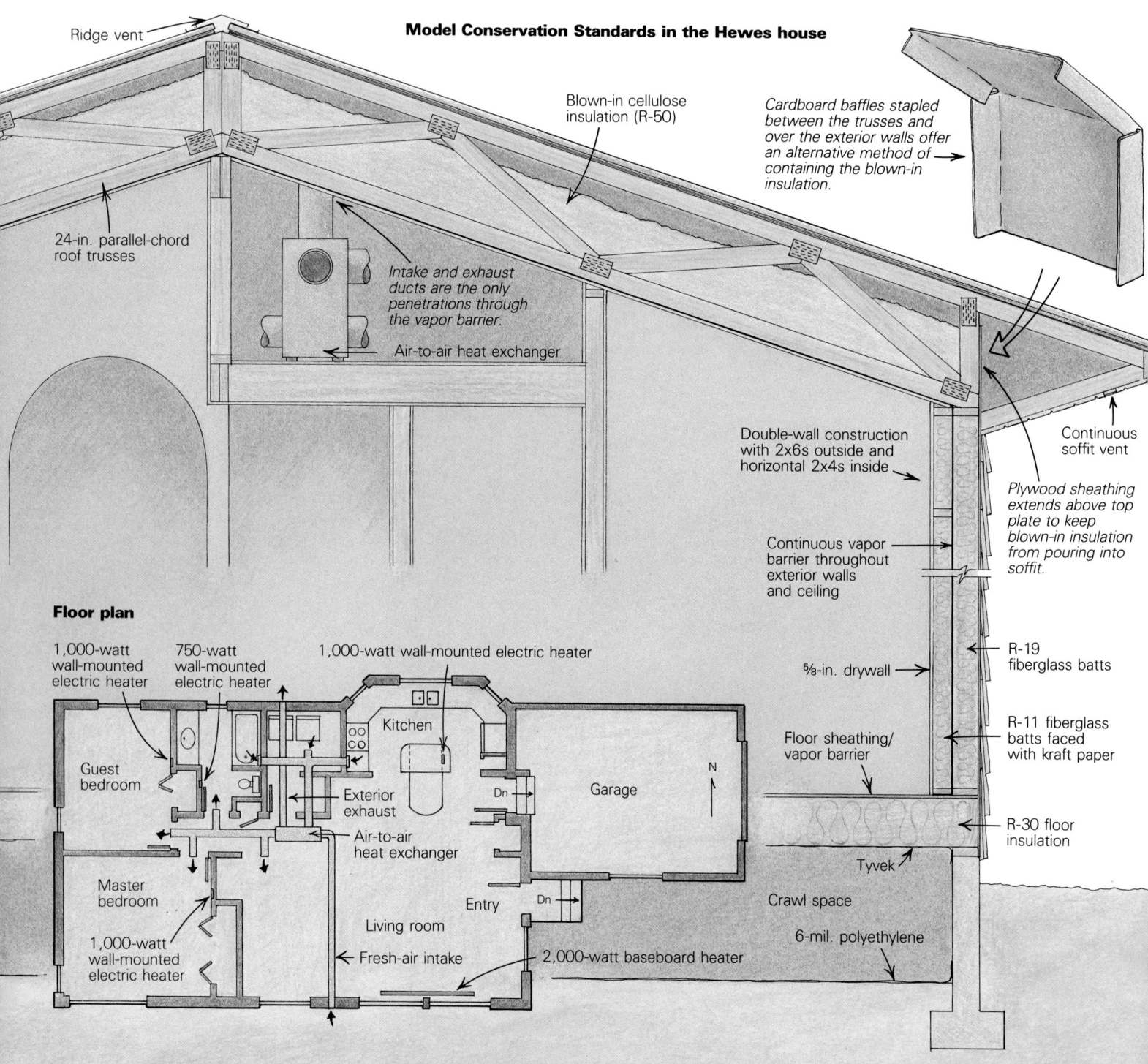

Model Conservation Standards in the Hewes house

Ridge vent

Blown-in cellulose insulation (R-50)

Cardboard baffles stapled between the trusses and over the exterior walls offer an alternative method of containing the blown-in insulation.

24-in. parallel-chord roof trusses

Intake and exhaust ducts are the only penetrations through the vapor barrier.

Air-to-air heat exchanger

Double-wall construction with 2x6s outside and horizontal 2x4s inside

Continuous soffit vent

Plywood sheathing extends above top plate to keep blown-in insulation from pouring into soffit.

Continuous vapor barrier throughout exterior walls and ceiling

⅝-in. drywall

R-19 fiberglass batts

R-11 fiberglass batts faced with kraft paper

Floor sheathing/ vapor barrier

R-30 floor insulation

Tyvek

Floor plan

1,000-watt wall-mounted electric heater

750-watt wall-mounted electric heater

1,000-watt wall-mounted electric heater

Kitchen

Guest bedroom

Exterior exhaust

Air-to-air heat exchanger

Dn

Garage

N

Master bedroom

1,000-watt wall-mounted electric heater

Entry

Living room

Fresh-air intake

Dn

2,000-watt baseboard heater

Crawl space

6-mil. polyethylene

Surprisingly bright and cheery for a superinsulated building, the Hewes house is also especially quiet, which as far as the owner is concerned, justifies the airtight construction and the air-to-air heat exchanger.

the north-side soffit. To reduce noise, we mounted the unit on rubber cushions and used insulated ducts. A humidistat, installed next to the thermostat, turns the exchanger on high speed if humidity exceeds 60%.

Where the heat-exchanger ducts penetrated the vapor barrier, we sealed an extra piece of poly to the vapor barrier and to the duct as a flange. To make things easier, we put blocking around the duct to support the poly so we could seal the flange to it (see *FHB* #9, pp. 56-59).

The house retains its heat so well that a few baseboard units (5,750 watts total), along with the air-to-air heat exchanger, provide enough heat and air circulation without the cost of a furnace and ductwork.

The electricity used by the baseboard units in the Hewes house is metered separately from other uses, and the average interior temperature is recorded daily by an automatic device (photo at right). Along with the owners of other test houses, Hewes fills out a data card every week and mails it to an engineering firm that's collating the test results.

Economics—The cost of building the Hewes house to the Model Conservation Standards was about $3/sq. ft. more than normal construction costs for a well-built house in this area. This is probably the minimum to expect, since the Hewes house was a small, simple design.

In northeastern Washington, the electric rates are low—only 3.7 cents per kilowatt hour. After the first year of occupancy, Hewes reported electric usage for the baseboard units of 3,539 kilowatt hours, which amounted to $131, while maintaining an inside temperature of 70°F.

Based on industry predictions for the future, it should take about seven years before the savings in heating costs will surpass the principal

and interest payments on the initial expense of building to Model Conservation Standards. From then on it only gets better, especially when considering the increased resale value of the home. At the higher electric rates of the Northeast, the savings from such a house would pass the principal and interest payments much faster.

The MCS debate—Over the past three years, the data from these test homes have been questioned. This was not a strictly controlled experiment. The construction methods were new, and

All of the MCS houses have special electronic devices so that their owners can monitor temperature readings and energy use. This information is recorded on a data card and mailed each week to an engineering firm.

the builders involved had different levels of experience and skill. The most controversial measures, relative to cost effectiveness, are the airtight construction (i.e., the continuous vapor barrier) and the air-to-air heat exchanger.

Circumstances have changed dramatically in the four years since the Model Conservation Standards were written. Dropping oil prices have cut out-of-state revenues for Washington power plants. Where three years ago utility companies in the state were pushing for energy conservation, one local utility was recently offering rebates to home owners on the purchase and installation of hot tubs.

Acknowledging these new circumstances, the final 1987 MCS standards have been lowered in order to be more easily accepted by the area's building-code officials and to avoid some of the cost-effectiveness arguments. The final standards, in the eastern Washington area, are R-38 ceiling, R-24 walls, R-30 floors and an air-infiltration rate of .35 air changes per hour. These result in an electrical use of 4.5 kWhr/sq. ft. The Hewes house, with more insulation and an air-infiltration rate of .1 air changes per hour, results in a use of 2.83 kWhr/sq. ft. This is 37% more efficient than the latest MCS standards.

But while the controversy continues to rage over these issues, Bill Hewes is quite happy with his tight little house. Besides the low heating costs, it's also very quiet. Outside noises can't easily penetrate the double walls, truss-roof construction, triple glazing, ⅝-in. drywall and all that insulation. The air is clean, not too humid, and can easily be freshened up without losing heat simply by dialing up the rate of flow on the air-to-air heat exchanger. □

Gerry Copeland is an architect/builder in Spokane, Wash.

Skidompha House
A small home and studio built without blueprints

by David Sellers

In the summer of 1974, I got a call from silversmith Nancy Barrett, who wanted me to design a house for her in Maine. She wanted a small combination house and studio that wouldn't require a well, septic system, heating system or electrical lines. She wanted to build it herself, didn't want a mortgage or any of the standard utility bills, and had $9,000 to spend. I told her it was impossible. She laughed and asked if that meant I wasn't interested.

In 1974 the oil embargo had just hit, passive solar hadn't yet caught on, *Popular Science* was featuring articles on windmills from Australia, and Sellers & Co. was in its eighth year of design-build. As an example of the kind of thing we'd been doing, our crew that summer had built a house in Topeka, Kans., with the nation's first Clivus Multrum, a homemade, active-solar collector, a cistern and a greenhouse. Nancy's project seemed like a real challenge, so I visited the site and agreed to help. This was the agreement: there would be no design fee because there was no money. We would design the house on the site, and we would also take the framing contract for $6,000, including materials. Nancy would supply all the clams, lobsters and pies the crew could eat while we were building.

The seed—Nancy wanted an idea of what the house would look like in advance. Not an outrageous request, but there was no money for design time. This was when the "seed" idea came up. I feel that with creative people on the job site there doesn't need to be much in the way of instructions, drawings and plans. What there needs to be is a seminal idea that anyone can use as a guide for solutions to whatever problems come up. It would be like a DNA molecule of the final house. I decided not to design the house at all but to design the seed instead. All I needed to do was establish the core structural concept and locate major elements like the entrance, stairs and kitchen; the specifics would spill out as we went.

I cut some scaled-down lumber and made a model of the simple idea that eventually became Nancy's house (photo bottom right). The model took half a day. There were no drawings. I sent a Polaroid to Nancy, who approved the design and signed us on.

I had recently started North Wind Power Company, and knew quite a bit about wind generators. I felt that the integration of a windmill in a house deserved some attention.

With no money in the budget for design time, David Sellers quickly built a small model (above) for his client's approval. It was used during some of the framing, but was destroyed before most of the house (top) went up. Sellers feels that once the general idea of a house is established, creative builders can work out the details as they go.

It had to be up above the trees and open to the prevailing winds off the ocean. This seemed to be a perfect place for a vertical axis windmill. Although it would take years for the technology to catch up to the point where it could supply proper hardware, we made the place where it would eventually go.

The seed began to take on the form of a tower with a triangular lookout top (Nancy wanted to be able to see the ocean), and three extended braces, or buttresses (photo facing page, right). These braces are large triangular stress-skin panels, anchored to the tower at the center of the house and to three separate, remote concrete foundations. Two buttresses would enclose the greenhouse, and the third would become a fire stair.

The idea was that there would be an apartment on the ground floor with a three-story open space entirely covered by skylights. The silversmith's studio would fit on the second floor, overlooking the first, with an extra bedroom on the third floor, a guest room on the fourth, the windmill on the fifth, and a roof deck on top. This was about as far as it went before construction.

Building without blueprints—Six of us left Vermont at midnight for the six-hour drive to the coast of Maine. I was the only one who had seen the property. Lumber was to arrive at 7 a.m., along with the backhoe. The concrete was scheduled for 11. We arrived at 6 a.m., dug the holes, made the forms, poured the concrete and set up camp on the first day.

I have a theory that the kindest little old lady in town makes the best pies, and that she probably works in the library. So during our work break, I went to the town library in Damariscotta, put my theory to the test, and walked out having placed an order for two homemade pies delivered to the site every day for that week. The library was called the Skidompha Library after the local Indians. We adopted the name for the house, and made Skidompha T-shirts. Nancy arranged for lobsters, clams and scallops straight off the boat every day, as well as corn on the cob and barrels of melted butter.

The next day we began building the seed—the tower with the braces—using the model as a guide. At the end of the second day, a load of lumber fell on the model, and we had nothing but the real thing thereafter.

We broke into three crews of two. The first

From the top of the house, you can look straight down through acrylic glazing into the main living space (top). To get to the observation deck, you have to pass through a plywood door on the third floor (above right), and climb a ladder. One kitchen wall is a large, curved acrylic window (above left). Much of the glazing in the house has leaked. In 1974, installation details for Plexiglas hadn't been worked out, and much of the hardware that is now common wasn't available. The sheet-metal flashing here is a stopgap until the window's installation detailing can be changed.

The seed plan for the house called for a tower with braces to support a vertical-axis windmill. The braces took the form of plywood box beams, one of which was also put to use as an outside stairway. The wave-pattern door was bandsawn from scraps. The interior stairs curl up in the extension under the curved skylight.

crew framed up the rest of the tower, the buttresses and the walls; the second crew sheathed; and the third crew followed up closing in windows, putting up stairs, and so forth. All six of us would meet at intersections of walls, beams and columns to solve whatever problems existed. We used the structure, the site and our materials to guide the solution. If a problem was difficult, we let rafters, beams and other structural members hang out wild into space to guide the solution. Six days and 100 lobsters later, we were finished.

The stairs were an interesting design problem, which wasn't figured out in advance, of course. We looked at the walls we had framed up for the tower and buttress, and figured the stair would go somewhere in the corner. Instead, it began to emerge as an outgrowth—as a volume chubbing up around the door. Since the stair didn't seem to want a top, we made Plexiglas skylights to cover it. This design solution would have been impossible to draw up—even after we built it. It was very simple and direct if you were there, hammer in hand.

Nancy wanted the front door to be solid looking to discourage intruders. To make the door on site, we used scraps of framing lumber cut on the bandsaw to resemble the nose of a floor sander. The resulting undulations somehow related to the ocean waves.

The triangular windows were lots of fun. Twice as we went up with the framing, we left large triangular holes for windows. These were covered in two different ways. One was a fly's eye dome of triangles framed up on the spot using the 48-in. maximum size of Plexiglas as the only limitation. The other was a double triangle. Here, with an 8-ft. by 8-ft. square of Plexiglas cut on the diagonal, we designed a slight 6-in. bow to strengthen the pieces. They were each partial cones and became very rigid. This was another design solution that would have been impossible to imagine, let alone draw up beforehand.

An ongoing project—Nancy's house was built for remarkably little money, at a time when some of the technologies we used were

From *Fine Homebuilding* magazine (October 1983) 17:76-79

The Skidompha house (facing page) looms out of the woods near the Maine coast. One of Nancy Barrett's requirements was that she be able to see the ocean from it. From the deck at the top of the house (right), she can.

in their infancy. These two factors have resulted in some problems. The first one is storage, one of Nancy's primary requirements. With a small house, the interior spaces eventually must be adjusted to store the accumulations of a lifetime. Storage has to fit the space—Nancy will have to build hers under stairs and in balconies and work areas—but beyond these constraints, it's simply a matter of cash.

Another problem, also related to lack of funds, is that the south-facing glazing has no thermal shutters or shades. The rest of the house is well insulated, but it gets awfully cold in the winter, and it overheats in summer. Movable insulation and louvers would take care of this.

The skylight system is the third major problem. It leaks. In 1974, the details for using acrylic in this application hadn't been worked out, and the hardware we use today (see "Acrylic Glazing," *FHB* #10) simply wasn't available. We were, frankly, experimenting. Over the years, we've been back several times for short visits to give Nancy a hand on finish, improvements and more lobsters. One session we almost lost the whole deal. Nancy called saying the skylights were leaking. Three of us went up and looked over the situation. The skylights had leaked so badly that Nancy was living in a tent in the living room. It was a nice day, so we removed all the skylights to install an improved detail while Nancy went out for lobsters.

Before we had a chance to put the roof of skylights back on, a heavy rainstorm came through, soaking everything. We had no choice but to work through it to close in the roof. Nancy came back in horror to find her house open to the sky, rain pouring in and three naked men scrambling to put the skylights back on. She left the lobsters, mentioned something about being at the local bar and drove away. When she returned, late that night, the skylights were on, a roaring fire in the stove was drying the place out, and everything was okay.

Choosing to go with something in its early stages of development requires taking the long view. Do I get a computer now and get in on the ground floor, or do I wait until they are cheaper and better next year? Nancy likes to experiment, and she likes the process, so she went for the early computer. The difficulties have been undeniable, but, as she says, the pluses outweigh the minuses.

The architect as craftsman—This project was my chance to check my theory on the architectural profession and its directions. I feel that the architect was wrong when he left the construction site and established the system in which the contractor does the work based on set drawings, thereby eliminating on-site

innovation, individuality and, finally, high-quality craftsmanship.

Today, contemporary residential architecture (and most other architecture as well) is an embarrassment to the craftsman, enormously costly to the client, and a compromise to the architect, who is removed from the construction itself and is at the mercy of cost and bids. I believe that, given a good crew of interested craftsmen, economical, sensible and delightful solutions to problems can be evolved on the site with common tools, materials and good sense—better and more appropriate solutions than those drawn up before the fact, in the office.

When you look at the great buildings of the past with the amazing windows, beautiful roof shapes and spectacular beam connections, you have to wonder if most of it wasn't evolved while standing in the middle of it. When you see the full-scale set of relationships in front of you—as we did when we stood in Nancy Barrett's living room looking at the hole in the wall where the stair was to go—the real choices shout at you. Those which on paper may seem worthy of attention are pale compared to the rich possibilities presented by the hole in the wall, the board in your hand and the tools available.

Once a structure is started, it begins to speak. It's like a big cauldron of soup. If you can overcome your preconceived notions of what it should taste like and respond to what it is, the richness of subtleties reaches out and asks for recognition. Chartres Cathedral is a great example. The central idea is a strong, powerful image. It's strong enough to accommodate the variations and subthemes seen and felt by the craftsmen, whose focus became one of a long vision (the DNA of the cathedral) elaborated on and clarified by the freedom of the short vision (the specific craft). This is the joy of building. You don't need the blueprints. This is why people are attracted to remodeling old barns. The theme is so strong and the structure so clever that sympathetic options for alterations abound.

Building like this is more a process of discovery and invention than of controlled composition. When you are standing in the middle of a pile of materials with the responsibility of turning them into something, all your juices flow and you can feel the power of ideas calling. When there is a clear idea—call it the DNA—when all the parts relate to the whole, it becomes magic. The whoopee of inspiration shows up in the chisel mark or embellished corner. These become the memory and fantasy catalysts. You're sitting reading a book, your eye drifts to the edge of the wall and off goes your mind to some great dream.

The craftsman was kicked off the construction site between 1920 and 1935 as the architect went into his office. We've gone on a 50-year excursion and are coming back. The value is too great, the joy too irresistible. A new era of master builder and craftsman is returning. It's going to be spectacular. □

David Sellers lives in Warren, Vt.

Living in an ongoing project

When it came time for me to go independent and have my own place, I saw few houses anywhere that appealed to me, except for Sellers' designs. So with very little money and lots of zeal, I contacted Dave. The worst he could say was no. When I visited him in Vermont and saw more of his houses, I was convinced I would like whatever he came up with. The only requirements were that it go up high enough to see the ocean, and that it have plenty of storage space. Dave liked the idea of having so few restrictions, and since the Prickly Mountain crew like lobster, they decided to do it.

When I first saw the model, I thought a few of David's ideas were a little strange. Like having the bathroom with tub in the middle of the living room, with nothing but windows on one wall. But I didn't voice my objections, because I liked his designs so much that I let him have a free hand. In fact, I still don't have a real bathroom (the outhouse works fine), but after I lived in the house a few summers trying to figure out where the bathroom should go, the living-room area under the south-facing Plexiglas turned out to be the perfect place for the hot tub.

The third floor, which was to be part of my studio, turned out to be the warmest room in the house. I use it as a guest room in the summer, and I sleep there myself in cold weather. I sleep on the fourth floor in the summer, with a view of the sky through a fantastic window the crew installed in a November nor'easter.

The house is an ongoing project, as there are no bankers or mortgages involved, and living in it unfinished has given me more and better ideas of space than I otherwise would have had. The negatives are the ones David talks about in the article. First, a lack of storage space. I finally made room for one closet after five years, but it's tough having other carpenters work on the house because few of them think the way Dave does, and he and his crew always seem to want to tear out whatever anyone else has built for me. Second, the acrylic skylights leak. Third, the house gets too hot in summer and too cold in winter because of all the southern glazing. I like my house's design a lot, and if I had to do it again, I'd consider choosing Dave as an architect. But I'd try to assert just a bit more control. *—Nancy Barrett*

poo, we installed a commercial liquid-soap dispenser (both from Kroin Inc., Charles Square, Suite 300, Cambridge, Mass. 02138).

Jeff was so pleased with the color and texture of the mosaic tile that he thought it was a shame to hide them in the shower. The next thing I knew, they were creeping out of the shower to cover the sink and medicine cabinet and even made their way out the door and into the sleeping area where they concealed the front of the built-in dresser (photo below).

By this point in the project, curves and circles had become the dominant design theme. When we installed the large door at the head of the stairway to maintain privacy upstairs, we realized that it swept a semicircular arc through the room. But while the door had to stop, the arc didn't. We curved the walls of the stairwell to complete the circle. To accentuate the circular forms, we dropped the ceiling above the door and replaced the rose-colored carpet beneath it with a circle of deep blue.

The transition between the upstairs and downstairs posed a challenge. The second floor was finished in silver, pink and deep blue, while the walls of the main living area were tinted a greyish-green accented with auburn-colored trim. Both sets of colors converge on the stairwell. The auburn stripe running along up the stairs on one wall rises from the baseboard to form a huge circle, painted on the wall that separates the two levels and the two colors.

The guest rooms—Curiosity about our project made visits from relatives imminent, so the two guest rooms on the first floor became our next project. These rooms had originally been added by a previous owner, and the layout was unusable.

The first order of business was to move the existing bathroom from its original location off of the kitchen to its rightful place between the guest rooms. To conserve floor space, we used pocket doors leading into the bathroom. The walls and ceiling, including the tub area, were finished with 4-in. wide T&G redwood, installed horizontally and sealed with seven coats of satin polyurethane. By lowering the ceiling from 8 ft. to 6-ft. 8 in., we made this tiny space feel much larger.

In both guest rooms, the walls that adjoin the bathroom stop short of the ceiling. The extra 12-in. space above the walls was used to make a display shelf for plants, art objects and lights. In the smaller of the two rooms, we built in a platform bed with a set of drawers beneath it (photo top).

The main living area—In the middle of the living area there was a brick chimney that needed to be concealed. As we considered how to handle this problem, we were also thinking about where to put our grand piano, which we were anxious to retrieve from storage. The curve of the piano suggested the solution. We built a semicircular wall surrounding the chimney against which the piano

With drawers below and shelves at the head, a built-in bed saves space in the small guest room (above). The walls stop short of the ceiling to create space for the display shelf on top. The mosaic tiles that line the circular shower (below) on the second floor flow out of the bathroom, into the sleeping area and across the front of a built-in dresser. In the reading area beyond, a built-in couch backed by storage cabinets overlooks a wooded ravine.

The two-tiered soffit and circular wall in the main living area hide a 4-in. drain pipe that runs along the ceiling, and they also provide a sympathetic curve for the grand piano to nestle against. The semicircular shelves on the opposite wall were lag-bolted to a sheet of fiberboard, which was then hung and finished like a piece of drywall.

Instead of building a tunnel for the kitchen sky-light (above), the space between the ceiling and the roof was left open to create a ledge for plants. On the cabinets, the black squares at the intersections of the stripes indicate where to push to open the doors. The serpentine couch (right) was built with ¾-in. plywood and urethane foam, then upholstered with carpet. Pine frames stretched with linen diffuse the lights installed in the dropped ceiling.

Building the playhouse

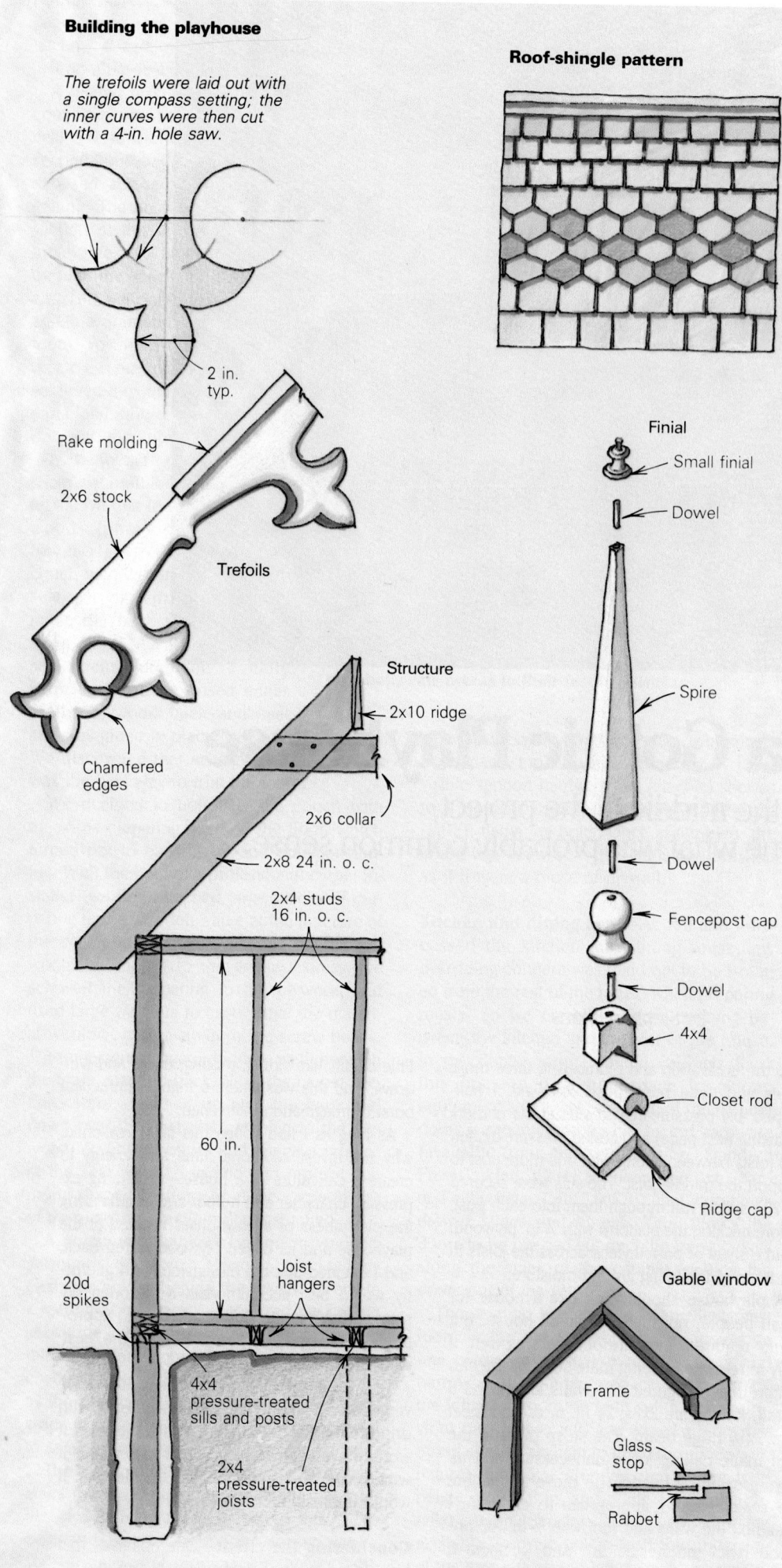

The trefoils were laid out with a single compass setting; the inner curves were then cut with a 4-in. hole saw.

2 in. typ.

Rake molding

2x6 stock

Trefoils

Chamfered edges

Structure

2x10 ridge

2x6 collar

2x8 24 in. o. c.

2x4 studs 16 in. o. c.

60 in.

20d spikes

Joist hangers

4x4 pressure-treated sills and posts

2x4 pressure-treated joists

Roof-shingle pattern

Finial

Small finial

Dowel

Spire

Dowel

Fencepost cap

Dowel

4x4

Closet rod

Ridge cap

Gable window

Frame

Glass stop

Rabbet

---

windows or shutters of playhouses, in spite of the moderate peril to their miniature fingers. I wanted small, lightweight windows that the kids could play with without maiming one another. "Barn sash" is what the guy behind the desk at the lumberyard called it. I ordered a pair of the smallest ones available—17x21, with four lights. Hung as inward-opening casements and latched with small barrel bolts, the windows allow preschoolers to open and close to their hearts' content. As a precaution, I fitted plexiglass to each light on the inside, securing it with glazing points.

The windows in the front and rear of the house, beneath the gables, are decorative as well as functional. Consistent with the Gothic motif, they have pointed tops. As you might imagine, building-supply catalogs seldom list pentagonal windows, so I built the frames from scratch. I cut rabbets in 5/4 clear white pine, then half-lapped the corners and glued everything up (drawing left). There's a muntin down the center, secured with dowels top and bottom, that forms a two-light sash. Yes, I can think of better ways to build windows than with lap joints, but not when the windows have five sides and not when family members and neighbors are already asking when the project will be finished.

The windows and the doorway have 1x drip molding along their top edges, raked at 45°. Such molding is typical of Carpenter Gothic detailing and provides an example of how an ostensibly functional design element can be decorative. I ripped the stock on my table saw, then chamfered the edges with a router.

In the interest of economy—The vertical emphasis in Carpenter Gothic design almost presupposes use of board-and-batten siding. In the interests of economy, I simply ripped ⅜-in. AC plywood sheets into "boards" 7 in. wide (I wanted to use up every scrap of plywood that was lying about), and secured them over the sheathing with galvanized nails and a bead of construction adhesive down the middle. The battens are 1½ in., chamfered at the edges, and butted against 2x molding at the sills and eaves.

Construction of the playhouse door was what one might describe as "fast and dirty" raised-panel technology. The rails and stiles are 5/4 clear white pine, and the panels are 3/4 stock. I did all of the mortising and cutting of grooves for the panels with the dado blade on my table saw. Tenons were formed with the dado blade as well; with the stock squared-up in the miter gauge, I made multiple passes across the blade. I raised the panels with a router, a ¾-in. straight bit and an edge guide, making two successive passes on each face to form a simple stair-step pattern. Also with the router, I stop-chamfered the rails and stiles, a decorative shortcut I deemed reasonable in light of the labor-intensive technique required in creating traditional forms of molded edges.

The door is 54 in. tall and 24 in. wide, with four panels. The center stile is 18 in. high, which puts the latch at a comfortable height

Drawings: Frances B. Ashforth

for small kids. To my delight (and quite frankly, a little to my surprise), the door was square and flat when the clamps came off. When installed, it was an immediate hit, providing Son in particular with a source of exotic amusement almost equal to unrestrained operation of the casement windows.

Homegrown Gothic details—Probably the most prominent decorative feature of the playhouse is the vergeboard (sometimes called a bargeboard). I considered various patterns from photographs and Victorian stylebooks, and ultimately decided on the trefoil decoration, a border design borrowed from the "crockets," which appear along the edges of Gothic spires and pinnacles. Trefoils, I discovered, are easily executed in wood, if one has reasonable patience and a sturdy drill press. All curves were laid out with a single setting of the compass (drawing facing page). Although the outer curves required freehand use of the sabersaw, the inner curves were merely cut out with a 4-in. hole saw and then connected with sabersaw cuts. I used a triangular file to emphasize the angles between the leaves of the trefoils, then shaped the inner curves and edges of the cuts with a router and a chamfering bit.

Like the vergeboard, the two finials along the ridge probably look like they entailed more work than they actually did. Each is nothing more than an elongated pyramid set atop a piece of fence-post decoration set atop a base of square stock (drawing facing page). I glued up clear 2x stock for the pyramids and cubes, then ripped everything to shape (the pyramids required a simple tapering jig). I bored out recesses in the underside of each pyramid so they would look less like having been "stuck

on," although that's exactly what I did. A tiny turned finial rests atop each pyramid. The ball-finials are more commonly used to dress up the tops of fence posts, and they're available from anybody's home-improvement center.

Dowels hold everything together, the accurate placement of which was enhanced by careful employment of a brad-point bit in ye trusty drill press. I cut a V-shaped chunk out of the bottom of each base so it would fit the ridge boards. As a final touch, I routed a V-groove in lengths of closet pole and secured them at the ridge.

A cheerful band of shingles—I like the effect of the band of hexagonal shingles across the playhouse roof, but I can't claim to have invented the idea. Like other design elements I used, the fancy shingles are suggested in one of the stylebooks of A. J. Downing. The shingles are cedar, and 24 in. long. Fortunately, I found a few bundles of generally uniform width—uniformly narrow, that is, in scale with the playhouse. The courses of rectangular shingles are 8 in. to the weather, and I stained them with grey opaque stain as I went. Four courses, cut into hexagonal shapes, form a decorative roof band. Though you can buy fancy-butt shingles, I made these by ripping standard shingles to a width of 5 in. before lopping off the corners on the table saw. I stained the shingles with two shades of green, and added more color to the last course of regular shingles along the ridge.

A lasting impression—I chose paint for the playhouse to emphasize the decoration and trim. Victorian houses frequently had contrasting colors, although my yellow siding may be more cheerful than authentic. Daughter actu-

ally had requested purple paint for the whole place. But she seemed satisfied enough if we diluted the hue to a shade of lilac, and applied it only to the front door.

The interior of the playhouse, with studs and rafters exposed, is decorated only with a coat of white primer. As time allows, I'll spruce it up a bit, although I have no ambitions to make the inside of the playhouse conform to the heavy coat of Victorian frosting that decorates the exterior. For now, the interior is plain but kid-proof.

And the kids themselves? They remained very patient with their father as he got in the way and spent ever more time with what must have seemed *his* house rather than theirs. When a little older, perhaps they'll appreciate his attention to the project on their behalf, and recognize the part of the kid that is in most fathers. □

Stephen Elkins is a tax attorney with a large corporation in Philadelphia. Photo by the author.

Suggested reading
● Installing wood shingles, see *FHB #12*, pp. 52-57; reprinted in *Construction Techniques I*, The Taunton Press.
● Decorative shingles, see *FHB #54*, pp. 42-45.
● Gothic Revival architecture, see: A. J. Downing, *The Architecture of Country Houses* (reprint), Dover, New York, 1969. Calder Loth and J. T. Trousdale, Jr., *The Only Proper Style*, New York Graphic Society, Little Brown and Company, New York, 1975. W. H. Pierson, Jr., American Buildings and Their Architects Series, *Technology and the Picturesque—The Corporate and Early Gothic Styles*, Doubleday & Co., Garden City, New York, 1978.

Carpenter Gothic

The fourth and fifth decades of the 19th century saw Gothic decoration appear on a considerable amount of domestic architecture in America. That a young and vigorous nation, forward-looking and ambitious, should take interest in an architectural style that reached its European peak around 1475 might seem a little peculiar. But there were ample reasons for a "Gothic Revival." They included a greater desire for ostentation on the part of an increasingly status-conscious society, and a fascination with the kind of romance and medievalism served up in the highly popular novels of Sir Walter Scott.

Early Victorian Gothic borrowed its design from ecclesiastical architecture of the same name, which had evolved in the late Middle Ages. After the rise to prominence of classic architecture, Gothic had to be

"rediscovered," notably by English eccentrics at the end of the 18th Century who applied it to their own houses.

Gothic architecture in America had talented proponents. Among the most able was architect Alexander Jackson Davis, who produced brilliant, sometimes extreme examples of Gothic design in the 1830s and 1840s. The first of Davis' Gothic designs was "Glen Ellen," completed at a site near Baltimore in 1833. The most extravagant of Davis' designs were executed in stone, but Gothic decoration was freely adaptable to wood. In fact, Gothic motifs translated into wood so easily and allowed such flexibility in design, that "Carpenter Gothic" represented a stylistic point of departure.

While the elements of Carpenter Gothic were diverse, certain motifs describe the style.

Foremost is vertical emphasis, manifested by exaggerated elevations and steep rooflines (16-in-12 is not uncommon). Further emphasizing height is board-and-batten siding. Immediately recognizable as Gothic is the pointed-arch design of windows and doorways.

The vergeboards, which enliven gables and dormers of Carpenter Gothic houses, are frequently the most obvious decorative elements. Their design may feature stylized leaves, rosettes, quatrafoils, high-relief carving or geometric elements. Typically, the vergeboards will include a narrow finial at the apex of the gable, terminating well above the roofline.

According to Andrew Jackson Downing, a friend of Davis and a highly influential author of books on architecture and landscape design, Gothic designs

were not only suitably picturesque, but practical as well. Because elements could be arranged asymmetrically, the Gothic style allowed greater flexibility in the design of floor plans than classical patterns. Greek Revival, in particular, required strict adherence to classical proportions and detail. Downing found that pompous. Carpenters probably found it tedious. Moreover, the frame construction of Carpenter Gothic was economical, offering a cost-effective means of asserting one's refined taste publicly, through basically a utilitarian edifice. While intense, Carpenter Gothic decoration imposed no unreasonable demands on the ordinarily skillful workmen of the day, who with pattern-book drawings and practical facility produced the delightful examples that memorialize their skill. —*S. E.*

Small House In Virginia

Cantilevers, careful planning and lots of glass make this cozy house feel spacious

by Bruce Gordon

My decision to build a 460-sq. ft. house resulted from circumstances I share with many people—a lack of time and money. I owned a great piece of land, and wanted to stop supporting a landlord without committing myself to a large, long-term mortgage. But with a time-consuming young business to run, I knew that building a large custom house would occupy all my spare time for a few years. On the other hand, I knew I could build a small house in a few months, without a mortgage, and then could live on and enjoy my land. I had no immediate plans for a family, so a cozy house for one—or maybe two— was the solution.

Designing the house required special attention to details, so that no space would be wasted and my desire for comfort would be fulfilled. I carefully considered the use of space in the house I was renting and found that most of the floor area was lost to poor traffic flow, to useless corners and other dead space. To minimize wasted space, I decided to keep my utility areas on the house's perimeter, and use an open plan to foster the illusion of spaciousness. The only separate room is the bath (floor plan, below).

I had managed to get a lot of ⅜-in. tempered glass, imperfect but cheap surplus from a manufacturer. The sheets ranged from 4½ ft. by 8 ft. to 6½ ft. by 9½ ft., and since they couldn't be cut, I had to design around them. As a result, the house has almost half as much glass as floor space. I am conscious of the outdoors, not of the small enclosed volume, and I feel close to the elements.

The glass isn't the only salvage in the house. My design incorporated other materials I had stockpiled over the years. Many of the doors and windows are secondhand, the loft floor joists are from an old cabin floor, and the kitchen cabinet tops are old bowling-alley lanes. The paneling is old barn siding. I used local roughsawn lumber for some framing and siding, and roll roofing, which I have since replaced with cedar shakes.

I chose a steeply sloping site for my home, to take advantage of a spectacular view of the Moormans River, the winter sun to the south and mountain views to the west. I tucked the house in under a canopy of hardwoods for summer cooling, and left open areas to the north for parking and gardens.

To save money and add a little pizzazz, I kept the perimeter of my pole foundation small, and cantilevered nearly one-third of the house beyond it (photo below). These extensions help make the house feel larger by virtually thrusting people out into the leafy surroundings. In the downhill section of my block basement, where the natural grade gave me standing room, I located the water heater, pressure tank and washing machine. This small utility room is also used for storage.

At the front door, I extended the north roof overhang 4 ft. beyond the building line to create a covered entry porch with a large area for storing firewood. The extension helped the building's proportions as well.

I cantilevered a 6-ft. by 8-ft. deck off the southeast corner, where it is sheltered from the cool northwest breezes, so I can use it on sunny days well into winter and in early spring. The tiny deck would be clogged by even one lawn chair, so I built benches

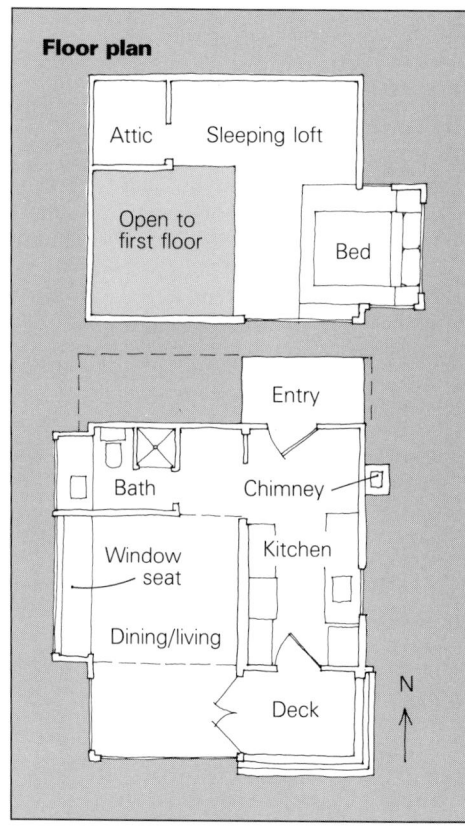

Floor plan

Attic · Sleeping loft · Open to first floor · Bed

Entry · Bath · Chimney · Window seat · Kitchen · Dining/living · Deck

N

From *Fine Homebuilding* magazine (February 1983) 13:64-66

around its perimeter. Eight people can sit comfortably against the railings.

Inside, I located the woodstove against the east wall, just to the left of the entry, which is in the windowless north wall. The stove is under the loft floor, and it keeps the first floor warm, but the heated air escapes to the high ceiling before people can fall asleep in an overheated living room.

My outside chimney of concrete masonry with flue block stays cold and collects creosote. It's possible to buy flue blocks webbed with air spaces, and if I were building another exterior chimney I would use these rather than solids, because they're much lighter and easier to handle when you're tottering around on scaffolding. I would also fill the space between the flue block and flue liner with fiberglass insulation to keep creosote from building up so fast. The best idea, of course, is to build your chimney inside the house so it can act as a heat sink and a radiator.

The galley kitchen (photo next page, bottom) doubles as one of two passages to the deck. I used glass shelves and a glass rack across the window over the sink. They provide the necessary storage without blocking the light, or the view. The exposed ceiling joists are only 7½ ft. off the floor, but the white underside of the loft floor makes the space feel a lot higher. Open shelving between the kitchen and the living room (photo right) also makes the kitchen seem larger.

The 4-ft. wide hall closet is the only fullheight clothes storage in the house, but with two clothes poles there's plenty of room to hang things up.

The bathroom is as small as a full bath can be. It's 5 ft. by 5 ft., but doesn't feel cramped. One reason is the large window opposite the door, under which the sink sits on an extended sill (photo next page, center left). Another reason it feels spacious is that the 2½-ft. by 2½-ft. shower has a glass wall. This solution wouldn't be feasible if I had neighbors, but on my site, privacy is no problem. The mirror is hidden in the back of a framed picture that swings out from the wall to the left of the sink. A 4-ft. by 4-ft. by 4-in. deep medicine cabinet in the wall yields plenty of storage.

The living/dining area is 10 ft. by 15 ft. My dropleaf table comfortably seats six, but folds to only 1½ ft. by 4½ ft. The couch, really a window seat that extends 30 in. beyond the building line (photo bottom right), also serves as a guest bed.

A stairway to the loft would have been a real space hog, so I built a ladder that rolls to a vertical position against the wall (photo next page, center right). Its handrail folds flat against one of the stringers to save space. A functional ladder for everyday use should never be vertical, nor should the treads over-

Rough structural elements are played off against elegant detailing in the kitchen, above right. The counter's backsplash is copper, while the exposed posts and beams are salvage. The windowseat, right, rests beneath a window made from discarded industrial glass.

Photos: Susan Mortell

The ceiling of the loft, left, is a single piece of heavy tempered glass. When the ladder to it, center right, is not in use, it can roll to a vertical position and be tucked out of the way.

A glass wall makes the 5-ft. by 5-ft. bathroom, center left, feel bigger than it really is. The mirror swings out over the sink. It's backed with a print, which is displayed against the wall when the mirror isn't needed.

The galley kitchen, bottom, is one of two paths to the deck. Gordon's company built all the cabinets. Glass shelves over the sink let the sunlight shine through.

lap each other by more than ½ in. A 10-in. rise with 4-in. treads is about right. I usually go up and down without using the handrail, and the only inconvenience comes when I have to cart something that takes two hands. My railing and stringers rise 3 ft. above the top tread, and they provide safe handholds for getting on and off.

The ceiling of the loft slopes from 7 ft. down to 2 ft., and there's plenty of room for low items like blanket chests and stereo speakers (photo top left). There is also enough full-height wall space for a couple of bureaus and some bookshelves. The built-in bed sits on a raised platform 8 ft. wide, cantilevered 4 ft. out from the east wall of the house. Though small, this second-story cantilever creates valuable extra space in the loft.

For the skylight over the bed, I simply set my rafters in the standard manner, laid a heavy bead of caulk on the rafter tops (mono tape would have been better), and slipped the glass up under a copper base flashing at the gable and wall. The glass overhangs the rafters by about 2 in. on all sides, a detail I wouldn't attempt with thinner glass. I fabricated metal brackets at the rafter tails to lock the glass in place. All of this sounds simple, and was—except for the difficulties of placing a 5-ft. by 8½-ft., 200-lb. piece of glass on a cantilevered section 20 ft. in the air.

My skylight gives up a lot of radiant heat, and it lets the sun in to wake me up at the crack of dawn, but I don't mind. The stargazing is great, and I love to watch the sunrise. If these drawbacks bothered me enough, I could install a shade. I don't have to worry about overheating in the summer, because of the canopy of green leaves overhead.

If you're designing a small house, you have to plan a space for each possession. Not providing for one necessary chair, a TV or a stereo may leave you with a serious problem later. Although small-house design forces attention to space-related details, it also allows some unusual design freedoms. For example, a ratio of 50% glass to floor space is practical only in such a small house, where a woodstove heats adequately.

Only another small-house dweller knows the special cozy comfort of living shipshape. And there's one other important benefit—you can clean house in one hour. □

Bruce Gordon is a partner in Shelter Associates of Free Union, Va.

Treehouse

by Alfred Wells

Most boys stop dreaming of building a treehouse at a reasonable age, but my dreams became more grandiose as the years went by. By the time I was 60 my fascination had gotten out of control. I had visions of spending the whole summer way up in a big treehouse overlooking a lake.

Miracles do happen. Today my treehouse sits comfortably among several large trees. It's 10 ft. to 15 ft. above the ground, which slopes down to a small lake in the Berkshire hills of northwestern Connecticut. It has a large loft, 150 sq. ft. of first-floor space, and 400 sq. ft. of deck.

When my family crew and I began building, our first problem was the support system. The design called for six trees 10 ft. to 40 ft. apart, and we finally settled on five oaks and one maple, each about 1 ft. in diameter.

We spiked together three 40-ft. 4x12 beams out of 2x12s, then bolted each beam to two trees about 20 ft. apart. The house was built on these beams, which were long enough to support nearly 10 ft. of deck at each end.

We were afraid of killing the trees, so in each case we notched out only 2 in. to 3 in. of wood and used a single long bolt at each connection. To distribute the load and to prevent swaying in the wind, we added 2x8 braces between the tree trunks and the overhanging beams.

Friends often worry that the platform and house will rise unevenly as the trees grow. My reply is that if you carve a heart on a tree 3 ft. above the ground and return 50 years later, the heart will still be 3 ft. above the ground. That's how trees grow.

Once the three main beams were in place, the rest of the construction was fairly conventional, except that we used pressure-treated lumber. We placed 2x8 joists on the beams, and 2x6 decking went over the joists.

The treehouse and the deck railings were attached to the platform, not to any of the trees. The platform itself is as steady as a rock in a storm; the trees sway from the platform up as though the platform were the earth. We left a generous space between the treehouse roof and the trees so that branches would not bang against the roof in the wind.

We nailed up the diagonal T&G sheathing green. It has since shrunk, and there are now annoying gaps. Eventually we shall put insulation panels covered with brightly colored material between the studs to keep out the cold.

A woodstove, an old gas refrigerator, and running water contribute to the pleasures of life aloft. We are now debating how to upgrade the privy, which is tucked away behind a clump of mountain laurel.

Obtaining planning permission was worrisome. As we expected, our application was refused because "the foundations do not conform with existing regulations." We appealed.

On a lovely sunny day, the members of the appeals board drove up the five-mile dirt road that rises 1,000 ft. to our lake. They looked at the six healthy trees, climbed up the steps to the deck, noted that the house was stable despite a strong wind, and then drove back down to the village. We won our appeal. We often wonder what would have happened if we had applied for planning permission before construction (as we should have done) and not afterwards. □

N
Tree
Lake
Bedroom
Sofa/bed
Ladder
Loft above
Woodstove
Beam
Future W.C.
Floor plan
Up

Alfred Wells is an architect in international service with the United Nations. Photo by the author.

Small House in Ski Country

Cutouts and curves open up space on a tiny lot

by Graeme Means

When my prospective clients Marty and Shannon Rodgers showed me the four surveyor's stakes on the lot they intended to buy in Aspen, Colo., I thought that they sure had a small house in mind. Then they told me that those stakes—which looked to be at the corners of the house—really indicated the limits of the property. They had said that their lot wasn't any too big, but this was tiny. It was not only tiny, it was at the base of a mountain. I cast a sideward glance at the Rodgers, but their faces seemed

pretty serious, so I looked a little harder at this garage-size piece of land.

True, it was just a few minutes walk to the center of town, and downtown Aspen is a pretty chic place. And yes, Shadow Mountain, located to the southwest, provided a great big backyard, which is an amenity few city lots of any size have. From the center of the site, I could see the ski slopes of Aspen Mountain to the east. I figured that having views like these is like having an ocean-front lot, or better. The Colorado sun

brightened the soft fall colors in the sage and grasses, and I started to realize the potential for building on this lot.

How the lot got its size—The silver-mining town of Aspen was laid out in the early 1880s as a grid of lots each 30 ft. wide by 100 ft. long. The Rodgers' lot began in this configuration, but before the decade was over, it was bisected by the Midland Railroad, which was put in to haul out silver ore. This history is still apparent in the abandoned railroad grade nearby and the abundant mine tailings. After the split, the leftover piece was shaped like a trapezoid, only about ⁴⁄₄₀ of an acre, or 1,100 sq. ft. in size. A previous owner had received a variance from the planning board to reduce the usual building setbacks from 10 ft. on the front, 5 ft. on the sides and 15 ft. on the rear to 5 ft. on all sides (drawing, right). This left us a trapezoidal building envelope 20 ft. wide, with 19½-ft. and 31-ft. sides, and about 740 sq. ft. in area—that's big enough for a one-bedroom apartment. By zoning standards, we could build a total floor area of only 882 sq. ft. (heated space) and had to provide one off-street parking space. Although 882 sq. ft. is small, it seemed like a lot to squeeze into a 740-sq. ft. footprint, but my clients wanted as much square footage as they could get.

Marty and Shannon had planned the house as a speculative project that they would live in for about a year and then sell when it was time for them to make a planned move to another state. They were wise to recognize potential in a piece of land that others had rejected as unworkable, because it was unlikely another property of such diminutive size and price would be listed in Aspen when it came time to sell. The Rodgers knew that a house with special appeal would stand out even more in a flat real-estate market, so they asked for a house where they could have some fun with interior design. They also wanted this house designed in a hurry so construction could start before winter and be over before spring. Since it was September when the Rodgers found the lot, and since in Aspen serious winter weather shows up by November, we began designing right away.

Carving a house from a trapezoid—The shape of the house is very much a function of the shape of the lot and site conditions. To use the allowable square footage efficiently, we began with a trapezoidal footprint that followed the legal setback lines. Even though we could build to the edge of this envelope, we found that only a three-story house could handle both a parking space and the maximum floor area. We began to shape the house by deciding how interior spaces should relate to the site.

The major views, the most privacy (very important for a tiny lot) and the southern sun were all on one side, facing the mountain. The longer sides of the lot were crowded by a building on the east and a steep, shaded hillside on the west (photo facing page). The north side faced a quiet street of houses and lodges. Our strategy was to locate the most heavily used spaces on the sunny, private southeast corner, so I took a slice off that point of the trapezoid to make the dining room, a sitting area for the bedroom and a sunning deck. I rounded the edge of the point to soften the look of the house (photo above right). Then we assigned the stairway and front door to the north, or street side. I recessed the door both for protection from rain and snow and to call out its function as an entrance, and curved the glass-block stairwell to add distinction to a house that otherwise turns away from the street.

Cost considerations and height limitations set by zoning laws led us to choose a flat single-ply

Third-floor plan

Second-floor plan

First-floor plan

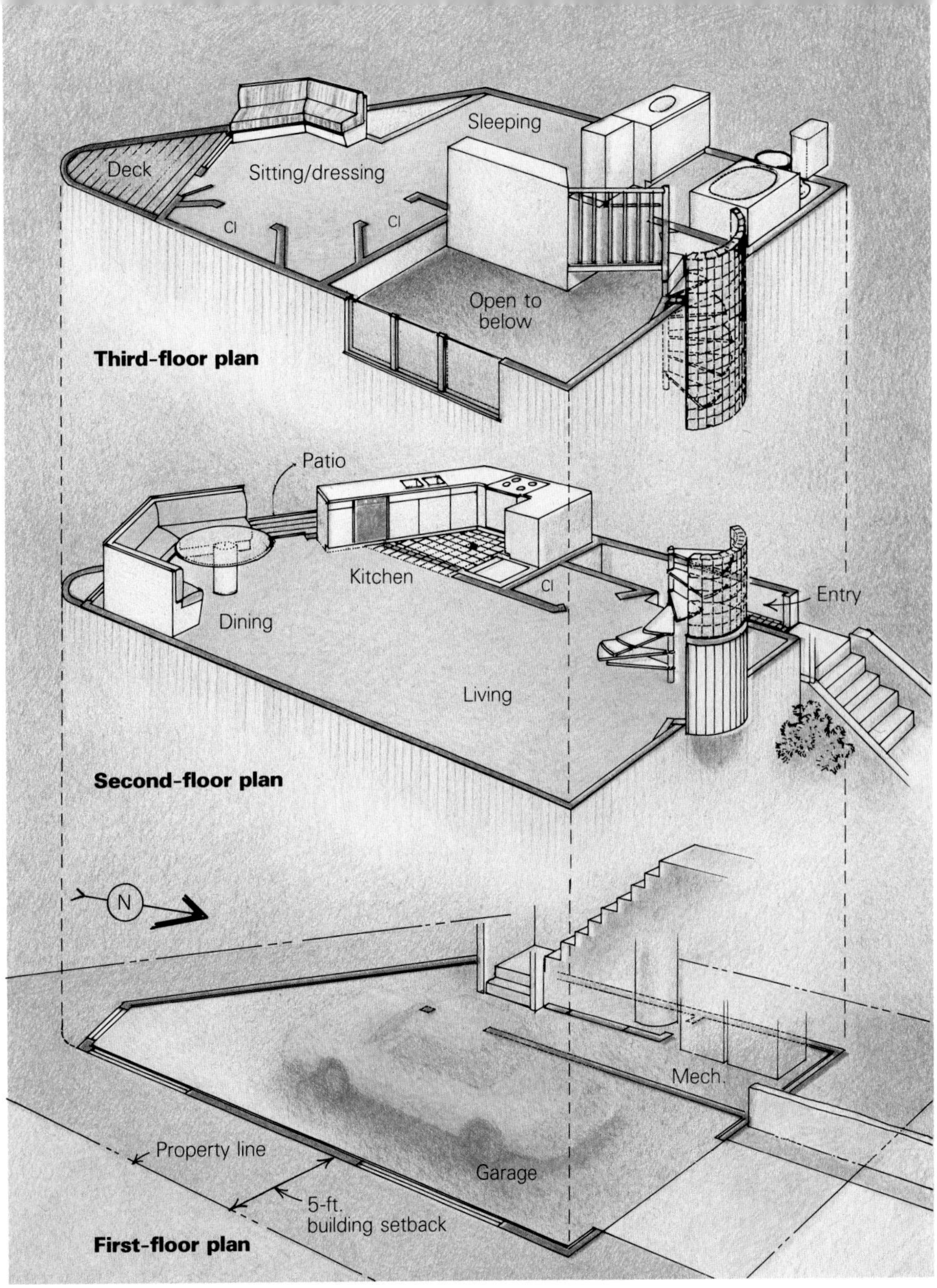

A curved corner. **With the best view of Aspen Mountain, the most privacy and the southern sun all found on one corner of a small lot, the author stacked up the floors, then rounded off a corner of the house to make a deck and dining room. A flat roof allows the house to grow all the way to the zoning height limit; sloped metal roofing over the living area relieves the roof and ceiling profiles. The pale grey and shiny blue of the house stand out against both snow and woods as manmade, yet they also pick up the color of cloudy and clear skies.**

membrane roof for most of the house. Properly installed flat roofs with roof drains perform very well in snow country by eliminating ice dams, by preventing sliding-snow conditions and by doing away with the problem of dripping icicles. A blanket of snow on the roof can even serve as extra insulation. We added small pitched metal roofs over the kitchen and at the northeast corner, both to make a sloped ceiling inside and to relieve the look of an entirely flat roof. We refined these roof shapes and other exterior details by working with cardboard models, which I find much more useful than drawings for showing both my clients and me what the house really will look like.

The form of the house is purposely in contrast to its setting, both manmade and natural. The severe, rectilinear outline stands sharply against Shadow Mountain, and its form and color liven up a street of conservative and largely undistinguished houses and lodges. It speaks, perhaps, of design influences important to Aspen but not

Drawing: Gary Williamson; Photo this page: Graeme Means

completely at home in this little part of town. For this reason the house has its critics who consider it an unwelcome intrusion, but to others it represents change and excitement.

Make only big plans—We began to develop the layout of interior spaces by talking about how to design a small house that didn't look small inside. One way would be to squeeze in the number of rooms of an average house—but at a smaller scale—to achieve the sense of separation and intricacy that the normal-sized house would have. But such a house might also feel claustrophobic, so we tried the opposite approach. If we made each level one continuous space, that space would be similar in scale to a room in a generously sized house. We would let light flow freely throughout the space to reinforce the feeling of openness, and to emphasize continuity, we would open the two living levels to each other at various places. Although this design would allow noise to carry between levels, we didn't consider this a problem since only two people would live in the house.

Using this approach to stretching a small house, we developed the plan from the ground up (drawing, p. 149). From inside the garage, you climb a stair that arrives at a landing three steps below the main-floor level, then takes a 90° turn up to the living room. To enter the house from the street, you walk up a set of exterior concrete steps, which is fitted out with a metal pipe handrail, and come to the front door just outside the lowered landing. This change in level acts as a buffer, keeping mud, cold air and a direct view away from the living room. The living area is compact and accommodates the basic sofa, a coffee table and chairs, a small woodstove and an open closet, which has cabinets for stereo equipment and books and keeps the room free of clutter (photo facing page).

Across from the living room, a round dining table with built-in upholstered seating occupies the sliced-off corner of the house (photo bottom right). The generous window opens to the sunny, southern exposure and mountain vista. There's a little patio outside the back door for dining or lounging when weather permits. A small kitchen (photo top right)—but big enough for two because it angles widely toward the open end—is opposite the dining area and partly hidden from the living room by a wall.

We located the bathroom at the top of the spiral stair so that guests can use it without walking through the upstairs sleeping area. The corner of the bathroom separates the bed from the stairwell for privacy and deflects any noise and headlight glare coming through the glass-block wall (top photo, next page). A sitting area with a dressing table and flanking closets fits into the sunny southeast corner of the upper level (bottom photo, next page). Just outside, in the curved prow of the house, is a small screened deck perfectly placed for private sunbathing or for admiring the view.

Sleight of hand—One design trick to use when space is tight is to borrow space and light from another space. In this house, a well between the sleeping corner upstairs and the

From *Fine Homebuilding* magazine (Spring 1988) 45:60-64

The floor of the bedroom level above is cut away to give the living room height and light (facing page). The landing and front door (the darker door to the left of the coat closet) are separated from the living area by a change in level. A compact kitchen (above) includes all the necessary appliances and just enough counter space. The kitchen is open to the dining and living areas, yet set off by its black and white floor and walls. A triangular cutout in the ceiling shares light with the bedroom on the floor above. The bank of cabinets angles out toward the dining area (below).

Dividing a small space. A short wall and dropped beam define the built-in sleeping area on the third level (above). The bathroom behind the wall buffers light and sound from the glass-block stairwell. On the right, a dresser is built into the half-wall that overlooks the living area. At the other end of the dropped beam, a built-in sitting/dressing nook fits into the sliced-off southeast corner of the house (below).

kitchen below scoops up light for the upstairs from the window over the kitchen sink, and at the same time makes the kitchen seem more spacious (top photo, previous page). There's also a large chunk cut out of the ceiling over the living room next to the spiral stair to make the living area a two-story space with a sloped ceiling (photo, p. 150). The hall overlooking the living area isn't just a balcony but serves as dresser and storage space.

A few colors and simple changes in ceiling height and angle take the place of walls in defining spaces for sleeping and dressing. Downstairs, the living area is free of columns because the floor around the cutout is hung from the roof structure by an exposed steel rod.

Simple and thrifty—The curves and cutouts were designed for high impact but low cost. Marty and Shannon were firmly tied to a square-foot price that was very low for the well-to-do town of Aspen. We met the budget, though, with modest materials and a simple design.

The shape of the house from exterior walls to roof framing was kept clean and straightforward. To minimize the cost of the curved walls, we used vertical siding on the exterior, indented the windows to eliminate trim on the face of a curve and trimmed the curves with sheet metal instead of wood. We kept the number and size of walls, and especially doors, to a minimum, specified drywall and standard wood stud framing and used prehung, painted flush doors with stock trim. Built-in seating in the dining room and bedroom sitting areas is constructed of simple painted plywood, with upholstered seats and backs. We made built-in bedroom furniture from inexpensive and unfinished store-bought furniture, which we cut to fit and painted with the other woodwork.

Like a diamond—Building the house in severe winter weather was rough going. But in February, contractor Paul Rasmussen and his crew finished under the budget and the Rodgers were able to move in.

When I look at the house now, I think that its spiral stair and glass-block light well are the most successful parts of the project. Spiral staircases are space-saving features, and in this case, light from above and below the stair makes the levels flow together, creating the illusion that the house is bigger than it is. Glass block prevents the glare and heat gain that a comparable expanse of glass block on the south would generate, so there's never a need for shading devices. Although energy-use guidelines for cold climates discourage the use of north-facing glass, the weathertightness and size of the house make for modest heating bills, even with electric heat.

The life this wall breathes into the house definitely offsets the costs involved. When you walk up the stair, you get a constantly changing, prism-like view of the street scene beyond. The sun's rays on early summer mornings and car headlights at night shine through the block as vibrant sparkles of light. From the outside, its shimmering, curved surface illuminates the otherwise plain front facade. Every time I bicycle by, the glass block sparks my imagination. □

Hands-On Down East

Careful design and craftsmanship in a Maine house built by its owners

by Mark Alvarez

There's nothing unusual about this house; it's the combination of things that makes it special." Cabinetmaker Stan Griskivich's assessment of the house he and his wife Toni designed and built on Cousins Island, Yarmouth, Me., is accurate only to a point. Spaces, structural elements and simple systems do combine to make the house work as it was planned to. But there's more: Stan's own finishwork. The handcrafted cherry kitchen cupboards are warm and rich (page 154, lower right). The pine balustrade and cherry balcony rail (page 154, upper left) are put together with evident skill and care (page 154, lower left). And the thermal shutters that cover each window at night are trim and handsome (page 154, upper right). The Griskivich house, which they built for under $30,000 in 1978, is noteworthy because of its well-planned efficiency. It is extraordinary because of Stan's craftsmanship.

Stan and Toni had bought the plans for their first house through a magazine. They both admire traditional New England architecture, and that's what they got—a handsome, conven-

tional, all-electric, 1,200-sq.-ft. saltbox that included three bedrooms and two baths.

They soon realized it wasn't for them. "We decided on the plans even before we knew where we were going to build," says Stan. "That's no way to approach a custom-built house." The rooms were too small for the way they lived, and energy bills were too big. With electric heat, it still took four cords of wood to see them through the long Maine winter.

When they decided they wanted something different, the Griskiviches bought another piece of land, then designed and built their new house themselves. This time 1,200 sq. ft. enclosed fewer rooms, but larger and brighter spaces. The house is heated by the sun and less than two cords of wood a year. "Our first house," says Stan, "was designed for the average family. This one is designed for Stan and Toni Griskivich."

Design development—Nevertheless, designing the new house did pose a problem. Stan and Toni knew what they wanted and what their site would allow, but how could they reconcile their

love of colonial architecture with the requirements of passive solar gain and their desire for large, open spaces? They couldn't.

"Passive solar requires all that glass on the south side," says Stan. "You can make a house look colonial on the north, east and west sides, maybe, but on the south you just can't." His first design was a characteristic one for a New England owner-builder: a 1½-story rectangular shape with a shed roof—simple, straightforward and, for passive solar heating, efficient. Toni didn't like it. "It didn't look like a house to me," she says. "I still liked the colonial saltbox design of our first house."

Stan's next attempt was a breakthrough. He divided the house into two 16-ft. by 24-ft. modules, and set the eastern segment back six feet to give the morning sun a path into the western module, where the kitchen, bedroom and dining areas would be. And a greenhouse would fit nicely into that 6-ft. setback (see plan). But it was still a shed design. "It was better," says Toni, "but I still wasn't comfortable with it."

Finally, Stan tried a saltbox shape on the

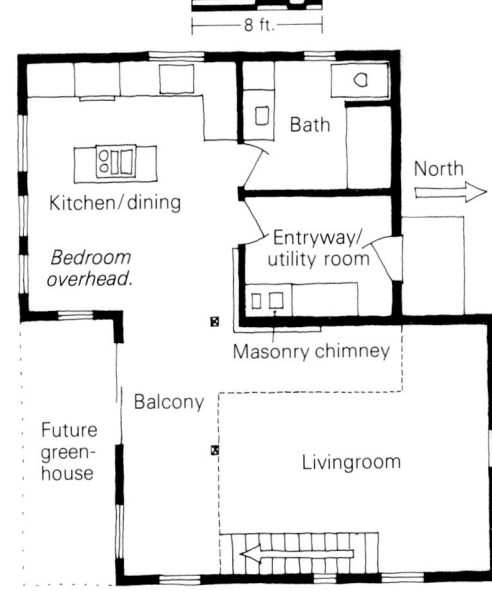

The eastern module of the Griskivich house is a shed design, opening wide to the southern sun. The western module is a saltbox, which will carry solar panels.

First floor plan

8 ft.

Bath

Kitchen/dining

North

Bedroom overhead.

Entryway/ utility room

Masonry chimney

Balcony

Future greenhouse

Livingroom

Stan's finishwork is the glory of the Griskivich house. The dovetail (left) joins cherry balcony railings. The living area's slate floor and chimney mass (upper left) soak up heat, which thermal shutters (folded back, upper right) help keep in the house. Sunlight playing warmly over cherry kitchen cabinets (lower right) lends a feeling of comfortable elegance to an essentially informal room.

western module. The roof's pitch would break up the mass of wall and glass that Toni objected to, and—a bonus—it could someday support solar hot water panels. The result is a saltbox/shed hybrid that performs as the Griskiviches wanted, and satisfies them aesthetically.

Energy—The Griskivich house is fully wired for electric heat. The system hasn't been turned on since it was tested at installation. From the start, Stan and Toni planned with the sun in mind. The eastern, living room module was given a slab floor, which Stan covered with dark red slate. The winter sun penetrates to the full 24-ft. depth of the house; the slab absorbs its warmth during the day, and gradually surrenders it back to the house after the sun goes down. The large chimney mass does the same.

The only significant change they would make

if they were building again would be to lay a slab in the kitchen and dining module as well. It now has a floor of wide pine boards over a carefully installed rock bed that was originally planned as storage for heat from warm air drawn by fan from the ceiling of the second story. The simple slab mass of the livingroom works so well that the storage system has never been hooked up. "The simpler the system," says Stan, "the more efficient it is."

The Griskiviches estimate that they get over 50% of their heat from the sun. For the rest, they rely on wood burned in one of their two stoves. One, a range that Toni occasionally cooks on, is perfect for chilly fall or spring evenings. The other, a big Lange brought from their first house, takes over in the winter. It cranks out too much heat for so small and efficient a house, and may soon be replaced by a smaller woodburner. So

far, Stan and Toni have been burning dead, diseased or misshapen trees from their own land, but they will soon have to begin buying the 1½ to 2 cords of wood they burn each year.

Stan's site-built thermal shutters are important components of the heating system. Combined with double glazing, they offer an R value of about 8, which goes a long way toward keeping heat in and cold out at night. They replace curtains and, when folded back neatly during the day, they contribute to the cozy house's ordered, shipshape appearance.

Most of the double-glazed windows are owner-built and are fixed in place. They cost about $80 each, as compared to around $250 for commercial units. Store-bought sliding glass doors lead outside from the living room, and a Velux roof window over the bed affords a starry view at night. □

Making Thermal Shutters
by Stan Griskivich

A passive solar house has a lot of glass on its south side. But the windows that let sunlight in all day can let heat out just as easily at night. Even if you don't have large expanses of glass, you lose heat and money through uninsulated windows after dark. Thermal shutters cut heat loss by between 70% and 85%. These are a refinement of a design developed several years ago by Charlie Wing of Cornerstones owner-builder school and use no fiberglass or foam. Instead, they work on the same insulating principal as a Thermos bottle: reflective surfaces facing each other across a dead air space. They provide an R value of about 8, at a material cost of around $3 per sq. ft.

Materials
⅛-in. Farmline Thermoply, made by Simplex Products, Box 10, Adrian MI 49221 (517-263-8881). Also called "white face," it comes in 4x8 sheets, with one foil face and one white.
1½-in. by 1½-in. stock
Glue (Franklin Titebond or similar)
½-in. to ⅝-in. wire brads (#17 or #18), or narrow crown staples
4d finishing nails
Hinges (I use 3-in. loose pin hinges.)
Weatherstripping (Closed-cell vinyl foam is best.)
Latches (Acorn square-bolt latches or similar)
Wood putty (Darworth's Wood Patch or similar)

Tools
Table saw or radial-arm saw with carbide-tipped blade
Backsaw
Miter box
Straightedge
Utility knife or fine plywood blade
Electric or pneumatic stapler (I use a DuoFast Model E)
Hammer
Butt chisel or router
Screwdriver
Nail set

Measuring and cutting
1. Measure the inside of your window casing. Subtract ¼ in. to determine frame (rail) lengths. This provides the clearance the shutter needs to swing. Most shutters are bifold or trifold, so divide by 2 (bifold) or 3 (trifold) for the length of the horizontal rails.
2. Cut rails to length, and miter their ends. I use a radial-arm saw, and do both in a single operation. You can do it with a backsaw and miter box.
3. Saw two ⅛-in. slots just over ½ in. deep in the frames, ¼-in. in from their edges (see drawing). The little extra depth in the slots (about ¹⁄₃₂ in.) leaves room for play if other measurements are close, but not perfect. Most carbide-tipped blades leave a kerf just the right size, but check your cut to be sure. Cutting these slots is the only operation you'll need a power tool for. I use a table saw, but a radial-arm saw would work just as well.
4. Cut Thermoply sheets squarely, 2 in. smaller all around than the outer dimensions of the shutter panel. For example, a panel that has rails cut 48 in. by 18 in. would take Thermoply 46 in. by 16 in. Use a fine plywood blade or a utility knife and straightedge.

Assembly
1. Squeeze Franklin Titebond or a similar glue into the kerfs of a long rail. With the rail sitting slots-up on your bench, insert a sheet of Thermoply into each kerf, with foil sides facing in. Set another long rail down, apply the glue, and insert the opposite edges.
2. Lay the panel flat, squeeze glue into the slots of a short rail, and slide the kerfs over the sheets of Thermoply on one of the short sides. Do the same with the final rail on the opposite end.

The glue will not bond wood to sheet. Its job is to assure a dead airspace.
3. To fasten the frame to the Thermoply panels, I use ½-in. to ⅝-in. narrow crown staples and a *heavy-duty* electric stapler powerful enough to countersink the staples. #17 or #18 wire brads work just as well. Use a nailset to countersink the brads.

Drive brads or staples near corners first, getting each joint tight and square before adding more fasteners every 8 in. or so around the rails. Then flip the frame over and fasten the other sheet of Thermoply the same way.
4. Use two 4d finishing nails to fasten each miter. Offset them slightly so you won't nail one into the other (below).

Finishing and installation
1. Plug staple or brad holes. Wait until dry, then sand with 120-grit paper.
2. Finish, paint or stain the rails. The white surface of the Thermoply is washable, and handsome as it is. If you want to, though, you can paint it, paper it, stencil a design on it or cover it with fabric. If you do, remember that on trifold shutters one of the panels that faces the window at night will be exposed to the room when folded back.
3. Assuming you've made both panels of a bifold shutter, or all three of a trifold, stand two panels on edge, butting them face to face. On a bifold, butt the sides that will face the window when the shutter is closed. On a trifold start the same way, then butt the room sides of the second and third panels. Decide where to position the hinges (usually 6 in. to 8 in. from top and bottom, for vertical shutters). Lay hinges in place, and outline them with a sharp pencil. Use a router or butt chisel to mortise out these areas to a depth equal to the hinge's thickness.
4. When the panels are connected, the whole assembly must be attached to the window casing. First fasten hinges to the shutter, as above. Then put a piece of ⅛-in. Thermoply scrap on the windowsill to assure proper clearance. Stand the shutter on it, and mark hinge placement on the casing. Chisel out as before, and attach hinges.
5. Weatherstripping is vital to keep air from circulating behind the shutter. Exactly how you install it depends on the type of window you're dealing with. As a rule, you can nail ⅜-in. to ½-in. wood strips to the window jambs, and fasten weatherstripping to it. The shutter should close snugly against it. Weatherstrip between shutter panels, too, so no air can leak between butted rails.
6. Finally, to install latches at top and bottom to keep the shutter closed, I use Acorn square bolts at the sill, and a simple turn button at the top. □

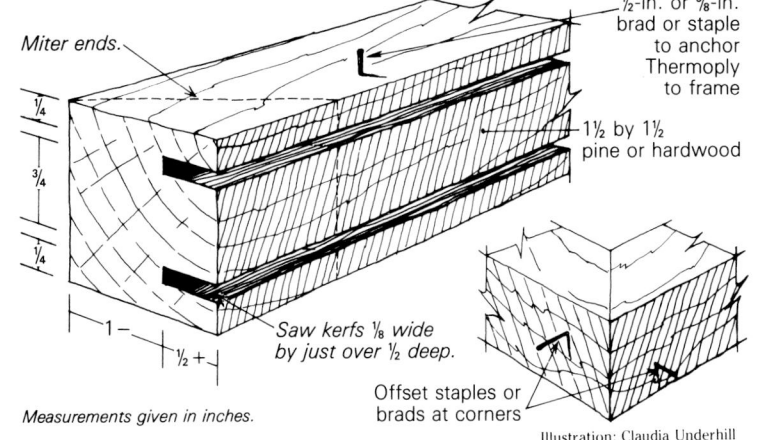

Miter ends.

½-in. or ⅝-in. brad or staple to anchor Thermoply to frame

1½ by 1½ pine or hardwood

Saw kerfs ⅛ wide by just over ½ deep.

Measurements given in inches.

Offset staples or brads at corners

Illustration: Claudia Underhill

A New View

A San Francisco owner-builder fashions a light-filled cottage from a claustrophobic shack

by Sudi Scull

A flexible floor plan. Gratz's house is mostly one large room that can be easily rearranged. An armoire on casters houses the stereo, records, the TV and fold-up dining chairs. It can be moved around to anchor different furniture groupings. In the foreground, the gas range top is let into an extra wide counter, which gives the cook some workspace in front of the burners.

With the help of a compass and a flashlight, Geoffrey Gratz inspected the exterior of his house-to-be one summer night in 1978. He took the flashlight to assess the condition of the run-down building; the compass was to ascertain solar exposure. Gratz is a born botanist, and if the site wasn't promising for a sunny garden, then the house wasn't for him.

To say that Gratz's budget was tight would be putting it mildly. San Francisco is an expensive place to live, and even in 1978 house prices were well along their path toward six figures. But Gratz is also a patient man, and he knew what he wanted: a small house that needed work. With a budget of $45,000, he planned on doing most of the renovation work himself. Fortunately, his carpentry skills had been honed in theatrical set design and construction.

Fog is a fact of life in San Francisco, but there are a few neighborhoods that remain sunny even when the rest of the city is socked in. Two of these neighborhoods, Potrero Hill and Bernal Heights, have a few older homes that have fallen into disrepair. Gratz got to know the real-estate agents who work in these areas, and it paid off. One night he got a call from an agent saying that a decrepit house on a nice hillside lot was about to be listed. Gratz jumped on his bike to make a late-night inspection. Sure enough, the house was indeed rundown, but it looked sound, and

From *Fine Homebuilding* magazine (Spring 1987) 38:46-48

the site was definitely a winner. The 50-ft. by 100-ft. lot was at the end of a cul-de-sac. Its long dimension followed the contour of the hill, and a 60-ft. pine tree grew near the lot's eastern edge. The rest of the property was a tangle of untended vines. Gratz gave the agent a deposit. The owner accepted his bid, and the house (left photo below) was his for just under $30,000.

Opening up the house—Most small houses suffer from a lack of storage space, but at about 600 sq. ft., this one had an abundance of closets. In fact, much of the house was given over to hallways and storage nooks (see original plan below). Circulation patterns robbed the tiny house of much-needed living space. Its ceilings were so low that Gratz could touch them, adding to the claustrophobic nature of the rooms.

A bonus, which Gratz hadn't counted on, was a sweeping view of the city to the north (photo top right). But the only way to appreciate the view was from the deck—a rickety affair made from discarded forklift pallets. Gratz brought in three dumpsters and filled them with the deck, ceilings and partition walls from the house. Most of the old exterior siding was also removed in preparation for new cedar shingles.

Fortunately, the basic structure of the building was still sound, and Gratz was left with a gabled shell 15 ft. wide and 40 ft. long. He moved into the gutted space and set up a hotplate.

A multi-purpose room—To gain a bit more interior space and bring in more light and view, Gratz decided to transform an 18-ft. section of single-story gable roof into a two-story shed roof (photo top right). The high shed faces north, toward the city, and contains a sleeping loft (drawing, below right).

To extend the roof, Gratz first added a ridge beam beneath the rafters for extra support. Then he removed the rafters on the north side of the beam. The shed rafters were then simply nailed alongside the south-side rafters, extending the south roofline to create a two-story wall on the north side of the house.

To maximize the view and let in plenty of light, Gratz installed a glass sliding door in the north wall, and glazed the spaces between the

Built in 1910, Gratz's house in the hills of San Francisco was a rundown shack with a sagging ridge and a rickety deck when he bought it in 1978. Photo: Geoffrey Gratz.

To make space for a sleeping loft, Gratz extended the roofline, creating a two-story shed that faces north toward a sweeping view of the city, top. Most of the north wall is enclosed with glass to take advantage of the panorama. A new deck atop the garage, above, extends the full length of the house.

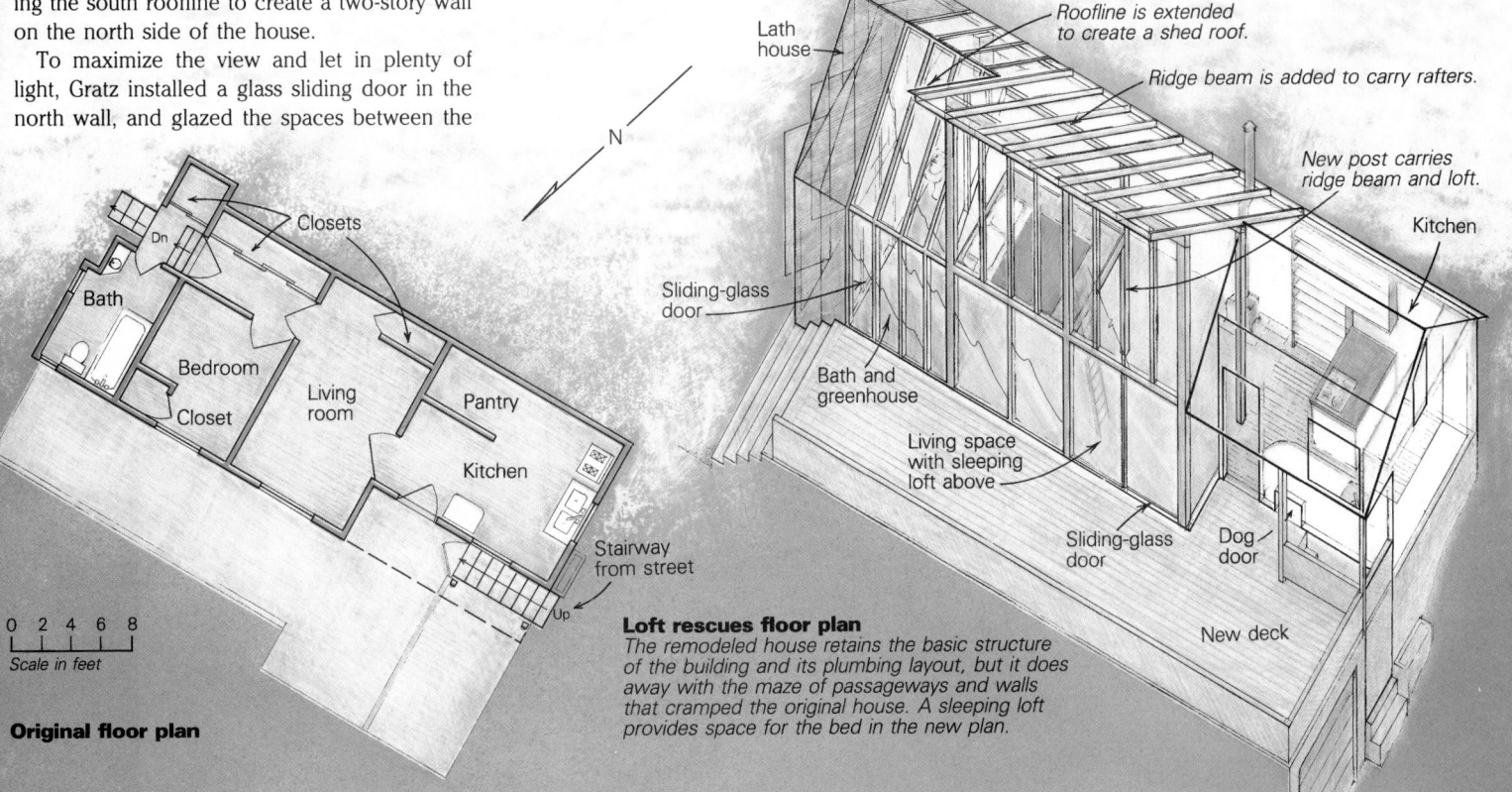

0 2 4 6 8
Scale in feet

Original floor plan

Labels: Closets, Dn, Bath, Bedroom, Closet, Living room, Pantry, Kitchen, Stairway from street, Up

Loft rescues floor plan
The remodeled house retains the basic structure of the building and its plumbing layout, but it does away with the maze of passageways and walls that cramped the original house. A sleeping loft provides space for the bed in the new plan.

Labels: Lath house, N, Roofline is extended to create a shed roof., Ridge beam is added to carry rafters., Sliding-glass door, New post carries ridge beam and loft., Kitchen, Bath and greenhouse, Living space with sleeping loft above, Sliding-glass door, Dog door, New deck

spherical casters provides movable storage for the stereo, television, records and folding chairs. To hold all this weight, Gratz took the armoire apart and reassembled it around a sturdy plywood carcase.

Gratz occasionally does theatrical lighting for Bay Area troupes, and this puts him in a good position to pick up castoff light fixtures. These low-volt fixtures have transformers built right into them. Rewiring and replacing the transformers is costly, so theaters usually buy new ones. Gratz rebuilt 20 of the fixtures, and installed them in the kitchen and living room. The fixtures are fitted with a variety of lamps, from tight spotlights to wide floods, and they allow a full range of lighting effects in the room.

Kitchen corner—The new kitchen is in the same corner as the old one was, but it's arranged to allow views of the city and the living room. For storage, Gratz lined the west wall with built-in closets for clothing and shelves for kitchen gear and supplies (photo bottom left).

Gratz wanted to use concealed hinges on the doors, but he realized that conventional doors this large would place a weighty burden on the hinges. To lighten the doors, he made their frames out of ¾-in. thick wood rails and stiles and filled the voids with ¾-in. thick styrene honeycomb, a strong, lightweight material that resembles cardboard with a waffled core (see *FHB* #36, p. 89). Gratz then used contact cement to bond white plastic laminate to both sides of the doors. In this application, the laminate is both the finished surface and the structural element holding the doors together. At the north end of this wall of cabinets is a tiny refrigerator. There's a freezer in the garage.

The kitchen corner is one of high contrasts, with sleek plastic laminates in white and brushed stainless steel playing off the dark wood ceiling and floor. A 42-in. deep peninsula topped by a maple chopping block protrudes from the south wall. It houses the cooktop, and unlike many kitchens with maple counters, the wood actually gets used as a work surface. The cooktop is set back from the edge of the counter, leaving a usable area in front of the burners. Deep drawers below the counter slide on full-extension drawer glides. Some of them hold kitchen implements, while others are filled with socks and T-shirts. It's a combination kitchen/dressing room. A portable convection oven is used for baking.

Greenhouse bathroom—A sliding-glass door at the east end of the living room leads to a bathroom that doubles as a greenhouse (photo top left). This quarry-tile and wood room has a roof made of wired glass, and in it Gratz's collection of orchids, bromeliads, ferns and succulents flourishes. The room is made to get wet, so the floor is pitched toward a central drain. Copper pipes at the ridge deliver water to sprinkler heads that generate a fine mist for the plants.

The bathroom's east wall is also glass, allowing a good view of the plants in the adjoining lath house. This space, devoted solely to gardening, has an exterior wall made of redwood lath that filters the sunlight, often when the rest of the city is cloaked in fog. □

An interior of contrasts. **A recycled pedestal sink and toilet have found a new home in the greenhouse bathroom, above. A drain in the floor under the rug carries away runoff when the plants are watered. The kitchen nook, below, is finished in white and brushed stainless-steel. The small refrigerator over the sink has a matching plastic-laminate door insert.**

studs. The door leads to a new deck that runs the entire length of the house.

Under the newfound headroom provided by the shed, Gratz installed a simple loft made of 2x8 joists and plywood decking. The loft is supported by walls on two sides, and by a post on one corner. Access is by way of an oak ladder.

With the bed out of the way in a permanent spot, the rest of the room could be treated in a flexible way. Apart from the loft, the cast-iron fireplace is the only fixed feature in the living space. A hammock can be stretched between the two posts as a guest bed or a place to read. The sofa and chairs are lightweight rattan pieces that can be easily moved, and they generally spend the winter grouped around the woodstove—the only source of heat in the house. Meals are served on a table placed beneath the sleeping loft. The low ceiling creates an intimate alcove in a room that is otherwise open to the rafters.

In keeping with the nomadic nature of the furnishings, an antique armoire on heavy-duty

Index